普通高等学校邮轮服务与管理专业系列规划教材

The English Teaching Course on the Practice of International Cruise Ships

国际邮轮实务英语教程

程丛喜　等著

化学工业出版社

·北京·

《国际邮轮实务英语教程》是普通高等学校邮轮服务与管理专业系列规划教材之一。内容主要包括学习该课程的意义和目标、国际邮轮业发展概论、国际邮轮业多种文化环境中工作和生活的基本情况、国际邮轮工作应知应会的专业英语知识及相关技能、对客服务的技巧、对健康与安全的法定要求、卫生和环保实务与管理及安全实务与管理等，是广大学生和邮轮乘务人员从事国际邮轮业的必备用书。该教材和国际邮轮实际工作紧密结合，既可作为高等院校旅游管理类专业、英语专业、海乘专业的双语教学用书，又可作为职业培训或相关专业的参考用书，对学生就业国际化具有重要的现实意义。

图书在版编目（CIP）数据

The English Teaching Course on the Practice of International Cruise Ships/程丛喜等著．—北京：化学工业出版社，2016.4（2022.7重印）

普通高等学校邮轮服务与管理专业系列规划教材

ISBN 978-7-122-26454-1

Ⅰ.①T…　Ⅱ.①程…　Ⅲ.①旅游船-旅游服务-英语-高等学校-教材　Ⅳ.①H31

中国版本图书馆CIP数据核字（2016）第044442号

责任编辑：王　可　蔡洪伟　于　卉　　装帧设计：刘丽华

责任校对：边　涛

出版发行：化学工业出版社（北京市东城区青年湖南街13号　邮政编码100011）

印　　装：北京七彩京通数码快印有限公司

787mm×1092mm　1/16　印张16　字数389千字　2022年7月北京第1版第4次印刷

购书咨询：010-64518888　　售后服务：010-64518899

网　　址：http://www.cip.com.cn

凡购买本书，如有缺损质量问题，本社销售中心负责调换。

定　　价：36.00元

顾问名单

马　勇　湖北大学旅游发展研究院院长
薛兵旺　武汉商学院旅游与酒店管理学院院长
黄其新　江汉大学商学院副院长
毛　焱　湖北经济学院旅游与酒店管理学院副院长
鄢向荣　武汉交通职业学院旅游与商务学院院长
徐　江　江汉大学文理学院英语系主任
李　军　武汉中部对外经济技术合作有限公司总经理
赖润星　欣欣旅游董事长
徐　勇　武汉恒大酒店总经理
陈青云　腾邦欣欣产业园总经理
魏　宁　武汉凯文海乘酒店管理有限公司培训总监
郑道成　武汉丽莎海乘酒店管理服务有限公司总经理
朱　飞　武汉恒大酒店餐饮部经理
吴宏伟　武汉委托帮教育科技有限公司董事长
陈　欢　武汉中部对外经济技术合作有限公司培训总监

前言

邮轮，也称游轮、海上酒店、海上度假胜地和海上城镇等，是集“吃、住、行、游、购、娱”为一体的水上流动酒店或海上度假胜地，除了具备陆地上酒店或度假胜地的一般功能外，还具有交通运输功能。随着世界经济的发展、人们生活水平的不断提高，全球邮轮旅游市场规模一直稳步增长，潜力很大。自20世纪80年代以来，国际邮轮业以年均8%的速度递增，远远高于国际旅游业的整体发展速度，近几年来，更是呈加速增长的态势。据CLIA统计，2014年全球乘坐邮轮出行的乘客达到2300万人次，2015年达到2500万人次，预计2020年为3000万人次；上海国际航运研究中心2015年8月发布的《2030年中国航运发展展望》也预测，2030年，中国每年邮轮旅客量将达到800万至1000万人次，成为全球第一大邮轮旅游市场。国内沿海邮轮和内河邮轮特别是长江邮轮旅游也日益成熟和完善。邮轮业的迅猛发展对邮轮乘务人员无论从数量上还是质量上都提出了更高的要求，尤其需要既有理论知识又有实际操作技能，还要熟悉邮轮知识和精通外语的复合型人才。经过深入调查研究和实地考察，邮轮专业人才无论是在国际上还是在国内都具有良好的就业前景。

国际国内邮轮业的快速发展为邮轮人才的培养和教育创造了良好的条件，提供了绝好的契机。为了适应邮轮教育发展的需要，作者根据自己20多年的科研教学及国内外邮轮实际工作经验，在参考大量海内外有关邮轮资料的基础上，特撰写此教材。该教材内容主要包括学习该课程的意义和目标、国际邮轮业发展概论、国际邮轮业多种文化环境中工作和生活的基本情况、国际邮轮工作应知应会的专业英语知识及相关技能、对客服务的技巧、对健康与安全的法定要求、卫生和环保实务与管理及安全实务与管理等，是广大学生和邮轮乘务人员从事国际邮轮业的必备用书。该教材和国际邮轮实际工作紧密结合，既可作为高等院校旅游管理类专业、英语专业、海乘专业的双语教学用书，又可作为职业培训或相关专业的参考用书，对学生就业国际化具有重要的现实意义。

本教材主要由武汉轻工大学程丛喜教授撰写并统稿，其他参与本书撰写的人员名单与具体内容是周霄（武汉轻工大学，Part 2 中的 2.5.1）、邓念梅（三峡大学，Part 2 中的 2.5.3）、刘保丽（武汉生物工程学院，Part 2 中的 2.5.4 及 2.5.5）、陈顺良（武汉交通职业学院，Part 2 中的 2.5.6 及 2.5.7）、刘丽莉（武汉职业技术学院，Part 3 中的

3.3.1)、孙婧婍（武汉船舶职业技术学院，Part 6 中的 6.2 及 6.3）、林华英（武汉航海职业技术学院，Part 5 中的 5.13）、李良辰（长江大学工程技术学院，Part 3 中的 3.3.7 及 3.3.8）、赵为佳（江汉大学文理学院，Part 3 中的 3.3.2），感谢他们为本书付出了辛勤的劳动！

撰写此书的过程中，得到了湖北省教育厅、湖北省旅游局、中交协邮轮游艇分会、武汉市旅游局、厦门市旅游局、湖北省旅游学会、武汉轻工大学、武汉中部对外经济技术合作有限公司、武汉丽莎海乘酒店管理服务有限公司、武汉凯文海乘酒店管理有限公司等相关领导及专家的大力支持和帮助，在此表示衷心的感谢！由于水平所限，本书撰写过程中的疏漏之处在所难免，敬请广大同行和读者指正。

程丛喜

2016 年 1 月

目录

Part 1 Information for Studying This Course

Part 2 Overview of the Cruise Industry

Part 3 Working on the Cruise Ship

Part 4 Customer Service

Part 5 Hygiene and Environmental Protection on the Cruise Ships

Part 1

Information for Studying This Course

1.1 Background for Studying This Course

The cruise ship industry is a new industry, It's also one of the fastest growing job sectors in the world. Five to ten new luxury liners are being built every year, and with that growth there has been an equally impressive boom in the number of available cruise ship jobs. While many of these employment opportunities are aboard luxury cruise ships, students can also find employment on smaller vessels that include everything from eco-tour ships to steamboats and romantic sailing yachts. More and more people begin to join this industry, it's very attractive to Chinese young people on employment and salary.

In the past, there were not many Chinese crew ready for the employment on the cruise ships of international standard, because:

(1) The language was a major obstacle for the Chinese crew to enter the international cruise ship market.

(2) Generally speaking, the Chinese crew lacked the necessary skills for working on the international cruise ship because such type of cruise ships had never existed in China before.

But this situation has changed greatly. Now Chinese government has taken a lot of measures to improve English education, Chinese students' English level has been raised a lot. In addition, more and more students begin to work on the Yangtze River cruise ships, coastal cruise ships, and even some international cruise ships, although their skills are not up to the international standard, indeed improved a lot.

Our Chinese crew have a lot of merits to be employed on the international cruise ships.

(1) the value of salary With the still relatively lower cost of living in China, specially for those people in the inland, the salary offered for them on board will have much higher value than that in the developed countries and this itself is a very efficient motivation for the Chinese crew. It goes without saying that Chinese crew will value their job very much and this will certainly reflect in their work output, performance, etc.

(2) the availability China has a huge population with an average annual income of US $ 3200 per person, it is not difficult to imagine that the high wages offered on the cruise ship can definitely and easily attract thousands of highly qualified, motivated young boys and girls to join the cruise industry.

(3) the working attitude of Chinese crew Most of Chinese crew are influenced by the eastern culture and have strong service consciousness. With suitable training, it will not be difficult to mould them into what are required in the international cruise industry.

(4) the discipline of Chinese crew China is a socialist country and it is therefore normal to find most of people are well disciplined and obedient to the superior. In addition, most of the cruise ship training institutes or academies are under semi-military management to ensure the crew sent on board will be disciplinary-minded.

In conclusion, the conditions are ready for Chinese crew to enter the international cruise industry. So our urgent matter is to develop China's cruise ship education to meet all the requirements of the international cruise ship industry and other relevant regulations. If we train our Chinese crew according to the international standards of cruise ships, It's not difficult for them to obtain employment in the international cruise ship industry.

Notes

1. It's also one of the fastest growing job sectors in the world. 这也是世界上增长最快的就业部门之一。
2. There has been an equally impressive boom in the number of available cruise ship jobs. 邮轮工作岗位也有一个可观的相应增长。
3. From eco-tour ships to steamboats and romantic sailing yachts 从生态旅游船到汽艇和浪漫的帆船游艇
4. a very efficient motivation for the Chinese crew 中国船员的一个非常有效的动机
5. reflect in their work output, performance 反映在他们的工作效率和表现中
6. disciplinary-minded 有纪律意识的

New words & expressions

sector [ˈsektə] n. 部分，部门，扇形 v. 使分成部分，把……分成扇形

luxury [ˈlʌkʃəri] n. 奢侈，华贵 adj. 豪华的

liner [ˈlainə] n. 班船，班机，衬垫

aboard [əˈbɔːd] adv. 在船（飞机、车）上 prep. 上（船、飞机、车）

boom [buːm] n. 繁荣，激增，暴涨 v. 兴隆，大事宣传

employment [imˈplɔimənt] n. 雇用，使用，利用，工作，职业

steamboat [ˈstiːmbəut] n. 汽船，轮船

romantic [rəˈmæntik] adj. 传奇式的，浪漫的，空想的，夸大的

yacht [jɔt] n. 游艇，快艇，轻舟 vi. 驾游艇，乘游艇

obstacle [ˈɔbstəkl] n. 障碍，妨害物

relatively [ˈrelətivli] adv. 相关地

motivation [ˌməutiˈveiʃən] n. 动机

output [ˈautput] n. 产量，输出，输出量

availability [əˌveiləˈbiliti] n. 可得性，可得到的东西（或人员），可用性，有效性

average [ˈævəridʒ] n. 平均，平均水平，平均数，海损 . adj. 一般的，通常的，平均的

mould [məuld] n. [亦作 mold] 肥土，壤土，模具 v. 用土覆盖，发霉，铸造

discipline [ˈdisiplin] n. 纪律，学科 v. 训练

obedient [əˈbiːdiənt] adj. 服从的，孝顺的

superior [sjuːˈpiəriə] n. 长者，高手，上级 adj. 较高的，上级的，上好的，出众的，高傲的

marine [məˈriːn] n. 舰队，水兵，海运业 adj. 海的，海产的，航海的，船舶的，海运的

academy [əˈkædəmi] n. （高等）专科院校，研究院，学会，学术团体，学院

urgent [ˈəːdʒənt] adj. 急迫的，紧急的

requirement [riˈkwaiəmənt] n. 需求，要求，必要条件，需要的东西，要求必备的条件

relevant [ˈrelivənt] adj. 有关的，相应的

board n. 木板，（供特殊用途的）木板，甲板，膳食费用，会议桌，部 vt. 提供膳食

in conclusion 最后，综上所述

on board 在船（火车，飞机，汽车）上

Exercises

1. What were the weak points of Chinese crew in the past?

2. What are the strong points for Chinese crew to obtain employment in the international cruise ship industry now?

1.2 The Target for Studying This Course

After studying this course, the students should:

(1) Understand the nature of the cruise industry, the hotel department on board, the working and living conditions in a multi-cultural environment.

(2) Be aware of the statutory requirements of health and safety when working on board a cruise ship.

(3) Reach to the level of written and spoken English comprehension and obtain the ability to communicate so that safety instructions, and job procedures in both written and verbal English are understood.

(4) Demonstrate that they can express themselves and inquire basic questions concerning their employment and safety.

Notes

1. the nature of the cruise industry 邮轮产业的性质
2. in a multi-cultural environment 在多种文化环境中
3. the statutory requirements of health and safety 健康和安全的法定要求
4. safety instructions 安全指令

New words & expressions

multi-cultural 多种文化的

environment [in'vaiərənmənt] n. 环境，外界

statutory ['stætjut(ə)ri] adj. 法令的，法定的

bring up v. 教育，培养，提出，（军队等）调上来，（船）抵达目的地

instruction [in'strʌkʃən] n. 指示，用法说明（书），教育，指导，指令

procedure [prə'siːdʒə] n. 程序，手续

verbal ['vəːbəl] adj. 口头的

communicate [kə'mjuːnikeit] v. 沟通，通信，（房间、道路、花园等）相通，传达，感染

demonstrate ['demənstreit] vt. 示范，证明，论证 vi. 示威

Exercises

1. What is the target for the students to study this course?
2. What does "the hotel department" mean?

Part 2

Overview of the Cruise Industry

2. 1 What Is a Cruise Ship

Generally speaking, a cruise ship or cruise liner is a passenger ship used for pleasure voyages, where the voyage itself and the ship's amenities are a part of the experience, as well as the different destinations along the way, it is a "floating hotel" which merges dining, accommodation, transportation, travel, shopping and entertainment, etc. into an organic whole, so also called "maritime hotel" . Transportation is not the prime purpose, as cruise ships operate mostly on routes that return passengers to their originating port, so the ports of call are usually in a specified region of a continent.

The short names for different ships:

S. S. —Steam Ship

M. V. —Motor Ship

C. S. —Cruise Ship

Name: Allure of the Seas

Owner: Royal Caribbean Cruises Ltd.

Class and type: Oasis-class cruise ship

Gross Tonnage: 225,282 tons

Length: 362m (1,187 feet)

Max Beam: 60. 5 (198 feet)

Draft：9. 3m（31 feet）

Height：72m（236 feet）above waterline

Decks：16 passenger decks

Cruising Speed：22. 6 knots（41. 9km/h）

Capacity：5412 at double occupancy，6296 maximum

Crew：2384

Maiden Voyage：1 December 2010

Number of cabins：2704

Notes

1. The short names for different types of ship

S. S. —Steam Ship

M. V. （M. S. ）—Motor Vessel（Motor Ship）

C. S. —Cruise Ship

2. Conversion of Length Units

1foot＝12 inches＝30. 48cm

1inch＝2. 54cm

1nautical mile＝1. 852 kilometers＝1. 150 miles

3. Max Beam　横梁，（舰船船身等的）最大宽度

4. originating port　出发港

5. ports of call　停靠港

6. Allure of the Seas　海洋魅力号

New words & expressions

overview［ˈəuvəvjuː］n. 一般观察，总的看法

liner［ˈlainə］n. 班轮，班机

voyage［ˈvɔiidʒ］n. 旅行，航海，旅程 vi. 航行，旅行

amenity［əˈmiːnəti］n. 便利设施，愉快，礼仪，举止，（环境等的）舒适

accommodation［əˌkɔməˈdeiʃən］n. 住处，膳宿

merge [mə:dʒ] v. 合并，并入，结合，吞没，融合

originate [ə'ridʒineit] vt. 创始，创作 vi. 起源于，来自；产生；起航

specify ['spesifai] vt. 指定；详述 vi. 明确提出，详细说明

continent ['kɔntinənt] n. 大陆，陆地 adj. 克制的，节欲的，贞洁的

allure [ə'luə(r)] n. 诱惑力，魅力 vt. & vi. 引诱，诱惑；吸引

oasis [əu'eisis] n. （沙漠中的）绿洲，乐土，宜人之地，慰藉物

gross tonnage [grəus 'tʌnidʒ] 总吨数

beam [bi:m] n. 梁，栋梁，束，光线 vi. 发出光与热；面露喜色

draft [drɑ:ft] n. 吃水深度，拖，拉，一网（鱼），气流

waterline ['wɔ:təlain] n. （船的）吃水线，水线

knot [nɔt] n. 结，绳结，蝴蝶结，[航] 节（＝海浬/小时），浬，海里 vt. & vi. 把……打结，捆扎

capacity [kə'pæsiti] n. 载客量，容量，才能 adj. 充其量的，最大限度的

maiden ['meidn] n. 未婚女子，处女 adj. 首次的，初次的，没有经验的

motor vessel ['məutə'vese] 内燃机船

conversion [kən'və:ʃən] n. 转换，变换，转化

nautical mile ['nɔ:tikəlmail] n. 海里（合 1. 852 千米）

Exercises

1. What is a cruise ship?
2. What's the cuising speed of Allure of the Seas?
3. How many kilometers is one nautical mile equal to?

2.2 Some Information on the Cruise Ships of Different Times

2. 2. 1 SS Prinzessin Victoria Luise

The popularity of trans-Atlantic sea passage gradually declined with the arrival of the airplane. People could fly to more destinations in a fraction of the time it took on an ocean liner, so shipping companies changed their business model to focus on tourism instead of passenger transportation. In 1900, the American-Hamburg Company built the first ship specifically designed for cruises. The Prinzessin Victoria Luise measured 406 feet (124 meters) long by 52 feet (16 meters) wide, and was 4,409 gross tons with the speed of 15 knots and twin-screw. Built as a cruise ship, she did make some sailings to NY and wrecked near Plum Point, Jamaica, in 1906.

2.2.2 MV Princesa Victoria

MV Princesa Victoria (ever named Dunnottar Castle, Victoria, the Victoria) was built as Dunnottar Castle by Harland & Wolff at Belfast and entered service in July of 1936, owned by the Union-Castle Mail Steamship Company Ltd., London. She was ever completely rebuilt and reengined by Wilton-Fijenoord, Rotterdam 1959 and changed to be owned by Incres Lines, Monrovia. In the history, she was ever sold and remaned on several occasions. She measured at 14,583 gross tons, 174.4m long by 21.8m wide (572 feet long by 71.9 feet wide). She was powered with16, 800 BHP to drive twin screws at a speed of 18 knots. Her capacity is 696 passengers. She was one of the most popular and "modern" cruise ships of her era. During the ship's 1959 conversion at Rotterdam, she became one of the most spacious ships in the world. The Victoria's 250 seat auditorium was among the largest afloat for many years.

2.2.3 MV Aurora

Aurora is a cruise ship with a classic British design. Yet life on board feels distinctly cosmopolitan. French chic. Moorish elegance. International glamour. Built by Meyer Werft in Germany, the Aurora was delivered to P&O Cruises in April 2000. The Aurora has an overall length of 270m and of 242. 6m between perpendiculars. It has a moulded beam of 32. 2m and a 33. 6m maximum beam. Its draught is 7. 9m. It has an air draught of 52m and a height of 115 feet. The Aurora has a gross tonnage of 76, 152t, a net tonnage of 40,037t and a deadweight of 64,450t. The Aurora has a maximum passenger capacity of 2,290. These passengers are all looked after by 936 officers and crew. It has 12 bars, 3 pools (1 with sky dome), 1 cinema, 1 cyber study, 1 open deck grill restaurant, 1660-seat theater, 1 spa and 1 gym, etc. In short, it is just like a small town even including a golf simulator.

2.2.4 MS Oasis of the Seas

MS Oasis of the Seas is one of the World's largest cruise ships with a gross tonnage of over 220,000t when it launched in 2009, it is was built by Royal Caribbean in Finland. The ship is not only set to be the largest vessel at sea, but also the most expensive at a cost of 230,000 US dollars per berth, valued at $1. 24 billion. It is 1, 180 feet long, 154 feet wide and 240 feet high -one and a half times taller than the O2 Arena and longer than four football pitches. It spans 16 decks and carries over 5,400 passengers. An area resembling New York City's Central Park is located in the center of the ship offering inside cabins an "outside" view, it spans the entire length of a football field, featuring trees, flower gardens and pathways as well as a town square, restaurants, shops and bars. Concerts and street performances are also staged there. The ship also boasts the first moving bar at sea. The Rising Tide Bar spans three decks and moves between the Central Park and public areas below. Royal Caribbean International president and chief executive Adam Goldstein said: "Central Park is a true evolution of a cruise ship design and allows us to provide our guests with not only a more varied selection of balcony accommodations, but also a public venue that will be a central element of the ship during the day and at night." Generally MS Oasis of the Seas is just like a floating city including a lot of advanced facilities.

2.3 How Many Cruise Ships Are Active in the World Today

At present, over 400 maritime cruise ships have been put into operation in the world, obviously this number doesn't include the cruise ships on all rivers of the world.

2.4 How Many New Cruise Ships Have Been or Will Be Put into Operation

With the development of the world's economy and improvement of people's living standard, a lot of huge cruise ships have been or will be put into operation.

Year	Quantity	Year	Quantity
2001	16	2008	9
2002	11	2009	11
2003	10	2010	10
2004	8	2011	8
2005	10	2013—2014	29
2006	10	2015	20
2007	10		

Notes

1. trans-Atlantic sea passage　横跨大西洋的海上航道
2. twin-screw　双螺旋桨的，双推进器的
3. Wilton-Fijenoord，Rotterdam　位于鹿特丹的威尔顿费诺德公司
4. on several occasions　屡次，好几次
5. 242. 6m between perpendiculars　垂线间距离 242. 6 米
6. air draught　净空高度，即外桅杆最高点至水面的高度
7. It has a moulded beam of 32. 2m and a 33. 6m maximum beam.　它的型宽是 32. 2 米，最大宽度是 33. 6 米（型宽指的船舶最宽的地方，通常指船中，这个宽度不包括外板厚度，定义中指的是船体“型”表面的宽度）。
8. sky dome　天幕，穹顶
9. golf simulator　高尔夫模拟球场
10. offering inside cabins an“outside” view　为内侧房间提供外景
11. more varied selection of balcony accommodations　更多对阳台舱室的多样化选择

New words & expressions

Victoria [vik'tɔːriə] n. 维多利亚

popularity [ˌpɔpju'læriti] n. 普及，流行，声望

decline [di'klain] vi. 下倾，下降，下垂 v. 拒绝，衰落 n. 下倾，下降，衰败，衰落

a fraction of　一部分

wreck [rek] n. 失事船（或飞机），残骸，（船，飞机的）失事 vt. 破坏，拆毁

Jamaica [dʒə'meikə] n. 牙买加，牙买加甜酒

Monrovia [mən'rəuviə] 蒙罗维亚（①利比里亚首都 ②美国一城市）

reman [riː'mæn] vt. 为（舰队等）重新配备人员，使重新鼓起勇气

reengined ['riːdʒind] adj. 换过发动机的

aurora [ɔː'rɔːrə] n. 黎明的女神，极光

Belfast [bel'faːst] n. 贝尔法斯特

auditorium [ˈɔːdiˈtɔːriəm] n. 听众席，观众席，〈美〉会堂，礼堂

Rotterdam ['rɔtədæm] 鹿特丹 [荷兰西南部港市]

cosmopolitan [ˌkɔzmə'pɔlitən] n. 四海为家的人 adj. 世界性的，全球（各地）的

chic[ʃi(i)k] n. 别致的款式（尤指妇女的服饰）adj. 别致的

Moorish ['muəriʃ] adj. 摩尔人的，（建筑，家具等）摩尔人式的，摩尔人风格的

glamour ['glæmə] n. [亦作 glamor] 魔力，魅力 v. 迷惑

deliver [di'livə] vt. 递送，交付，引渡，瞄准，给予（打击）

maximum ['mæksiməm] n. 最大量，极大 adj. 最高的，最大极限的

perpendicular [ˌpəːpən'dikjulə] adj. 垂直的，正交的 n. 垂线

deadweight ['dedweit] n.（船的）总载重量，（车辆的）自重，固定负载，重负

dome 天幕，穹顶

simulator n. 高尔夫模拟球场

tonnage [ˈtʌnidʒ] n. 登记吨位，排水量

genesis ['dʒenisis] n. 起源

Finland ['finlənd] n. 芬兰 [欧洲]

the O2 Arena 伦敦千年穹顶（高 134 米）

football pitch 足球场

evolution [ˌiːvə'luːʃən] n. 进展，发展，演变，进化

venue ['venjuː] n. 会场，犯罪地点，（尤指）体育比赛场所

active ['æktiv] adj. 积极的，能起作用的，现行的

put into operation 使生效

Exercises

1. Would you please list the names of four cruise ships of different tomes and their tonnage?
2. How many cruise ships are active all over the world today?
3. How many cruise ships will be put into operation in 2015?

2.5 The Introduction of Some Main Cruise Ship Operators

2.5.1 Carnival Corporation & Plc

Carnival Corporation & Plc（"Carnival"）is an American/British cruise company and the world's largest cruise ship operator，with a combined fleet of over 100 vessels across 10 cruise line brands，with the fathom brand announced for launch in 2016. A dual listed company，Carnival is composed of two companies，Carnival Corporation and Carnival Plc，which arc combined and function as one entity, despite having separate listings on the New York and London stock exchanges respectively. As such, Carnival is the only company in the world to be listed on both the S&P 500 and FTSE 100 indices. The Carnival group has global headquarters in Doral, Florida in the United States and Southampton, Hampshire in the United Kingdom, with regional headquarters in Australia, Germany, Italy, United Kingdom and United States.

Carnival Corporation & Plc was formed in 2003, with the merger of Carnival Corporation and P&O Princess Cruises Plc. Carnival Corporation was originally founded as Carnival Cruise Lines in 1972. The company grew steadily throughout the 1970s and 1980s, making an initial public offering on the New York Stock Exchange in 1987. The capital generated was used to finance acquisitions, and between 1989 and 1999, the company acquired Holland America Line, Windstar Cruises, Westours, Seabourn Cruise Line, Costa Cruises and Cunard Line. The name Carnival Corporation was adopted in 1993, to distinguish the parent company from its flagship cruise line subsidiary. P&O Princess Cruises Plc was formed in 2000, following the demerger of the cruise ship division of the P&O group. Originating as the Peninsular and Oriental Steam Navigation Company in England in 1837, P&O operated the world's first passenger ships, the predecessor of modern cruise ships. Restructuring of the P&O group in the 20th Century led to its cruise operations being rebranded as P&O Cruises and P&O Cruises Australia, with the company acquiring Princess Cruises in 1974. Following the demerger in 2000, the company also acquired AIDA Cruises, as well as establishing the A'Rosa Cruises and Ocean Village brands.

Prior to the merger with Carnival Corporation, P&O Princess Cruises Plc had agreed a merger with Royal Caribbean Cruises Ltd. The decision to abandon the deal came after Carnival Corporation made a new bid with improved terms for British shareholders. It was agreed that P&O Princess Cruises Plc would remain as a separate company, listed on the London Stock Exchange and retaining its British shareholder body and management team. The company would simply be renamed Carnival Plc, with the operations of the two companies merged into one entity. Carnival Corporation and Carnival Plc, jointly own all the operating companies in the Carnival Group.

The Carnival Group now comprises 10 cruise line brands operating a combined fleet of over 100 ships, totalling over 190, 000 lower berths, and with new ships on order. A 10th brand, stylised as fathom, was announced in June 2015, and will commence operations in April 2016. In 2011 the combined brands of the Carnival Group controlled a 49.2% share of the total worldwide cruise market. The following operating companies have full executive control of the Carnival brands in their portfolio.

(1) Carnival

① Carnival Cruise Line

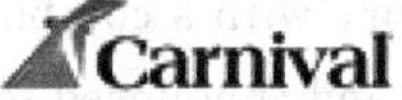

Headquarters in Doral, Florida, USA, operating twenty four vessels. In 1987, Carnival completed an initial public offering of 20 percent of its common stock on the New York Stock Exchange, raising approximately \$400 million in capital. The capital raised was used to finance acquisitions, so in 1993 the business was restructured as a holding company, under the name Carnival Corporation, with Carnival Cruise Line becoming it's principal subsidiary. Carnival continues to be the largest single brand in the Carnival Group today, operating twenty four vessels.

② Fathom (Cruise Line)

Fathom (corporately styled fathom) is a cruise line based in Doral, Florida, a suburb of Miami, USA. It is incorporated in the United Kingdom, and owned by Carnival Corporation & Plc. It will commence operations in 2016, the first ship in Fathom's fleet will be the *R*-class cruise ship. Fathom will operate what Carnival calls "social impact travel" journeys lasting seven days from Port Miami, Florida, to the Dominican Republic. The journeys will include volunteer activities with established organizations on the ground. Carnival announced Fathom's establishment on June 4, 2015. According to Arnold Donald, CEO of Carnival, "Fathom will cater to an under served market of consumers who want to have a positive impact on people's lives, and aren't always sure where to begin."

(2) Carnival UK

① P&O Cruises

P&O Cruises is a British/American cruise line based at Carnival House in Southampton, England, operated by Carnival UK and owned by Carnival Corporation & Plc. Originally a constituent of the Peninsular and Oriental Steam Navigation Company, P&O Cruises is the oldest cruise line in the world, having operated the world's first passenger ships in the early 19th century. It retains strong links with its sister company P&O Cruises Australia. P&O Cruises was de-merged from the P&O group in 2000, becoming a subsidiary of P&O Princess Cruises, which subsequently merged with Carnival Corporation in 2003, to form Carnival Corporation & Plc. P&O Cruises currently operates eight cruise ships with a total passenger capacity of 14,970 and a 5% market share of all cruise lines worldwide. Its most recent vessel MV Britannia joined the fleet in March 2015.

② P&O Cruises Australia

P&O Cruises Australia is a British-American owned cruise line with corporate headquarters at Carnival House in Southampton, England and operational headquarters in North Sydney, New South Wales, Australia. The sister company of P&O Cruises in the United Kingdom, it was previously a part of the Peninsular & Oriental Steam Navigation Company and has a direct link in history to the world's first passenger ships. As such, it is one of the oldest cruise lines in the world, and now becomes part of the Carnival Corporation & Plc, under the executive control of Carnival UK. It currently operates three ships, sailing from various ports in Australia and New Zealand.

③ Cunard

The second oldest brand in the Carnival group after P&O Cruises, Cunard Line originates from 1840 and celebrated its 175th anniversary in 2015. It was founded by Samuel Cunard, who was awarded the first trans-Atlantic mail contract in 1937 and established the British and North American Royal Mail Steam-Packet Company in 1840. Following the merger of Carnival Corporation and Carnival Plc in 2003, executive control of the Cunard brand was transferred to Carnival UK, with corporate and operational headquarters based in Southampton, England. It owns 3 cruise ships.

(3) Holland America Group

① Holland America Line

Holland America Line is a British American owned cruise line based in Seattle, USA. It has been owned by Carnival Corporation & Plc since 1989. Holland America Line originated as Plate, Reuchlin & Company, founded in Rotterdam, Netherlands in 1871. It ultimately sold its cargo operations, becoming exclusively a cruise ship company in 1973. From 1873 to 1989, it was a Dutch shipping line, a passenger line, a cargo line and a cruise line operating primarily between the Netherlands and North America. As part of this rich legacy, it was instrumental in the transport of many hundreds of thousands of immigrants from the Netherlands to North America. Since the formation of Carnival Corporation and Plc in 2003, Holland America Line has been one of the principal operating companies of the Carnival Group, operating fifteen vessels.

② Princess Cruises

Princess Cruises began in 1965. Now it is an American owned cruise line, based in Santa Clarita, California in the United States and incorporated in Bermuda, currently operating eighteen vessels. Previously a subsidiary of P&O Princess Cruises, the company is now one of ten cruise ship brands owned by Carnival Corporation & Plc and accounts for approximately 19% share of its revenue. Being based in America, executive control of Princess Cruises was transferred to Carnival Corporation following its acquisition of P&O Princess in 2002. The company was made famous by The Love Boat TV series, in which its ship, Pacific Princess was featured. In May 2013, the brand new Royal Princess became the flagship of Princess Cruises, and in May 2014 was joined by her new sister-ship Regal Princess.

③ Seabourn

Seabourn was founded in 1986 by a consortium of Norwegian investors. In 2002, the company was demerged from Cunard Line and reorganized as a stand-alone operating brand of Carnival Corporation & Plc. Seabourn Cruise Line is a luxury cruise line headquartered in Seattle, Washington, currently operating three vessels. The line operates all around the world, from short seven-day Caribbean cruises to exotic 100+ day cruises around the world. It is owned by Carnival Corporation, a part of the "World's Leading Cruise Lines" marketing group. Passengers typically range in ages from the 40s to the 60s, but children are still welcome. Seabourn operates small ships that can fit in many ports around the world. The cabins are suites and are equipped with great amenities available at sea.

(4) Costa Group

① Costa Cruises

Costa Cruises (Italian: Costa Crociere), is a British/American owned Italian cruise line, based in Genoa, Italy, and under control of the Carnival Corporation & Plc. Founded in 1854, the company originally operated cargo ships, in order to carry olive oils and textiles from Sardinia to Liguria. The company later converted its entire fleet to full-time cruising, and as an independent company became one of the largest cruise operators in Europe. The takeover of Costa Cruises by Carnival Corporation began in 1997, as a 50/50 deal between Carnival and the British tour operator Airtours. Carnival then began purchasing Airtours' shares in the company, becoming the sole shareholder in September 2000. Costa Cruises is now one of the largest brands within the Carnival Group and accounts for approximately 16% of its revenue, with 15 ships, headquarter in Genoa, Italy.

② AIDA Cruises

AIDA Cruises is a British/American owned German cruise line, with corporate headquarters in Genoa, Italy and operational headquarters in Rostock, Germany. It owns 10 cruise ships. The company entered the cruise industry in the 1960s. The company was acquired by P&O Princess Cruises in 2000. In 2003, P&O Princess merged with Carnival Corporation, to form Carnival Corporation & Plc, the worlds largest cruise holiday company. Following the merger, executive control of AIDA Cruises transferred to Costa Cruises Group, one of the main operating companies of the Carnival Group, with responsibility for the group's European brands. AIDA Cruises is now one of 10 brands operated by the Carnival Group accounting for 6.5% of its share of revenue and has its own executive team. AIDA ships cater to the German-speaking market and are renowned for their youthful style and casual service. As seagoing "club resorts", AIDA ships have many on-board amenities and facilities that attract younger, more active vacationers.

Notes

1. A dual listed company 双挂牌上市公司

2. despite having separate listings on the New York and London stock exchanges respectively 尽管分别在纽约和伦敦证券交易所单独上市

3. Carnival is the only company in the world to be listed on both the S&P 500 and FTSE 100 Indices. 嘉年华集团是世界上唯一的在标准普尔 500 指数和富时 100 指数上市的公司。

4. making an initial public offering on the New York Stock Exchange in 1987 1987 年在纽约证券交易所公开发行股票

5. finance acquisition 财务并购

6. the parent company 母公司

7. after Carnival Corporation made a new bid with improved terms for British shareholders 在嘉年华公司改进了条款为英国的股东提出了一个新的出价之后

8. a combined fleet 一个联合船队

9. new ships on order 订购的新船

10. the Dominican Republic 多米尼加共和国

11. an under served market of consumers 有待供应的消费者市场

12. It was instrumental in the transport of many hundreds of thousands of immigrants from the Netherlands to North America. 它在将成千上万的移民从荷兰运送到北美的过程中发挥了很好的作用。

13. The company was made famous by The Love Boat TV series. 这家邮轮公司因电视剧《爱船》而闻名。

14. a stand-alone operating brand of Carnival Corporation & Plc 一个独立运营的嘉年华邮轮集团旗下的品牌

15. Passengers typically range in ages from the 40s to the 60s 旅客年龄通常 40 岁至 60 岁

16. Seabourn operates small ships that can fit in many ports around the world. 世鹏邮轮公司经营的邮轮较小，适合在世界上的许多港口停靠。

17. in order to carry olive oils and textiles from Sardinia to Liguria 为了把橄榄油和纺织品从撒丁岛运到利古里亚

18. casual service 休闲服务

New words & expressions

carnival [ˈkɑːnivl] n. 狂欢节，嘉年华，节日，联欢

operator [ˈɔpəreitə] n. （某企业的）经营者，接线员，话务员，投机取巧者

fathom [ˈfæðəm] n. 英寻 vt. 理解……的真意，推测，领会，测深

entity [ˈentəti] n. 实体，实际存在物，本质

Doral 朵拉市（位于 Florida 州的东部，属于 Miami-Dade County）

Southampton [sauθˈæmptən] 南安普敦（英国英格兰南部港市）

Hampshire [ˈhæmpʃiə] n. 汉普郡（英国南部之一郡）

merger [ˈmɜːdʒə(r)] n. （两个公司的）合并，联合体，吸收

acquisition [ˌækwiˈziʃn] n. 获得，购置物，获得物，收购

flagship [ˈflægʃip] n. 旗舰，〈比喻〉最重要的一个，佼佼者

subsidiary [səb'sidiəri] adj. 附带的，附属的 n. 附属机构，子公司
demerger [ˌdiː'məːdʒə(r)] n. 中止合并关系，合并企业解散
peninsular [pə'ninsjələ(r)] n. 住在半岛上的居民 adj. 形成半岛的
oriental [ˌɔːri'entəl] adj. 东方的，东方人的 n. 东方人，东亚人
predecessor ['priːdisesə] n. 前任，前辈，原有事物，前身，〈古〉祖先
abandon [ə'bændən] vt. 放弃，抛弃，离弃，丢弃 n. 放任，放纵，完全屈从于压制
shareholder ['ʃeəhəuldə(r)] n. 股东，股票持有者
comprise [kəm'praiz] vt. 包含，包括，由……组成，由……构成
commence [kə'mens] vt. & vi. 开始，着手，获得学位
portfolio [pɔːt'fəuliəu] n. 公文包，代表作品集，证券投资组合，业务量
Miami [mai'æmi] n. 迈阿密（美国佛罗里达州东南部港市）
Dominican [də'minikən] adj. 多米尼加的，多米尼加人的 n. 多米尼加人
volunteer [ˌvələn'tiə] n. 志愿者，志愿兵 adj. 自愿的，志愿的 vt. &vi. 自愿去做
cater to ['keitə tuː] v. 供应伙食，迎合，面向
market share ['mɑːkit ʃɛə] 市场占有率
constituent [kən'stitjuənt] n. 选民，成分，构成部分 adj. 构成的，组成的，选举的
retain [ri'tein] vt. 保持；留在心中，记住，雇用，付定金保留
worldwide ['wəːldwaid] adj. 全世界的 adv. 遍及全球地
Britannia [bri'tænjə] n. 大不列颠，大不列颠之古拉丁文名
Sydney ['sidni] n. 悉尼（澳大利亚一城市）
Wales [weilz] n. 威尔士（英国的一部分）
originate from [ə'ridʒineit frɔm] 来自……，源于……，起源
transfer [træns'fəː] vt. 使转移，使调动 vi. 转让，转学 n. 转移，调动
Seattle [si'ætl] n. 西雅图
Netherlands ['neðələndz] n. 荷兰
ultimately ['ʌltimətli] adv. 最后，最终，基本上，根本
cargo ['kɑːgəu] n. （船或飞机装载的）货物，负荷，荷重
exclusively [iks'kluːsivli] adv. 唯一地，专门地，特定地，专有地，排外地
legacy ['legəsi] n. 遗产，遗赠
Santa Clarita（美国加州洛杉矶）圣克拉里塔市
Bermuda [bə(ː)'mjuːdə] n. 百慕大群岛（北大西洋西部群岛）
accounts for [ə'kaunt fɔː] 说明（原因、理由等），（在数量、比例上）占，对……负责
revenue ['revənjuː] n. 税收，（土地，财产等的）收入，收益，[复数] 总收入
consortium [kən'sɔːtiəm] n. 财团，组合，共同体，[法] 配偶的地位和权利
exotic [ig'zɔtik] adj. 异国的，奇异的，吸引人的 n. 舶来品，外来物，脱衣舞女
takeover ['teikəuvə(r)] n. （事业等的）接管，（经营权等的）接收，验收，收购
Genoa ['dʒenəuə] n. 热那亚（意大利西北部的州及其首府）
Rostock ['rɔstɔk] 罗斯托克（东德港市）
acquire [ə'kwaiə] vt. 获得，取得，学到
vacationer [və'keiʃnə(r)] n. 度假者，休假者

Exercises

1. What's the whole name of "Carnival"?
2. How many brands does "carnival" own at present? What are they?
3. How many cruise ships does "Carnival" have at present?
4. When was "Carnival" formed?
5. Which brand is the newest one of "Carnival"?
6. Where is the headquarter of Carnival Cruise Line?
7. How many brands are under the executive control of Carnival? What are they?
8. How many brands are under the executive control of Carnival UK? What are they?
9. How many brands are under the executive control of Holland American Group? What are they?
10. How many brands are under the executive control of Costa Group? What are they?
11. Where is Santa Clarita located?
12. When was Costa Cruises taken over by "Carnival"?

2.5.2 Royal Caribbean Cruises Ltd.

Royal Caribbean Cruises Ltd. is the world's second largest cruise company, operating the Royal Caribbean International, Celebrity Cruises, Pullmantur, Azamara Club Cruises and CDF Croisieres de France brands, with 40 ships and a passenger capacity of approximately 94,000, and TUI Cruises through a 50% joint venture. It also offers unique land-tour vacations in Alaska, Asia, Australia/New Zealand, Canada, Dubai, Europe and South America. These brands offer an array of onboard activities, services and amenities, including simulated surfing, swimming pools, sun decks, beauty salons, exercise and spa facilities, ice skating rinks, in-line skating, basketball courts, rock climbing walls, miniature golf courses, gaming facilities, lounges, bars, Las Vegas-style entertainment, cinemas and Royal Promenades, which include interior shopping, dining and an entertainment boulevard. The company will introduce three more ships by the end of 2015, when it will have a total capacity of approximately 100, 000 berths. The ships operate worldwide with a selection of itineraries that call on approximately 400 destinations.

(1) Azamara Club Cruises

Azamara Club Cruises is a cruise company that operates two ships, the *Azamara Journey* and the *Azamara Quest*. The company is a subsidiary of Royal Caribbean Cruises. It was founded in 2007 as Azamara Cruises and was rebranded in 2009. Both ships were refurbished in the winter of 2012-2013. Azamara Club Cruises sails to fascinating destinations all over the world throughout Northern & Western Europe, the Mediterranean, Asia, South America, the West Indies, Central America and the United States West Coast.

(2) Celebrity Cruises

Celebrity Cruises' iconic "X" is the mark of modern luxury, with its cool, contemporary design and warm spaces; dining experiences where the design of the venues is as important as the cuisine; and the amazing service that only Celebrity can provide, all created to provide an unmatchable experience for vacationers' precious time. In addition to offering vacations visiting all continents, Celebrity also presents immersive cruisetour experiences in Alaska, Australia/New Zealand, Canada, Europe and South America. One of the fastest-growing major cruise lines, Celebrity's fleet currently consists of 11 ships offering updated luxury vacations worldwide.

(3) Croisiere de France

CDF Croisières de France provides cruise holidays custom-tailored for the French market with French as the primary language used on board. Founded on September 2007 as a subsidiary of Royal Caribbean Cruises Ltd. , currently operating 2 cruise ships. The company offers an all-inclusive product, with not only accommodation and meals but also all drinks and tips included in the price of the cruise.

(4) Pullmantur Cruises

Pullmantur Cruises S. L. is a cruise line headquartered in Madrid, Spain. It began operations in the late 1990s as an offshoot of the Madrid-based travel agency Pullmantur, currently operating 2 cruise ships. Pullmantur Cruises, through its parent company, was purchased by Royal Caribbean Cruises Ltd. in 2006. Pullmantur Cruises is the largest Spain-based cruise line. The company mainly markets to Spanish passengers, although cruises on Pullmantur ships are also sold by some travel operators outside the Spanish-speaking world. Most of the company's ships operate an "all-inclusive" product, where some extras, such as brand alcoholic beverages, are included in the cruise price. However, as of October 2014, this is no longer the case as alcoholic beverage packages are now sold separately.

(5) Royal Caribbean International

Royal Caribbean International is a global cruise brand with 22 innovative ships, calling on more than 270 destinations in 72 countries across six continents. It also offers unique cruisetour land packages in Alaska, Canada, Dubai, Europe, and Australia and New Zealand. Royal Caribbean provides a world-class vacation experience with a wide range of signature onboard amenities, entertainment, and award-winning family programming. It has a 40-year history of providing guests the Royal Advantage-the most innovative cruise ships, exciting itineraries to popular destinations, and world-renowned friendly and engaging Gold Anchor Service. Royal Caribbean has been voted "Best Cruise Line Overall" for nine consecutive years in the Travel Weekly Readers' Choice Awards.

(6) TUI Cruises

TUI Cruises, in which Royal Caribbean Cruises Ltd. has a 50% investment in a joint venture, operates cruise holidays specifically tailored for the German market. TUI Cruises is a Germany-based, Joint venture cruise line of the German Tourist firm, TUI AG and the American cruise line operator, Royal Caribbean Cruises Ltd.. The company started operations in 2009, currently operating 2 cruise ships. The concept is for German-speaking customers who opt for premium cruise experience. Onboard product are custom-tailored for German tastes and encompasses food, entertainment and amenities. German is the main language used onboard their ships.

Notes

1. miniature golf courses 小型高尔夫球场
2. Las Vegas-style entertainment 拉斯维加斯式娱乐
3. Both ships were refurbished in the winter of 2012—2013. 在 2012—2013 冬季两艘船都进行了翻新。
4. the West Indies 西印度群岛
5. an unmatchable experience 一次无与伦比的经历
6. an all-inclusive product 一个一价全包产品
7. an offshoot of the Madrid-based travel agency Pullmantur 位于马德里的普尔曼旅行社的分支机构
8. calling on more than 270 destinations in 72 countries across six continents 停靠六大洲 72 个国家的 270 个旅游目的地
9. award-winning family programming 获奖的家庭节目
10. the Royal Advantage 皇家待遇（优势、利益）
11. for nine consecutive years 连续九年
12. a Germany-based, Joint venture cruise line 一个位于德国的合资邮轮公司

New words & expressions

joint venture [dʒɔint 'ventʃə] 合资企业

Dubai ['dju:bai] 迪拜（阿拉伯联合酋长国的酋长国之一）

miniature ['miniətʃə] adj. 小型的，微小的 n. 微型复制品 vt. 使成小型，缩写

promenade [ˌprɔmə'nɑ:d] n. 散步，通道，走廊 vt. & vi. 漫步，散步，骑马

itinerary [ai'tinərəri] n. 旅程，旅行日程，旅行日记 adj. 旅程的，巡回的，

rebrand [ˌri:'brænd] v. 给（产品或组织）重新命名（或包装），重塑……的形象

refurbish [ˌri:'fə:biʃ] vt. 刷新，使重新干净

fascinating ['fæsineitiŋ] adj. 迷人的，使人神魂颠倒的 v. 使……陶醉（fascinate 的 ing 形式）

celebrity [sə'lebrəti] n. 名人，知名人士，名流，名声，名誉

iconic [ai'kɔnik] adj. 符号的，图标的，图符的，偶像的

contemporary [kən'tempərəri] adj. 当代的，现代的 n. 同代人，当代人

immersive [i'mə:siv] adj. 身临其境的，拟真的

custom-tailor ['kʌstəm'teilə] vt. 定制，定做

market to ['mɑ:kit tu:] 向……推销

innovativ ['inəveitiv] adj. 革新的，创新的，富有革新精神的，创新立异

engaging [in'geidʒiŋ] adj. 迷人的，吸引人的 v. 雇佣（engage 的 ing 形式），预订

consecutive [kən'sekjətiv] adj. 连续的，连贯的，[语] 表示结果的

concept ['kɔnsept] n. 观念，概念，观点，思想，设想，想法，总的印象

opt for [ɔpt fɔ:] v. 选择

premium ['pri:miəm] n. 额外费用，保险费，附加费 adj. 高昂的，优质的

encompass [in'kʌmpəs] vt. 围绕，包围，包含或包括某事物，完成

Exercises

1. How many cruise ships does Royal Caribbean Cruises Ltd own?
2. What's the passenger capacity of Royal Caribbean Cruises Ltd's fleet?
3. How many destinations does Royal Caribbean Cruises Ltd's fleet call on?
4. How many cruise companies are under the executive control of Royal Caribbean Cruises Ltd at present? What are they?
5. When was Azamara Club Cruises founded?
6. How many cruise ships does Celebrity Cruises consist of?
7. Which market does CDF Croisières de France provide cruise holidays for?
8. Where is the headquarter of Pullmantur Cruises?
9. Would you please list six destinations of Royal Caribbean Cruises Ltd's fleet?
10. What is the main language used onboard the cruise ships of TUI Cruises?

2.5.3 Genting Hong Kong Limited

Genting Hong Kong Limited（"Genting Hong Kong"）is a leading global leisure, entertainment and hospitality enterprise, with core competences in both land and sea-based businesses including Star Cruises in the Asia-Pacific, it's a holding company that operates cruise and resort businesses. Its cruise business is branded Star Cruises and was established in 1993. Genting Hong Kong owns 28 per cent of Miami-based Norwegian Cruise Line. Combined together, Star Cruises is the third largest cruise line in the world. In March 2015, NYK announced that it was selling Crystal Cruises to Genting Hong Kong (GHK), the owner of Star Cruises and a major shareholder in Norwegian Cruise Line Holdings. In addition, Genting Hong Kong also owns an associate "Travellers International Hotel Group, Inc." ("Travellers"). Genting Hong Kong is based in Hong Kong and is listed on the Hong Kong Stock Exchange (SEHK: 0678) and the Global Quote of the Singapore Exchange Securities Trading Limited. Genting Hong Kong has a presence in more than 20 locations worldwide with offices and representation in Australia, China, India, Indonesia, Japan, Malaysia, the Philippines, Singapore, Sweden, Taiwan, Thailand, the United Kingdom and the United States. Norwegian Cruise Line Holdings Ltd. is listed on the NASDAQ Global Select Market under the symbol "NCLH" and Travellers is listed on the Philippine Stock Exchange under the ticker "RWM".

(1) Star Cruises

Star Cruises was founded as an associate of the Genting Group of Malaysia, incorporated in Bermuda on 10 November 1993 with its corporate headquarters in Hong Kong. Now Star Cruises is a member of Genting Hong Kong, is the third largest cruise line in the world after Carnival Corporation and Royal Caribbean Cruises. Star Cruises dominates the Asia-Pacific market and is owned by Genting Hong Kong, who also owns 28% of the Norwegian Cruise Line. The company is listed on the Hong Kong Stock Exchange and the Singapore Exchange. Its services cater to Asian passengers as well as to North Americans, Europeans and Australians interested in Asian destinations, currently operating 6 cruise ships.

(2) Norwegian Cruise Line

Norwegian Cruise Line is a diversified cruise operator of leading global cruise lines that operates a combined fleet of 21 ships. Norwegian Cruise Line Corporation Ltd. (Norwegian), a wholly owned subsidiary of Norwegian Cruise Line Holdings Ltd., is an American company operating cruise ships, headquartered in Miami-Dade County, Florida. It began operations in 1966 under the name Norwegian Caribbean Line. The company is best known for its freestyle cruising concept, which means that there are no set times or seating arrangements for meals, nor is formal attire required. Norwegian is a publicly traded company with 44.1% publicly listed on NASDAQ, with major shareholders including Genting Group (28.0%), Apollo Global Management (20.0%), and TPG Capital (7.9%) as of 30 June 2014. Norwegian Cruise Line controls approximately 8% of the total worldwide share of the cruise market.

(3) Crystal Cruise Lines

Crystal Cruise Lines, most commonly referred to as Crystal Cruises, is a luxury cruise line with its headquarters in Los Angeles in the United States. The line was established in 1988 as a wholly owned subsidiary of the large Japanese shipping company Nippon Yusen Kaisha (NYK), currently operating 2 cruise ships. In March 2015, NYK announced that it was selling Crystal Cruises to Genting Hong Kong (GHK), the owner of Star Cruises and a major shareholder in Norwegian Cruise Line Holdings. The transfer was expected to close within the second quarter of 2015. Crystal Cruises is the world's leading luxury cruise provider, having earned more "World's Best" awards than any other cruise line, hotel, or resort in history. Crystal Cruises offers extensive itineraries in Europe and the Mediterranean, North America, Panama Canal, Mexican Riviera, the Caribbean, South America, the Pacific Ocean, Asia, Africa, and the Baltic, ranging from five days to approximately 100-day World Cruises and regionally-focused Grand Cruises.

(4) Travellers International Hotel Group, Inc. ("Travellers")

Travellers International Hotel Group, Inc. ("Travellers"), an associate of Genting Hong Kong, opened its first land-based attraction, Resorts World Manila, in the Philippines in August 2009. RWM is the Philippines' first one-stop, nonstop vacation spot for topnotch entertainment and world-class leisure alternatives, Resorts World Manila is located across Terminal 3 of Ninoy Aquino International Airport. It houses three hotels: Maxims Tower, Marriott Hotel Manila and Remington Hotel. The Newport Mall is part of this resort and includes the Newport Cinemas (4 high-end cinemas) and the 1, 500-seat multi-purpose Newport Performing Arts Theater.. "Travellers" is listed on the Philippine Stock Exchange in November 2013.

Notes

1. Genting Hong Kong is based in Hong Kong and is listed on the Hong Kong Stock Exchange (SEHK: 0678) and the Global Quote of the Singapore Exchange Securities Trading Limited. 云顶香港有限公司总部设在香港，在香港证券交易所上市（股份代号：0678）并列在新加坡证券交易所有限公司的全球报价上。

2. Norwegian Cruise Line Holdings Ltd. is listed on the NASDAQ Global Select Market under the symbol "NCLH" and Travellers is listed on the Philippine Stock Exchange under the ticker "RWM". 挪威邮轮控股有限公司以代码"NCLH"在纳斯达克全球精选市场上市，而达富来集团以代码"RWM"在菲律宾证券交易所上市。

3. Star Cruises was founded as an associate of the Genting Group of Malaysia, incorporated in Bermuda on 10 November 1993 with its corporate headquarter in Hong Kong. 丽星邮轮公司成立时是马来西亚云顶集团的合伙人，公司于 1993 年 11 月 10 日在百慕大群岛正式成立，总部设在香港。

4. There are no set times or seating arrangements for meals, nor is formal attire required. 用餐无固定的时间和座位安排，也不用穿正规的服装。

5. Panama Canal 巴拿马运河

6. Mexican Riviera 墨西哥里维埃拉

7. RWM is the Philippines' first one-stop, nonstop vacation spot for topnotch entertainment and world-class leisure alternatives. RWM 是菲律宾首个一站式直达的度假胜地，提供一流的娱乐和世界级的休闲选择。

8. Terminal 3 of Ninoy Aquino International Airport 阿基诺国际机场 3 航站楼

New words & expressions

core [kɔː] n. 中心，核心 vt. 去（果）核，挖去……的果心

competence ['kɔmpitəns] n. 能力，技能，相当的资产

Indonesia [ˌindəu'niːzjə] n. 印尼（东南亚岛国）

Malaysia [mə'leiʒə] 马来西亚，马来群岛

Philippines [ˌfilə'piːnz] n. （用作单）菲律宾

quote [kwəut] vt. & vi. 引述，引用 vt. 报价，引述 n. 引用，报价，引号

ticker ['tikə(r)] n. 老式的股票价格收报机，庆祝、欢迎等场合所散发的五彩纸带

associate [ə'səuʃieit] vi. 联盟，陪伴同事 n. 合伙人，伴侣，非正式会员

incorporate [in'kɔːpəreit] vt. 组成公司，包含，使具体化 vi. 包含，吸收，合并，混合

dominate ['dɔmineit] vt. & vi. 控制，在……中占首要地位 vt. 支配，施加

diversified [dai'vəːsifaid] adj. 多样化的，多种经营的

freestyle ['friːstail] n. 自由式，自选动作 adj. 自由式的，自由泳的

attire [ə'taiə(r)] n. 服装，衣服 vt. 使穿上衣服，使穿上盛装

refer to [ri'fəː tuː] 涉及，指的是，适用于，参考

provider [prə'vaidə(r)] n. 供应者，提供者，（尤指）维持家庭生计者

Extensive [iks'tensiv] adj. 广阔的，广大的，范围广泛的，[物] 广延的

Baltic ['bɔːltik] adj. 波罗的海的，波罗的海各国的

Manila [mə'nilə] n. 马尼拉

topnotch ['tɔpnɔtʃ] n. 最高度 adj. 〈口〉最高质量的，第一流的

high-end 高端

multi-purpose [ˌmʌltiː'pəːpəs, -tai-] adj. 多用途的，多功能的

Exercises

1. How many companies are under the executive control of Genting Hong Kong Limited? What are they?

2. When was Crystal Cruises sold to Genting Hong Kong Limited?

3. What's the share of Genting Hong Kong Limited in Norwegian Cruise Line Holdings?

4. How many cruise ships is Star Cruises operating now?

5. When did Norwegian Cruise Line begin operations?

6. How many cruise ships does Norwegian Cruise Line own?

7. When was Crystal Cruises established?

8. Where is Travellers International Hotel Group, Inc. located?

2.5.4 Silversea Cruises

SILVERSEA

Silversea Cruises is a privately owned luxury cruise line with its headquarters in Monaco. It pioneered all-inclusive cruising with its first ship in 1994, Silver Cloud. Silversea's co-founders, owners and operators are the Lefebvre family of Rome, Italy. As of early 2014, the company had eight boutique cruise ships, each of which carries only 100 to 540 passengers. Silversea was founded in 1993 by a joint venture made up of V-Ships (previously known as Vlasov Group) of Monaco and the Lefebvre family of Rome. The joint venturers had previously been the co-owners of Sitmar Cruises. Silversea's business model was to operate ships in the small, all-suite, ultra-luxury category. According to John Bland, Silversea's President in 1993: …we have a different ship design. It's larger, very seaworthy and very comfortable for ocean crossings--but small enough to do the things you want a small luxury vessel to do, to get into small islands where big ships can't go, to travel up rivers like the Thames. The new line's all inclusive fares included such features as gratuities (none were allowed), beverages (including selected wines at lunch and dinner), port charges, travel insurance, and one or more complimentary shore events in every itinerary.

It was announced on June 18, 2012 that Silversea acquired Canodros S. A., the premier Ecuadorian tourism company that operates in the Galapagos Islands. The purchase of the line also includes the former Renaissance ship the Galapagos Explorer Ⅱ.

Silversea provides its guests an option called Personalized Voyages, a cruise industry first. This program allows guests to choose their own embarkation and disembarkation ports, essentially allowing them to create their own voyages. Guests can board days before or days after a cruise begins, but they must sail a minimum of five nights. The onboard time is charged on a daily rate that varies depending on the ports visited and the category of suite accommodation.

2.5.5 Disney Cruise Line

Disney Cruise Line is the trading name of Magical Cruise Company Limited, which operates as a subsidiary of the Walt Disney Company. The company was incorporated in 1996

and is domiciled in London, England, with their operational headquarters located in Celebration, Florida. Disney Cruise Line currently operates four ships: *Disney Magic*, *Disney Wonder*, *Disney Dream*, and *Disney Fantasy*. Disney Cruise Line also owns Castaway Cay, a private island in the Bahamas designed as an exclusive port of call for Disney's ships. In 2012, Disney Cruise Lines owned nearly 3% share of the worldwide cruise market. Disney Cruise Line offers a variety of destinations including Europe, the Panama Canal, the Caribbean, Alaska & United States Pacific Coast, Canada and New England, The Bahamas, and transatlantic destinations. On May 18th, 2015, Disney Cruise line announced that they would be returning to New York, Galveston, and Miami.

Recognized as the leader in family cruising, It extends the standards and values that Disney is known for across the globe. This includes aggressive hospitality, its special way of treating our guests, anticipating their needs and making them feel welcome. The fleet of majestic, family-friendly cruise ships combines grand elegance with fun activities to create a magical experience. Onboard, passengers will find a complete range of modern luxuries, innovative technology and all the comforts of home. Not only will passengers have the tools and resources they need to succeed in their position, they will set sail to some extraordinary destinations-including Disney's private island paradise, Castaway Cay.

The Disney Cruise Line Values:

- Honesty
- Integrity
- Respect
- Courage
- Openness
- Diversity
- Balance
- Teamwork
- Trust
- Fun
- Quality
- Success

2.5.6 Mediterranean Shipping Cruises

MSC Cruises is a Swiss-based, global cruise company with headquarters in Geneva. It is the world's largest privately-owned cruise company, employs 15,500 people worldwide and has offices in 45 countries. MSC Cruises (Italian: MSC Crociere S. p. A.) is part of the Mediterranean Shipping Company S. A. (MSC), the world's second biggest container shipping operator. MSC Cruises is the fourth largest cruise company in the world, after Carnival Corporation & plc, Royal Caribbean Cruises Ltd. and Genting Hong Kong with a 5.2% share of all passengers carried in 2015, currently operating 12 cruise ships with four classes of Lirica, Musica, Fantasia & Seaside, and seven new cruise ships under construction. MSC was founded in 1970 as a private company by Gianluigi Aponte when he bought his first ship, Patricia, followed by Rafaela, with which Aponte began a shipping line operating between the Mediterranean and Somalia. The line subsequently expanded through the purchase of second-hand cargo ships. By 1977, the company operated services to northern Europe, Africa and the Indian Ocean. The expansion continued through the 1980s; by the end of the decade, MSC operated ships to North America and Australia. In 1989, MSC purchased the cruise ship operator Lauro Lines, renamed to Mediterranean Shipping Cruises (MSC Cruises) in 1995, and subsequently increased the cruising business. In 1994, the line ordered its first newly constructed ships, which were delivered beginning in 1996 with MSC Alexa. They were built by Italian shipbuilder, *Fincantieri*. As of October 2014, Diego Aponte (son of MSC founder Gianluigi Aponte) was named president and chief executive of MSC, taking over from his father who was named group executive chairman. Gianluigi Aponte would continue to oversee all group related activities as well as supporting Diego in shaping the future of MSC. Having grown by 800 per cent between 2004 and 2014, MSC Cruises is today the market leading cruise company in the Mediterranean, South Africa and Brazil. MSC Cruises sails year-round in the our way of life.

2.5.7 Regent Seven Seas Cruises

Regent Seven Seas Cruises (RSSC), owned by Prestige Cruise Holdings is a cruise line, formerly known as Radisson Seven Seas Cruises. It is based in Miami, was formed in 1992 as a result of the merger between two one-ship lines-Radisson Cruises and Seven Seas Cruises. The company offers luxury cruises which visit over 300 ports world-wide. Regent Seven Seas specializes in ships with small passenger capacity and many included amenities. Apollo Management, an investment group, purchased Regent Seven Seas Cruises from Carlson Cos. for $1 billion in February 2008. Apollo Investments also owns Oceania Cruises and 50% of Norwegian Cruise Line. Carlson retains ownership of the master Regent brand, along with the operations of Regent Hotels & Resorts around the world. On September 2, 2014 that Norwegian Cruise Line purchased Prestige Cruise Holdings, the parent company of Oceania Cruises and Regent Seven Seas Cruises, for $3.025 billion, so now RSSC is a subsidiary of Norwegian Cruise Line Holdings Ltd.

In contrast to other cruise lines which price the cruising experience, to some extent, a la carte, Regent Seven Seas bills its cruises as "the most all-inclusive". Base fare on Regent Seven Seas ships includes most alcoholic beverages onboard ship and most shore excursions in ports of call, as well as all gratuities that would normally be paid to hotel staff on the ship. Fare also includes one night's hotel stay before boarding and airfare to and from the cruise's origin and destination ports.

Notes

1. It pioneered all-inclusive cruising with its first ship in 1994, Silver Cloud. 1994年它率先推出了它的第一艘全包价邮轮"银云号"。

2. the Lefebvre family of Rome 罗马的勒费布尔家族

3. port charges 港口（使用）费，入港费

4. Galapagos Islands 加拉帕戈斯群岛

5. the category of suite accommodation 套房住宿类别

6. Disney Cruise Line also owns Castaway Cay, a private island in the Bahamas designed as an exclusive port of call for Disney's ships. 迪斯尼邮轮还拥有漂流岛，这是巴哈马群岛上的一个私人岛屿，专供迪斯尼的邮轮使用。

7. aggressive hospitality 热情服务

8. to succeed in their position 在他们的岗位上取得成功

9. the Indian Ocean 印度洋

10. the market leading cruise company in the Mediterranean, South Africa and Brazil 在地中海、南非和巴西市场领先的邮轮公司

11. in the our way of life 以我们的生活方式

12. many included amenities 许多包括在内的设施

13. Regent Seven Seas bills its cruises as "the most all-inclusive". 丽晶七海邮轮公司宣称它的邮轮"无所不包"。

14. shore excursions 岸上游览

15. from the cruise's origin and destination ports 从邮轮的起点到目的地港口

New words & expressions

Monaco [ˈmɔnəkəu] n. 摩纳哥（欧洲西南部国家，位于法国东南，南临地中海）

co-founder [kəuˈfaundə] n. 共同创办人，共同创始人

boutique [buːˈtiːk] n. （女士）时装店，精品店，精品店

venturer [ˈventʃərə] n. 合资控制者，冒险者，投机者

seaworthy [ˈsiːwəːði] adj. （尤指船舶）适航的

gratuity [grəˈtjuːəti] n. 报酬，小账，小费，养老金

complimentary [ˌkɔmpliˈmentri] adj. 免费赠送的，表示敬意的，赞美的，恭维的

renaissance [riˈneisns] n. 文艺复兴

essentially [iˈsenʃəli] adv. 基本上，本质上，根本上，本来

minimum [ˈminiməm] n. 最低限度，最小量，最低消费 adj. 最低的，最小的，最少的

Disney [ˈdizniː] n. 迪斯尼（美国动画影片制作家及制片人）

magical [ˈmædʒikl] adj. 魔力的，不可思议的，迷人的，神奇的

domicile [ˈdɔmisail] n. 住处，永久住处 vt. 定居

fantasy [ˈfæntəsi] n. 幻想，空想的产物，非正式的货币 vt. & vi. 想象，幻想，奏幻想曲

Bahamas [bəˈhɑːməz] n. 巴哈马群岛

exclusive [iksˈkluːsiv] adj. 专用的，高级的，排外的，单独的 n. 独家新闻，专有物

Galveston [ˈgælvəstən] 加尔维斯敦（美国得克萨斯州东南部港市）

anticipate [ænˈtisipeit] vt. 预感，预见，预料，先于……行动 vi. 预言，预测

majestic [məˈdʒestik] adj. 宏伟的，壮丽的，庄重的，磅礴

integrity [inˈtegriti] n. 正直，诚实，完整，[计算机]保存，健全

openness [ˈəupənnəs] n. 空旷，开阔，公开，率真

Geneva [dʒəˈniːvə] n. 日内瓦城（瑞士西南部城市）

container [kənˈteinə] n. 容器，箱，匣，集装箱，货柜

Somalia [səuˈmɑːliə] n. 索马里

subsequently [ˈsʌbsikwəntli] adv. 其后，随后，接着，嗣后，尔后

shipbuilder [ˈʃipbildə(r)] n. 造船业主，造船工程师，造船公司

oversee [ˌəuvəˈsiː] vt. 监督，监视，俯瞰，错过，宽恕，省略

prestige [presˈtiːʒ] n. 威信，威望，声望，声誉，（财势的）显赫，信望

specialize in [ˈspeʃəlaiz in] 专攻，精通，以……为专业，专修

Apollo [əˈpɔləu] n. 阿波罗，太阳神，〈诗〉太阳，美男子

Oceania [ˌəuʃiˈæniːə, -ˈeiniːə, -ˈɑːniːə] n. 大洋洲，澳洲

in contrast to [in ˈkɔntræst tuː] 相比之下

bill [bil] n. 账单，钞票，清单，广告 vt. 给……开账单，为……发提（货）单，把……登录在账

airfare [ˈeəfeə(r)] n. 飞机票价

Exercises

1. How many cruise ships does Silversea Cruises own at present? What are the passenger capacity of these cruise ships?

2. Please list five characteristics of Silversea Cruises' cruise ships.

3. What are the main contents of Silversea Cruises' Personalized Voyages?

4. When was Disney Cruise Line incorporated? How many cruise ships does it have at present?

5. What are the values of Disney Cruise Line?

6. Which cruise ship corporation is the fourth largest one in the world?
7. What's the share of MSC Cruises in all cruise ship passengers of the world carried in 2015?
8. What's the former name of Regent Seven Seas Cruises?
9. What kind of cruise ships does Regent Seven Seas Cruises specialize in?

2.6 Where Do Passengers Mainly Come From

Generally speaking, most of cruise ships' passengers come from North America, Europe, East Asia, etc. According to the statistics of CLIA, the cruise ship passengers amount to 23 millions in the world in 2014, among which 11.3 millions come from the USA. In recent years, China's cruise passengers are increasing very rapidly, reaching to 1.4 millions person times and ranking the seventh all over the world in 2014. According to the forecasting of Shanghai International Shipping Research Center, the cruise ship passengers of China will reach to 8 to 10 millions, becoming the largest cruise ship market in 2030.

2.7 Where Do Passengers Like to Travel to

2.7.1 Mediterranean

It is located at the junction of Europe, Africa and Asia. Along the Mediterranean, the passengers can enjoy a lot of famous scenic spots, local people's customs and stories, for example:

(1) Sicily is famous for its Mafia story;
(2) Barcelona is famous for its bull fight;
(3) Monaco is famous for its casino;
(4) Rome is famous for its gladiator;
(5) Pisa is famous for its Pisa Tower.

2.7.2 Canary Islands

They are a series of small islands located in the northeast of the Atlantic Ocean and on the northwest of Africa, some belong to Spain, some belong to Portugal, they are ideal interesting places for spending winter holidays.

2.7.3 Scandinavia

It's in the north west of Europe including the countries Denmark, Norway, Sweden and Iceland.

2.7.4 The Caribbean Sea

It is located at the junction of America, Mexico and some other Carribbean countries.

A lot of cruise ship operators establish their headquarters in the port city Miami of Florida Peninsular.

2.7.5 Alaska

It's one state of the United States located in the north west of North America.

2.8 The Cruise Ship Employment

Now the international cruise ship industry is developing very fast, a lot of employees have already been employed in this industry, more and more new employees are needed in this industry.

No other job markets have been growing so rapidly in the past ten years as the cruise line jobs. Just for the last four years all leading cruise lines have doubled their fleets and number of employees. Many new cruise ship lines have emerged trying to get their share from the cruise market explosion. With all the cruise ships currently under construction the number of cruise lines employees worldwide is expected to triple by the year 2015. A cruise ship is a self-contained floating community that supplies pleasures and services for many passengers. There are hundreds of jobs and skills required to keep a cruise ship operational. Cruise lines hire employees all year round, the majority of these employees are hotel staff (crew) . They are looking for highly motivated, energetic, outgoing, friendly and professional employees with a positive attitude and strong commitment to customer service excellence. Contracts duration vary between 3 and 9 months and in most cases you have the option to extend the contract. Compared to other industries, cruise lines have a much higher employees turnover rate. Most people do not consider cruise line jobs as life-long career, some crew members get promoted, change ships or cruise lines, go on vacation, return to school, or just settle down back on land. For that and many other reasons cruise lines are always hiring and looking for new personnel. Cruise lines hire applicants from almost every country in the world.

2.9 Who Works Where

The cruise ship mainly consists of administration department, deck department, engine department, entertainment department, medical department and hotel department, different department has different number of staff, their rates are as follows:

1. Administration Department 3.49%
2. Deck Department 6.46%
3. Engine Department 9.63%
4. Entertainment Department 9.95%
5. Medical Department 0.32%

6. Hotel Department 70.15%

From the above rates, we can see most of the staff on the cruise ship are hotel staff (crew).

Notes

1. according to the statistics of CLIA 根据国际邮轮协会的统计

2. person times 人次

3. Shanghai International Shipping Research Center 上海国际航运研究中心

4. the junction of Europe, Africa and Asia 欧、亚、非三洲的交汇处

5. Just for the last four years all leading cruise lines have doubled their fleets and number of employees. 就在过去的四年里，所有领先的邮轮公司已经将船队和员工数量增加了一倍。

6. the cruise market explosion 邮轮市场扩张

7. a self-contained floating community 一个独立的流动社区

8. a positive attitude and strong commitment to customer service excellence 一个对优质客户服务的积极态度和强烈的责任感。

9. contracts duration 合同期

10. to extend the contract 延长合同

11. a much higher employees turnover rate 一个高得多的员工流动率

12. life-long career 终身职业

13. go on vacation 去度假

14. settle down back on land 在陆地上定居下来

15. administration department 行政部门

16. deck department 甲板部

17. engine department 轮机部

New words & expressions

amount to [ə'maunt tuː] 共计，意味着，发展成，折合

Mediterranean ['meditə'reinjən] n. 地中海，地中海沿岸的居民 . adj. 地中海的，地中海民族的

Canary Islands 加那利群岛（大西洋东北部）

Scandinavia ['skændi'neivjə, -viə] 斯堪的纳维亚（半岛）（瑞典、挪威、丹麦、冰岛的泛称）

Caribbean [kæri'bi(ː)ən] n. 加勒比海

Alaska [ə'læskə] n. 阿拉斯加州（美国州名）

Florida ['flɔridə] n. 佛罗里达（美国州名）

peninsular [pi'ninsjulə] n. 住在半岛上的居民 adj. 半岛（状）的（居民），形成半岛的

Miami ['mai'æmi] n. 迈阿密（美国佛罗里达州东南港市）

Mafia ['mæfiə; (us)'maːfiə] n. 黑手党，秘密政党

Barcelona [ˌbaːsi'ləunə] n. 巴塞罗纳（西班牙东北部港市）

Monaco ['mɔnəkəu] n. 摩纳哥（欧洲西南部国家，位于法国东南，南临地中海）

casino [kə'siːnəu] n. 娱乐场（供表演跳舞、赌博的地方），一种由二至四人玩的纸牌游戏

gladiator ['glædieitə] n. 古罗马公开表演的格斗者，精于辩论和格斗的人，职业拳击者

Pisa [ˈpiːzə] n. 比萨（意大利中部一城市）

employee [ˌemplɔiˈiː, imˈplɔii] n. 职工，雇员，店员

emerge [iˈməːdʒ] vi. 出现，浮现，暴露，摆脱

hire [ˈhaiə] vt. 聘用，录用，雇用 n. 租金，酬金，工钱

motivated [ˈməutiveitid] adj. 有动机的，有目的的 v. 作为……的动机，激发

energetic [ˌenəˈdʒetik] adj. 精力充沛的，充满活力的，精力旺盛的，有力的

outgoing [ˈautgəuiŋ] adj. 对人友好的，开朗的，出发的，乐于助人的，即将离职的

turnover [ˈtɜːnəuvə(r)] n. 周转，翻滚，翻倒，弄翻，营业额，成交量

applicant [ˈæplikənt] n. 申请人，求职人，请求者

personnel [ˌpəːsəˈnel] n. 人员，职员

administration [ədminisˈtreiʃən] n. 管理，经营，行政部门

Exercises

1. How many does the cruise ship passengers of the world amount to in 2014?
2. How many person times does China's cruise ship passengers reach to in 2014?
3. Where do passengers of the cruise ships mainly come from?
4. Where do passengers like to travel to?
5. Would you please list five interesting places and their interesting programs?
6. What kinds of employees are cruise lines looking for?
7. For what kinds of reasons are cruise lines always hiring and looking for new personnel?
8. What's the rate of staff and crew of the hotel department on the cruise ship?

2.10 The Benefits & Challenges of "Life at Sea"

2.10.1 Benefits of "Life at Sea"

(1) What does cruising mean to passengers?

Taking a cruise ship, the passengers can get a lot of benefits, for example:

① Enjoy luxurious surroundings;

② Meet new friends;

③ Enjoy fantastic scenery;

④ Enjoy entertainment galore including casino, cabaret show, sport, etc.

⑤ Relax themselves completely;

⑥ Value for their money;

⑦ Enjoy super food;

⑧ Enjoy exciting destinations;

⑨ Enjoy first class service.

(2) What are the benefits for cruise ship employees?

Working on the cruise ship, cruise ship employees usually can get a lot of benefits, for example:

① Travel the world;

② Meet new friends;

③ Obtain new experiences;

④ Save money;

⑤ Enjoy ship's facilities including crew gym, beauty room, crew club, etc. ;

⑥ Learn a lot of new skills;

⑦ Have free board & lodging, usually either a single stateroom or a shared stateroom with another employee;

⑧ Enjoy exciting destinations;

⑨ Have excellent opportunities of promotion;

⑩ Free air travel to and fro;

⑪ Free laundry;

⑫ Free medical insurance (which is required by maritime law);

⑬ Discounts at cruise ship stores and often at land based stores, bars and restaurants;

⑭ Reduced price cruise vacations for family, relatives and friends.

2.10.2 Challenges of "Life at Sea"

Although cruise ship employees can get a lot of benefits on the cruise ship, in the meantime you must face many challenges at sea, for example:

(1) Semi-military life You must be used to the semi-military life on the cruise ship. The time for working, meeting, eating, sleeping, drinking, having a break and even going ashore, etc. is ruled strictly, you must proceed all of these strictly according to time table, quite different from our daily life ashore.

(2) Seasickness Sometimes you will feel dizzy on board, don't want to eat and don't dare to eat and drink because of disgusting and vomiting caused by seasickness, in the meantime you must insist on working, but generally speaking, you can overcome these after some time.

(3) Eating Whether you like foreign food or not, you must get used to eating it, because no special Chinese food is offered for you.

(4) Sleeping Probably you will share rooms with some foreigners, you must overcome different sleeping habits, times, etc.

(5) Working A job on a cruise ship is a job with greater impact than most people think. Not just because of the long hours and hard work. It's a job that is hard to get away from. How many people sleep in the office or the factory after a hard day's work? That's exactly what cruise ship employees do. Home is work, work is home. There is no 9 to 5. There even aren't any weekends. But there are always passengers. Working on a cruise ship, makes you part of a team that has just one goal: five star service to the passengers. You should be able to speak good English, be prepared to work hard, be very dedicated and have passion for what you do. It takes a special kind of people who are able to cope with that.

(6) Different culture and religions Different culture and religions sometimes may cause misunderstanding and discrimination between us and some foreigners.

(7) Professionalism While it's not always easy to maintain professionalism through long hours of work, the management will expect you not only to take pride in your work but also to excel in your service every day.

(8) Appearance You don't mind a loose button? You like to shave once every three days? Get a job somewhere else. Like the rest of the hospitality industry, appearance is of utmost significance to your employers. You will be expected as an employee of the ship to be well turned out every single day of the tenure of your contract. Especially if you are to be in contact with the passengers.

(9) Keeping smile Not withstanding long hours and back breaking jobs, you will be required to provide service with a smile, a big smile. Your duty as a staff member on board includes making the passengers feel welcome and a cheerful face and pleasant attitude are its basic ingredients.

(10) Homeless You can't be there when a relative celebrates a birthday. You won't be at your sisters graduation. You might even be thousands miles away when your firstborn makes its first steps. There is no going home after a long day. The cruise ship is your home and the crew is your family as long as the voyage lasts.

When you are up to the above challenges, working on a cruise ship may be a perfect career choice. If you do this, you will have the experience of a lifetime.

Notes

1. Enjoy luxurious surroundings 享受奢华的环境
2. Value for their money 钱有所值
3. Enjoy entertainment galore 享受娱乐一应俱全
4. Free air travel to and fro 免费往返的航空旅行
5. Free laundry 免费洗衣服务
6. Semi-military life 半军事化生活
7. time table 时刻表
8. It's a job that is hard to get away from. 这是一个很难离开的工作。
9. be very dedicated and have passion for what you do 对你所做的工作要很有热情并具有奉献精神
10. to take pride in your work 对你的工作感到自豪
11. to be well turned out every single day of the tenure of your contract 在合同期的每一天要打扮得漂亮点
12. withstanding long hours and back breaking jobs 承受长时间的工作和劳累
13. You might even be thousands miles away when your firstborn makes its first steps. 当你的初生儿刚学走路的时候，你可能远在千里之外。
14. When you are up to the above challenges 当你能克服上述挑战的时候

New words& expressions

benefit [ˈbenifit] n. 利益，好处 vt. 有益于，有助于 vi. 受益

luxurious [lʌgˈzjuəriəs] adj. 奢侈的，豪华的

fantastic [fænˈtæstik] adj. 幻想的，奇异的，稀奇古怪的，荒谬的，空想的

galore [gəˈlɔː,-ˈlɔə] adv. 丰富地

cabaret [ˈkæbəret, ˈkæbərei] n. (有音乐，歌舞表演的) 酒店，酒店的歌舞表演

lodging [ˈlɔdʒiŋ] n. 寄宿处，寄宿，(通常用复数) 出租的房间、住房

stateroom [ˈsteitruːm] n. [船] 特等客舱，[火车] 高级包厢，政府公寓

promotion [prəˈməuʃən] n. 促进，发扬，提升，提拔，晋升

opportunity [ˌɔpəˈtjuːniti] n. 机会，时机

to and fro 往返

laundry [ˈlɔːndri] n. 洗衣店，要洗的衣服，洗熨

insurance [inˈʃuərəns] n. 保险，保险单，保险业，保险费

discount [ˈdiskaunt] n. 折扣

challenge [ˈtʃælindʒ] n. 挑战 vt. 向……挑战

proceed [prəˈsiːd] vi. 进行，继续下去，发生

disgust [disˈgʌst] n. 厌恶，嫌恶 vi. 令人厌恶，令人反感 vt. 使作呕

vomit [ˈvɔmit] n. 呕吐，呕吐物，催吐剂 vi. 呕吐，大量喷出 vt. 吐出，呕吐

impact [ˈimpækt] n. 碰撞，冲击，冲突，影响 vt. 撞击，对……发生影响

dedicated [ˈdedikeitid] adj. 专注的，献身的

passion [ˈpæʃən] n. 激情，热情

cope with (善于) 应付，(善于) 处理

discrimination [disˌkrimiˈneiʃən] n. 辨别，区别，识别力，辨别力，歧视

professionalism [prəˈfeʃənəˌlizəm] n. 职业特性，职业作风，专家的地位

management [ˈmænidʒmənt] n. 经营，管理，处理，操纵，驾驶，手段

take pride in 以……自豪，对……感到满意

excel [ikˈsel] v. 优秀，胜过他人

appearance [əˈpiərəns] n. 仪表，出现，露面，外貌，外观

the hospitality industry 招待业

utmost [ˈʌtməust] n. 极限，最大可能，极力 adj. 极度的，最远的

turn out 打扮

tenure [ˈtenjuə] n. (土地等的) 使用和占有，任期，(土地) 使用期限

withstand [wiðˈstænd] vt. 抵挡，经受住

ingredient [inˈgriːdiənt] n. 成分，因素

graduation [ˌgrædiuˈeiʃən] n. 毕业，毕业典礼，刻度，分等级

firstborn [ˈfəːstbɔːn] adj. 头生的 (子女)，初生的 n. 初生儿，长男，长女

voyage [ˈvɔidʒ] n. 航程，航空 vi. 航海，航行 vt. 渡过，飞过

Exercises

1. What are the benefits of “life at sea” for passengers?
2. What are the benefits of “life at sea” for cruise ship employees?
3. What are the challenges of “life at sea” for cruise ship employees? Please list six points.
4. How to be professional on board the cruise ships?
5. Would you please tell your understanding for working on board cruise ships?

Part 3

Working on the Cruise Ship

3.1 Ship's Terminology

3.1.1 Ship's View & Terms

(1) The pictures of different ships

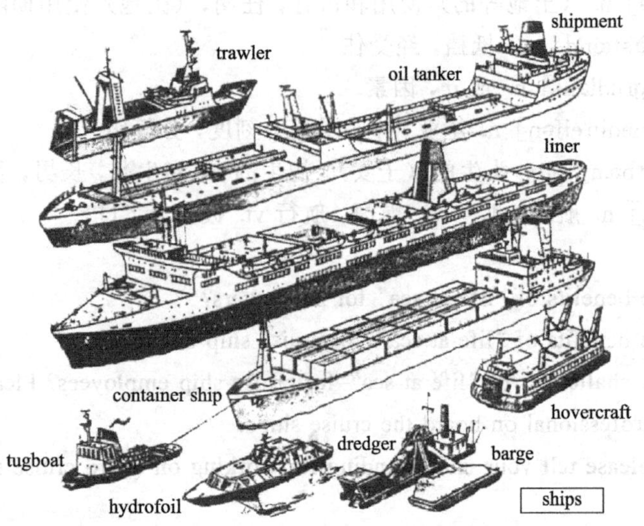

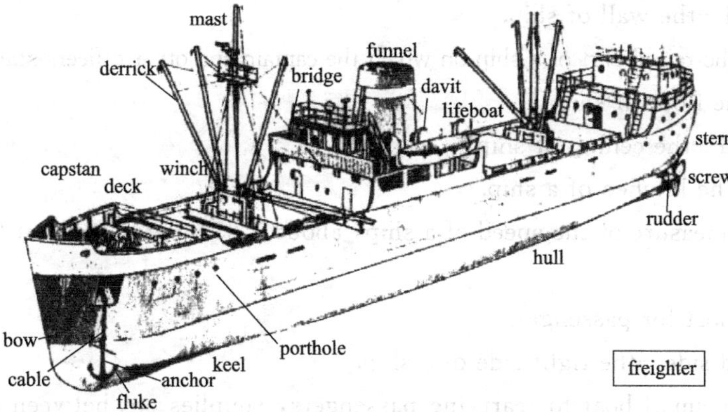

(2) The external and internal view of a cruise ship

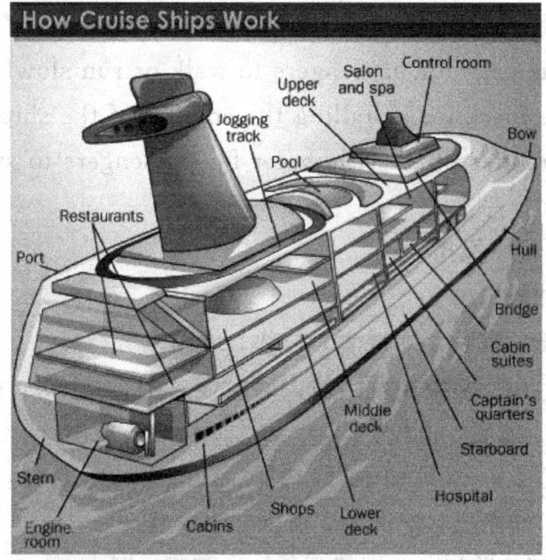

(3) The terms of the cruise ship

① bow—the forward part of a ship.

② stern—the back end of a ship.

③ mooring line—the line used for fastening a ship to land.

④ anchor—a piece of heavy metal, usu. a hook with two arms, at the end of a chain or rope, for lowering into the water to keep a ship from moving.

⑤ navigation bridge—the raised part of a ship on which the captain and other officers stand when on duty.

⑥ mast—a long upright pole of wood or metal for carrying flags or sails for ship.

⑦ funnel—a metal chimney for letting out smoke from a steam engine or steamship.

⑧ lifeboat—one of the small boats carried by a ship for escape in case of wreck, fire, etc.

⑨ gangway—an opening in the side of a ship and the movable board (gangplank) which is used to make a bridge from it to the land.

⑩ hull—the main body of the ship.

⑪ portholes—a small usu. circular window or opening in a ship for light or air.

⑫ windows—a space in a wall, esp. in a house, to let in light and air, which can be opened.

⑬ AFT—the rear of ship.

⑭ bulkhcad—the wall of ship.

⑮ bridge—the raised part of a ship on which the captain and other officers stand when on duty.

⑯ deck—the floor of ship.

⑰ Deckhead—the ceiling of ship.

⑱ galley—the kitchen of a ship.

⑲ knot—a measure of the speed of a ship, about 1.853 meters (about 6, 080feet) per hour.

⑳ PAX—short for passenger.

㉑ starboard side—the right side of a ship.

㉒ tender—a small boat for carrying passengers, supplies etc. between the shore and a larger boat.

㉓ port side—the left side of a ship.

㉔ jogging track—the path for passengers to walk or run slowly and steadily.

㉕ engine room—the place for installing the engines of the ship.

㉖ pool—a large container filled with water for passengers to swim on board.

New words & expressions

trawler [ˈtrɔːlə] n. [渔] 拖捞船

tanker [ˈtæŋkə] n. 油轮

liner [ˈlainə] n. 〈美〉班机，划线者，衬垫，班船

container [kənˈteinə] n. 容器（箱，盆，罐，壶，桶，坛子），集装箱

tugboat [ˈtʌgbəut] n. 拖船，拖轮

hovercraft [ˈhɔvəkrɑːft] n. 水翼船 n. 气垫船

dredger [ˈdredʒə] n. 挖泥机，挖泥船，捞网，撒粉器

barge [bɑːdʒ] n. 驳船，游艇 vt. 用船运输 vi. 蹒跚，闯入

hydrofoil [ˈhaidrəuˌfɔil] n. 水翼，水翼艇

freighter [ˈfreitə] n. 货船

derrick [ˈderik] n. 起重机，（钻井）井口上的铁架塔

winch [wintʃ] n. 绞盘

capstan [ˈkæpstən] n. 绞盘，起锚机

funnel [ˈfʌnəl] n. 漏斗，烟囱

davit [ˈdævit] n. 吊艇柱，吊柱

fluke [fluːk] v. 侥幸成功，意外受挫 n. 锚爪，意外的挫折，侥幸，倒霉

anchor [ˈæŋkə] n. 锚 v. 抛锚，锚定

keel [kiːl] n. 龙骨（船的脊骨），平底船 vt. 装以龙骨，使倾覆 vi. 倾覆

porthole [ˈpɔːthəul] n. 舷窗

hull [hʌl] n. （果实等的）外壳，船体

rudder [ˈrʌdə] n. 舵，方向舵

screw [skruː] n. 螺丝钉，螺旋，螺杆，螺孔，螺旋桨，吝啬鬼 vt. 调节，旋，vi. 转动，旋，拧

stern [stəːn] 船尾

gangway [ˈgæŋwei] n. 过道，（剧场，火车等）座间通道，（美国作 aisle）舷侧门，舷梯，跳板

bow [bau] n. 弓，乐弓，弓形，鞠躬，船首 v. 鞠躬，弯腰

portside n. 左舷，码头区 adj. 左边的，[美俚] 惯用左手的

starboard side 右舷

bulkhead [ˈbʌlkhed] n. 隔壁，防水壁

bridge [bridʒ] n. 桥，船桥，鼻梁，桥牌 vt. 架桥，渡过

deck [dek] n. 甲板，舰板，覆盖物，一副（纸牌）vt. 装饰，修饰，打扮，装甲板

deckhead [ˈdekhed] n. 头顶上之甲板，船舱之天花板

knot [nɔt] n. （绳等的）结，（树的）节，节（船速，=哩/小时）v. 打结

tender [ˈtendə] adj. 嫩的，温柔的，软弱的

jog [dʒɔg] n. 轻推，轻撞，漫步 v. 轻推，（使）蹒跚行进，（使）慢跑

track [træk] n. 轨迹，航迹，足迹，路 vt. 循路而行 vi. 追踪，走

quarter [ˈkwɔːtə] n. 四分之一，方向，地区 num. 四分之一，刻

Exercises

1. What's the bow?
2. What's the stern?
3. What's navigation bridge?
4. What's funnel?
5. What's gangway?
6. What's porthole?
7. What does AFT mean?
8. What does bulkhead mean?
9. What does knot mean?
10. What's tender?
11. What does bridge mean here?
12. What's jogging track on board?

3.1.2 The Terms about the Galley Line During Meal Service

① cook's hat specially used by cook in order to prevent cook's hair and sweat from falling into the food.

② cook's jacket—cook's uniform for working.

③ soup bowls—the bowls for holding soup.

④ plate covers—the covers for covering the plates to keep food clean and hot.

⑤ overhead heaters—an overhanging machine for heating air or water.

⑥ service counter—a narrow table or flat surface used for offering services.

⑦ bain marie—also known as a double-boiler, is a type of pot used to heat substances to a controlled temperature. It is useful in applications in which overheating must be prevented to yield desirable results.

⑧ No Smoking Notice—the notice for warning not to smoke.

⑨ notice board—a board on a wall which notices may be fixed to.

⑩ cooking tray—the tray used for cooking juicy foods such as tuna fish in the galley.

⑪ plastic gloves—a kind of gloves, used for protecting hand and keeping food clean.

⑫ waiter or restaurant steward—one of a number of men who serves passengers in the restaurant.

⑬ water fountain—a kind of device for drinking water.

⑭ service cook—the cook for offering service in the galley.

⑮ tray runner—a kind of equipment on which tray can slide.

⑯ plate's cover—the cover used for covering the plate to keep food clean and hot.

⑰ tray—a flat piece of wood or metal with raised edges used for carrying small articles, esp. cups, plates, food, etc..

⑱ galley—the kitchen of a ship.

⑲ fire sprinkler—a system of fire protection inside a building with water openings which are turned on by high heat.

⑳ ventilator—any arrangement or apparatus used for the passing of fresh air into and around a room, building, etc..

㉑ hot cupboard—the important pieces of equipment for any busy kitchen, capable of holding bulk food, plated meals or heating plates.

New words & expressions

counter [ˈkauntə] n. 计算器，计数器，计算者，柜台，筹码 adv. 相反地

overhead [ˈəuvəhed] adj. 在头上的，高架的 n. 天花板 adv. 在头顶上，在空中，在高处

stack [stæk] n. 堆，一堆，堆栈 v. 堆叠

notice board 布告牌

boiler [ˈbɔilə] n. 煮器（锅，壶的统称），汽锅，锅炉

substance [ˈsʌbstəns] n. 物质，实质，主旨

temperature [ˈtempritʃə(r)] n. 温度

application [ˌæpliˈkeiʃən] n. 请求，申请，申请表，应用，运用，应用程序

overheat [ˌəuvəˈhiːt] vt. 使过热 vi. 变得过热

yield [jiːld] v. 出产，生长，生产 vi. (～ to) 屈服，屈从 n. 产量，收益

desirable [di'zaiərəbl] adj. 值得要的，合意的，令人想要的，悦人心意的

tuna ['tju:nə] n. 金枪鱼 n. [动] 鲔鱼

steward ['stjuəd] n. （轮船，飞机等）乘务员，干事

bain marie [ˌbæn mə'ri:] n. 双重蒸锅，水浴，双重蒸锅，水浴器

runner [rʌnə(r)] n. 奔跑者，信使

sprinkler ['spriŋklə] n. 洒水车，洒水装置

ventilator ['ventileitə] n. 通风设备，空调机

galley ['gæli] n. 狭长船，大型划船，船上厨房，（印刷用的）长方活字盘，军舰

Exercises

1. What's the overhead heater?
2. What's the plate cover?
3. What's the bain marie?
4. What's the tray runner?
5. What's the water fountain?
6. What's the fire sprinkler?
7. What's the ventilator?
8. What's the hot cupboard?

3.1.3 About the Dining Room

(1) The terms about food service and buffet tables

① steward—means buffet assistant here.

② sneeze plate (guard)—an equipment used for protecting the food on the counter from a customer's nasal and oral discharges when the customer sneezes, particularly adapted for use in connection with a cafeteria style food service counter.

③ ice well—a trough filled with ice for keeping food and beverages cold.

④ sliced cucumber—the cucumber which are cut into slices.

⑤ mixed salad—a mixture of foods, usu. mainly vegetables, served cold and sometimes, esp, when other foods are added as the main dish at a meal: a green salad (=mostly of lettuce) .

⑥ cook's hat—used for covering cook's head to prevent the cook's hair and sweat into the food.

⑦ buffet plates—the plates for getting buffet food.

⑧ service cook—the cook for offering services in the galley.

⑨ small hat—the same as cook's hat.

⑩ plate—a flat, usu. round dish with a slightly raised edge from which food is eaten or served.

⑪ individual condiments—different powders or liquids used for giving a special taste to food.

⑫ hot roast meat—the meat cooked by dry heat, either in front of an open fire or in a hot iron box (oven).

⑬ cook's jacket—cook's unifom.

⑭ heat lamps—the lamps used for heating.

⑮ gravy—hot sauce.

⑯ carving knife and fork—the knife used for cutting in order to make a special shape; fork is an instrument for holding food or carrying food to the mouth, having a handle at one end with two or more points at the other, and usu. made of metal or plastic.

⑰ Heated food serving apparatus—An apparatus for both heating and serving food has both an interchangeable heat conducting food serving assembly and a heat exchange assembly

coupled to at least a portion of the interchangeable heat conducting food serving assembly.

⑱ dish cart—a cart used for holding dishes can be moved.

(2) The terms about the table set-up in the dining room

① napkin—a usu. square piece of cloth or paper used for protecting one's clothes and for cleaning one's hands and lips during a meal.

② dinner plate—used for taking food at dinner.

③ side plate—a small plate used for bread or other food that goes with a meal.

④ water glass—the glass for drinking water.

⑤ wine glass—the glass for drinking wine.

⑥ soup spoon—the spoon for drinking soup.

⑦ knife—a blade fixed in a handle used for cutting as a tool or weapon.

⑧ bread basket—a basket for holding bread.

⑨ fork—an instrument for holding food or carrying it to the mouth, having a handle at one end with two and more points at the other, and usu. made of metal or plastic.

⑩ chair—used for sitting at the table.

⑪ table cloth—a cloth for covering a table, esp. during a meal.

⑫ dessert spoon—the spoon used for eating dessert.

(3) The terms about waiter serving meal

① waiter—a person who serves food at the tables in the restaurant.

② waiter's cloth—used for taking hot plates.

③ meal—an amount of food eaten at one time.

④ wine— (any of many kinds of) alcoholic drink made from grapes.

⑤ gentleman—a man who behaves well.

⑥ lady—a woman, esp. a woman of good social position or of good manners or education.

⑦ salt and pepper—two kinds of condiments.

⑧ cocktail bar—the bar for making and offering cocktail.

⑨ tuxedo—dinner jacket.

⑩ companionway—the steps leading from the deck to the area below.

New words & expressions

sneeze [sniːz] n. 喷嚏 vi. 打喷嚏

equipment [iˈkwipmənt] n. 装备，设备，器材，装置

nasal [ˈneizəl] adj. 鼻的，鼻音的，护鼻的 n. 鼻音，鼻音字

oral [ˈɔːrəl] adj. 口头的

discharge [disˈtʃɑːdʒ] n. 流出物，排泄物，放电 vt. 卸下，放出 vi. 卸货，流注

cafeteria [ˌkæfiˈtiəriə] n. 自助餐厅

slice [slais] n. 薄片，切片，一份，部分，片段 v. 切（片）

gravy [ˈgreivi] n. 肉汁，不法利润，肉汤

roast [rəust] v. 烤，烘，烘烤，暴露于某种热力下以得温暖

apparatus [ˌæpəˈreitəs] n. 器械，设备，仪器

interchangeable [intəˈtʃeindʒəb(ə)l] adj. 可互换的

conduct [ˈkɔndʌkt, -dəkt] n. 行为，操行 v. 引导，管理，为人，传导

assembly [əˈsembli] n. 集合，装配，集会，集结，汇编

coupled [ˈkʌpld] adj 连接的，联系的

portion [ˈpɔːʃən] n. 一部分，一分

napkin [ˈnæpkin] n. 餐巾，餐巾纸，〈英〉尿布，〈美〉月经带

dessert [diˈzəːt] n. 餐后甜点

pepper [ˈpepə] n. 胡椒粉

cocktail [ˈkɔktei] n. 鸡尾酒，（第一道用杯盛的）开味食品 adj. 鸡尾酒的

condiment [ˈkɔndimənt] n. 调味品

tuxedo [tʌkˈsiːdəu] n. 男士无尾半正式晚礼服

companionway n. 升降扶梯，升降口

Exercises

1. What's the sneeze plate?

2. What's the ice well?

3. What's the heat lamps?

4. What's the gravy?
5. What's napkin?
6. What's bread basket?
7. What's tuxedo?
8. What's companionway?

3.1.4 About the Bar Set-up

① barman—also bartender, a man who serves drinks in a bar.

② spirits—an alcoholic drink (such as whisky or brandy) produced by boiling (distillation) from a weaker alcohol-containing drink or mixture.

③ Cup bar—a kind of measuring glass for drinks here.

④ highball glasses—the glasses for drinking an alcoholic drink, esp. whisky or brandy with soda.

⑤ cocktail decorations—used for making cocktail more beautiful.

⑥ mineral concentrate—the concentrated form of mineral.

⑦ waistcoat—a men's close-fitting garment without arms that reaches to the waist and is worn under the jacket of a 3-piece suit.

⑧ bow tie—a tie fastened at the front with a knot in the shape of a bow.

⑨ instruction notice—a usu. short written statement of information or directions to the public.

⑩ bar counter—a narrow table or flat surface for offering services in the bar.

⑪ cigarettes—finely cut tobacco rolled in a narrow tube of thin paper for smoking.

⑫ cocktail—a mixed alcoholic drink.

⑬ cocktail glass—used for holding short mixed drink.

⑭ orange slice—the orange which are cut into slices.

⑮ cherries—a type of small soft fleshy red, yellow, or black round fruit with a stone-like seed in the middle.

⑯ drip mat—put under a glass or a cup to absorb the drips and keep the table clean.

⑰ wine glasses—goblets for drinking wine.

⑱ umbrella—an arrangement of cloth over a folding frame with a handle, used for keeping rain off the head; Here it means a cocktail decoration shaped like an umbrella

⑲ bar counter—a narrow table or flat surface for offering services in the bar.

⑳ storage shelf—a frame for storing things.

New words & expressions

barman [ˈbɑːmən] n. 酒吧间招待员

bartender [ˈbɑːtendə(r)] n. 酒吧间销售酒精饮料的人，酒吧间男招待

alcoholic [ˌælkəˈhɔlik] adj. 含酒精的 n. 酗酒者，酒鬼

distillation [ˌdistiˈleiʃən] n. 蒸馏，蒸馏法，蒸馏物，精华，精髓

mixture [ˈmikstʃə] n. 混合，混合物，混合剂

graduate [ˈgrædjueit，-dʒueit] n. 量杯，量筒，（大学）毕业生，研究生

highball [ˈhaibɔːl] n. 掺有冰水的威士忌饮料，速度很快的火车

mineral [ˈminərəl] n. 苏打水，矿泉水，矿物，矿石

soda [ˈsəudə] n. 苏打，碳酸水

concentrate [ˈkɔnsentreit] n. 浓缩物 v. 集中，浓缩

waistcoat [ˈweistkəut] n. 〈英〉背心，马甲

garment [ˈgɑːmənt] n. 衣服，外衣，外表

cigarette [sigəˈret] n. 香烟，纸烟

tobacco [təˈbækəu] n. 烟草，烟草制品，抽烟

slice [slais] n. 薄片，切片，一份，部分，片段 v. 切（片）

fleshy [ˈfleʃi] adj. 肉的，肉体的，[植] 肉质的，丰满的

garnish [ˈgɑːniʃ] v. 装饰

surface [ˈsəːfis] n. 表面，外表，水面 adj. 表面的，肤浅的

drip mat 杯垫

goblet [ˈgɔblit] n. 高脚玻璃杯，酒杯

Exercises

1. What's spirit?
2. What's waistcoat?
3. What's cocktail?
4. What's storage shelf?
5. What's drip mat?
6. What's concentrate?
7. What are highball glasses?
8. What's bar counter?

3.1.5 The Terms about the Supply and Store of Food Products

① executive chef—the executive chef is in charge of everything related to the kitchen, including menu creation, staff management and business aspects. While the position requires extensive cooking experience and often involves actively cooking, it also involves a high level of management and business aspects of the kitchen. They can also be referred to as the "chef" or "head chef" .

② ship's storekeeper—responsible for the entire storage, ordering and distribution of all food supplies as directed by the executive chef.

③ provider—ship's supplier.

④ stores lists—the lists for recording ship's goods.

⑤ fresh vegetables—the plants for eating in good natural condition not long produced.

⑥ store pallets—the large metal plates for lifting heavy goods.

⑦ fresh fruit—a type of this object: fresh apples, oranges and grapes, etc.

⑧ porthole—the small usu. circular window or opening in a ship for light or air.

New words & expressions

executive [ig'zekjutiv] adj. 实行的，执行的，行政的 n. 执行者，经理主管人员

related [ri'leitid] adj. 叙述的，讲述的，有关系的

menu ['menjuː] n. 菜单

creation [kri'eiʃən] n. 创造，创作物

extensive [iks'tensiv] adj. 广大的，广阔的，广泛的

aspect ['æspekt] n. 样子，外表，面貌，（问题等的）方面

involve [in'vɔlv] vt. 包括，笼罩，潜心于，使陷于

be referred to 被称为……

storekeeper n. 店主，仓库保管员

distribution [ˌdistri'bjuːʃən] n. 分配，分发，配给物，销售，发送，发行

provider [prə'vaidə] n. 供给者，供应者，养家者

pallet ['pælit] n. 扁平工具，棘爪，货盘

Exercises

1. Please explain the executive chef.
2. Please explain the ship's storekeeper.
3. Please explain the store pallets.
4. What's the stores list?

3. 1. 6 About Cleaning on Board

The following terms relate to the proper way of cleaning a cruise ship's galleys, restaurants, crew mess.

(1) The terms about the cleaning of galley

① galley cleaner (utility)—do the cleaning and maintenance of assigned galley stations.

② protective hat—the hat for protecting head and food hygiene.

③ protective overalls—loose trousers often fastened over the shoulders by means of straps and worn esp. by men workers over other clothes for protection.

④ disposable apron—the apron which is intended to be used once and then thrown away.

⑤ cleaning sponge—the sponge used for cleaning.

⑥ work bench—work counter.

⑦ detergent—washing solution.

⑧ storage shelves—the shelves used for storing something.

⑨ clean garbage bin—clean dustbin.

⑩ cook—a person who prepares and cooks food.

⑪ cook's jacket—cook's uniform.

⑫ cook's trousers—cook's uniform.

⑬ cleaning cloth—the cloth used for cleaning.

⑭ plastic food tray—made of plastic used for holding food.

⑮ refrigerator door seal—a part of refrigerator door for keeping a gas or liquid in or out.

⑯ cleaning solution—a kind of chemical used for removing grease and dirt.

⑰ plastic food container—made of plastic and used for holding food.

⑱ work bench—a long worktable.

⑲ shelf support—the shelf which bears the weight of something.

(2) The terms about the plate house of galley

① dishwasher/pot washer—do the cleaning and stacking of all galley and passengers dishes, pots, pans etc..

② protective overalls—loose trousers often fastened over the shoulders by means of straps and worn esp. by men workers over other clothes for protection.

③ protective rubber gloves—made of rubber and used for protecting hand.

④ pre-wash spray—a spray with a high pressure.

⑤ plate—a flat, usu. round dish with a slightly raised edge from which food is eaten or served.

⑥ crockery rack—a framework with bars, hooks, etc., for holding plates and cups etc..

⑦ clean crockery—clean cups, plates, pots etc., esp. made from baked earth.

⑧ automatic dishwasher—a kind of machine which can wash dishes automatically.

⑨ detergent dispenser—a container from which detergent can be obtained by pushing or by pressing a handle.

(3) The terms about the three buckets, three sinks or pots wash systems

① wash bucket—the bucket used for removing grease and dirt.

② rinse bucket—the bucket used for washing in clean water so as to take away soap, dirt, etc..

③ sanitizing bucket—the bucket used for reducing microorganisms to a safe level.

④ wash bench—a long worktable used for washing.

⑤ tiled deck—the deck covered with tiles.

⑥ scupper—drain.

⑦ waste food disposal—the treatment of waste food.

⑧ washing sink—a large basin for washing.

⑨ rinse sink—a large basin for rinsing.

⑩ sanitizing sink—a large basin for sanitizing.

⑪ detergent dispenser—a container from which detergent can be obtained by pushing or by pressing a handle.

⑫ storage shelf—used for storing clean or dirty utensils.

⑬ gastronome tray—a kind of container used for food cooking.

New words & expressions

overall [ˈəuvərɔːl] adj. 全部的，全面的 n. [复] 工装裤

apron [ˈeiprən] n. 围裙，外表或作用类似围裙的东西，[机] 挡板，护坦

detergent [diˈtəːdʒənt] n. 清洁剂，去垢剂

utility [juːˈtiliti] n. 杂务，效用，有用

maintenance [ˈmeintinəns] n. 维护，保持，生活费用，扶养

assign [əˈsain] vt. 分配，指派 v. 赋值

protective [prəˈtektiv] adj. 给予保护的，保护的

hygiene [ˈhaidʒiːn] n. 卫生，卫生学

disposable [disˈpəuzəbl] adj. 可任意使用的

intend [inˈtend] vt. 想要，打算，意指，意谓

throw away 丢掉

counter [ˈkauntə] n. 计算器，计数器，柜台 adv. prep. 相反地

refrigerator [riˈfridʒəreitə] n. 电冰箱，冷藏库

seal [siːl] n. 封铅，封条，印 vt. 封，密封 n. 海豹，海豹毛皮

worktable [ˈwəːkteibl] n. 工作台，(有抽屉的) 缝纫桌

stack [stæk] n. 堆，一堆，堆栈 v. 堆叠

pan [pæn] n. 平底锅，盘子，面板

strap [stræp] n. 带，皮带 vt. 用带缚住，用带捆扎

pressure ['preʃə(r)] n. 压，压力，电压，压迫，强制，紧迫

bake [beik] v. 烘焙，烤，烧硬

framework ['freimwəːk] n. 构架，框架，结构

crockery ['krɔkəri] n. 陶器，瓦器

dispenser [dis'pensə] n. 分配器，药剂师，分配者，施予者，自动售货机

dishwasher ['diʃwɔʃə(r)] n. 洗碗机，洗碗的人

grease [griːs] n. 油脂，贿赂 vt. 涂脂于，〈俗〉贿赂

dirt [dəːt] n. 污垢，泥土

rack [ræk] n. 架，行李架，拷问台，小步跑，烧酒，破坏 vt. 放在架上

rinse [rins] v. （用清水）刷，冲洗掉，漂净 n. 漱洗，漂洗，漂清，冲洗

sanitize ['sænitaiz] v. 清洁

scupper ['skʌpə] n. 排水孔

drain [drein] n. 排水沟，排水 vt. 排出沟外，喝干，耗尽 vi. 排水，流干

disposal [dis'pəuzəl] n. 处理，处置，布置，安排，配置，支配

gastronome [gæ'strɔnəmi] n. 美食者，爱吃的人

sink [siŋk] vi. 沉下，（使）下沉 n. 水槽，水池，接收器

container [kən'teinə] n. 容器（箱，盆，罐，壶，桶，坛子），集装箱

Exercises

1. What does the galley cleaner do?
2. What's protective overalls?
3. What's cleaning sponge?
4. What's cleaning solution?
5. What's sanitizing solution?
6. What's pre-wash spray?
7. What's crockery?
8. What's scupper?
9. What's detergent dispenser?
10. What's gastronome tray?

3.2 Onboard Departments and Management Structure

3.2.1 Onboard Departments

The cruise ship structure is broken down into a number of different departments, these departments generally fall into the following categories.

(1) Deck Department The deck department is responsible for all safety, navigation and "driving" the ship.

(2) Engine Department The engine department is responsible for the ship's engines, water supplies and maintenance.

(3) Hotel Operations Department The hotel operations department is responsible for all the onboard hotel operation, including housekeeping, food and beverage, and reception duties. This department is in charge of all departments on board except deck and engine departments. Its main departments are as follows.

① Purser Department. Purser department is responsible for embarkation and clearance issues, front office reception, money matters of hotel departments and crew's affairs. Chief purser is in charge of the department.

② Housekeeping Department. Responsibility for the cabins or staterooms on a cruise ship fall under the housekeeping department. This division is responsible for making passengers comfortable while they are in their rooms, and includes the care of the cabins, room and messenger service, and laundry pickup and delivery.

③ Food and Beverage Department. The food and beverage division is responsible for all of the dining rooms, restaurant-bars, bars, the galleys (kitchens), cleanup and provisions. The Food and Beverage Director (Manager) runs this department.

④ Galley /Kitchen Department. Galley department is responsible for all of food preparation, dining and cleaning. The galley is usually divided into the hot galley and cold galley. The hot galley positions include all types of cooking-vegetables, fish, soup, and grill. The cold galley positions include baking, pastry, and buffets.

⑤ Cruise Staff Department. The cruise staff department is responsible for all of the activities and entertainment on board and ashore. The cruise director is in charge of the cruise staff. The size of this staff, like all of the other departments, is dependent on the size of the cruise ship.

⑥ Entertainment Department. The entertainment department is responsible for all onboard entertainment, including shows and cabarets. The cruise director is also in charge of all entertainers.

⑦ Medical Department. The medical department is responsible for the medical welfare of all passengers and crew. The department usually consists of one or two doctors and anywhere from one to four nurses depending on the onboard facilities.

⑧ Beauty Salon/Spa. The salons and spas department on board most of the luxury cruise ships offer passengers full service treatments ranging from aroma and aqua-spas, body wraps and mud baths, to facials, massages and hairdos. Some cruise lines operate the deparment themselves and some cruise lines tender out the department to some concessionaire companies.

⑨ Photo Department. The photo department is responsible for taking photos for both the passengers and crew. The skillful photographers can take various pictures for everyone, and they can also use advanced equipments to develop the films in time. Some cruise lines run their own photo department operations, some cruise lines tender out the department to some concessionaire companies.

⑩ Gift Shops Department. The gift shops department is responsible for the running of the onboard shops, which generally consist of a boutique, a cosmetic and fragrance counter, and a souvenir and gift shop. Some cruise lines operate their gift shop departments themselves and some cruise lines tender out the department to some concessionaire companies.

⑪ Casino Department. The casino onboard offers the classic shipboard games, roulette and blackjack, plus a range of slot machines. The casino is open whenever the cruise ship is at sea, it isn't permitted to open while the ship is in port. Children under the age of 18 are not permitted to enter the casino. Some cruise lines operate the deparment themselves and some cruise lines tender out the department to some concessionaire companies.

Notes

1. The cruise ship structure is broken down into a number of different departments, these departments generally fall into the following categories. 邮轮组织结构分成多个不同部门，这些部门一般分为以下几类。

2. "driving" the ship 驾驶船舶

3. water supplies and maintenance 供水和保养维修

4. room and messenger service 送餐和信使服务

5. laundry pickup and delivery 换洗衣物的收集和交还

6. cleanup and provisions 清洁和物质储备

7. hot galley and cold galley 热厨房和冷厨房

8. medical welfare 医疗福利

9. from aroma and aqua-spas, body wraps and mud baths, to facials, massages and hairdos 从香气和水温泉、身体裹泥巴浴到面部美容、按摩和做发型

10. tender out the department to some concessionaire companies 将这一部门向一些特许经营的公司招标

11. The casino onboard offers the classic shipboard games, roulette and blackjack, plus a range of slot machines. 船上赌场提供经典的游戏、轮盘赌和 21 点，还有一系列老虎机。

New words& expressions

break down v. 毁掉，制服，停顿，倒塌，中止，垮掉，分解，分类

category [ˈkætigəri] n. 种类，别，[逻] 范畴

responsible [risˈpɔnsəbl] adj. 有责任的，可靠的，可依赖的，负责的

maintenance [ˈmeintinəns] n. 维护，保持，生活费用，扶养

operation [ˌɔpəˈreiʃən] n. 运转，操作，实施，作用，业务，工作，手术

clearance [ˈkliərəns] n. 清洁，放行证，(船只的) 结关，出(入) 港证

housekeeping [ˈhauskiːpiŋ] n. 家务管理

beverage [ˈbevəridʒ] n. 饮料

fall under 被列为，归入…类

messenger [ˈmesindʒə] n. 报信者，使者

pickup [ˈpikʌp] n. 拾起，获得，拿取
delivery [diˈlivəri] n. 递送，交付，分娩，交货，引渡
provision [prəˈviʒən] n. 供应，（一批）供应品，预备，防备，规定
baking [ˈbeikiŋ] n. 烘焙，一次烘焙的量
pastry [ˈpeistri] n. 面粉糕饼，馅饼皮
dependent [diˈpendənt] adj. 依靠的，依赖的，由... 决定的，随... 而定的
entertainer [entəˈteinə(r)] n. 款待者，表演娱乐节目的人，演艺人员
welfare [ˈwelfɛə] n. 福利，安宁，幸福，福利事业，社会安全 adj. 福利的
entertainment [entəˈteinmənt] n. 款待，娱乐，娱乐表演
cabaret [ˈkæbəret，ˈkæbərei] n. （有音乐，歌舞表演的）酒店，酒店的歌舞表演
aroma [əˈrəumə] n. 芳香，香气，香味
aqua [ˈækwə] n. 水，溶液，水剂，水绿色，浅绿色 adj. 浅绿色的
facial [ˈfeiʃəl] n. 面部按摩，美容 adj. 面部的
hairdo [ˈheəduː] n. 〈美〉（好）发型，发式
tender out 提供，标出
concessionaire [kənˌseʃəˈnɛə] n. 受让人，特许权获得者
photographer [fəˈtɔgrəfə] n. 摄影师
boutique [buːˈtiːk] n. 专卖流行衣服的小商店
cosmetic [kɔzˈmetik] n. 化妆品 adj. 化妆用的
fragrance [ˈfreigrəns] n. 芬芳，香气，香味
salon [ˈsælɔːŋ] n. 沙龙
photographer [fəˈtɔgrəfə] n. 摄影师
casino [kəˈsiːnəu] n. 娱乐场（供表演跳舞、赌博的地方）
roulette [ru(ː)ˈlet] n. 轮盘赌，点线机，轨迹线，刻骑缝孔的齿轮
blackjack [ˈblækdʒæk] v. 以棒打，胁迫 n. 扑克牌的二十一点
slot [slɔt] n. 缝，细长的孔，硬币投币口，狭通道，足迹 vt. 开槽于，跟踪

Exercises

1. Generally speaking, how many departments is a cruise ship broken down into? What are they?
2. What are the main duties of deck department?
3. What are the main duties of entertainment department?
4. What are the main duties of hotel department?
5. What are the main duties of medical department?
6. What are the main duties of cruise staff department?
7. What are the main duties of casino department?
8. What are the main duties of beauty salon/spa department?

3.2.2 The General Management Structure

Different cruise ships have different types of management structures, the following is a typical one of them.

(1) The shipboard structure

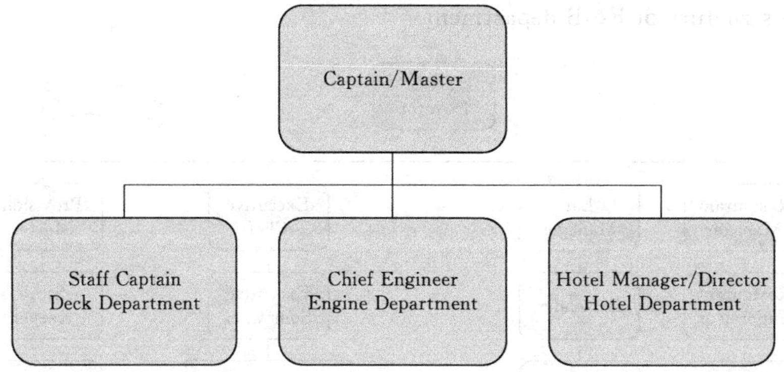

(2) The structure of hotel department

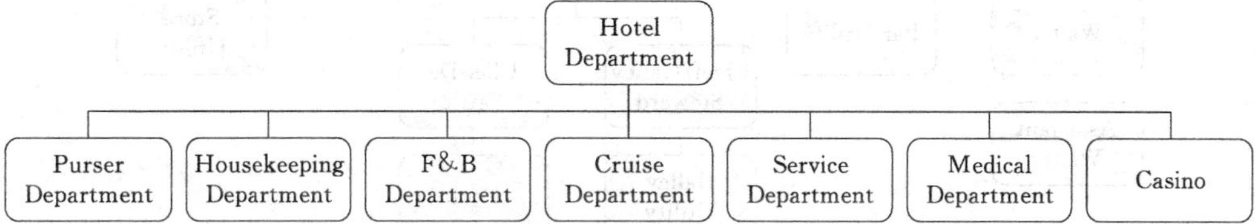

(3) The structure of purser department

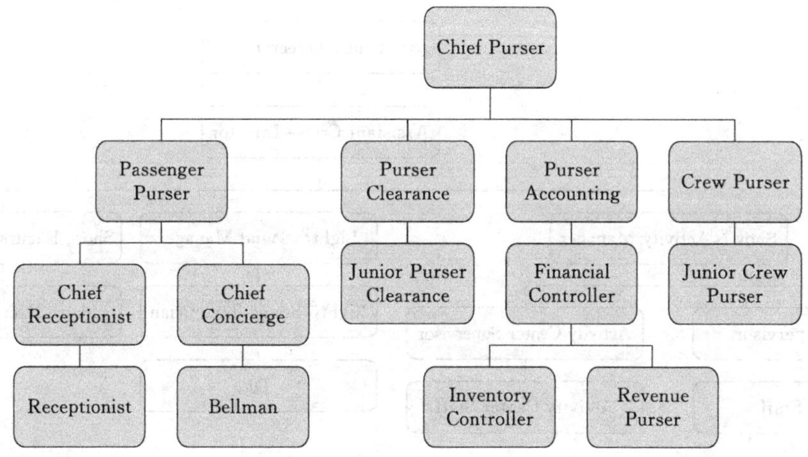

(4) The structure of housekeeping department

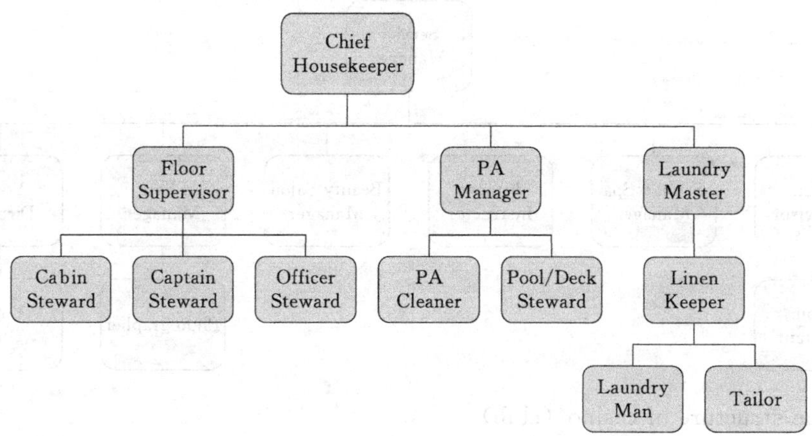

(5) The structure of F&B department

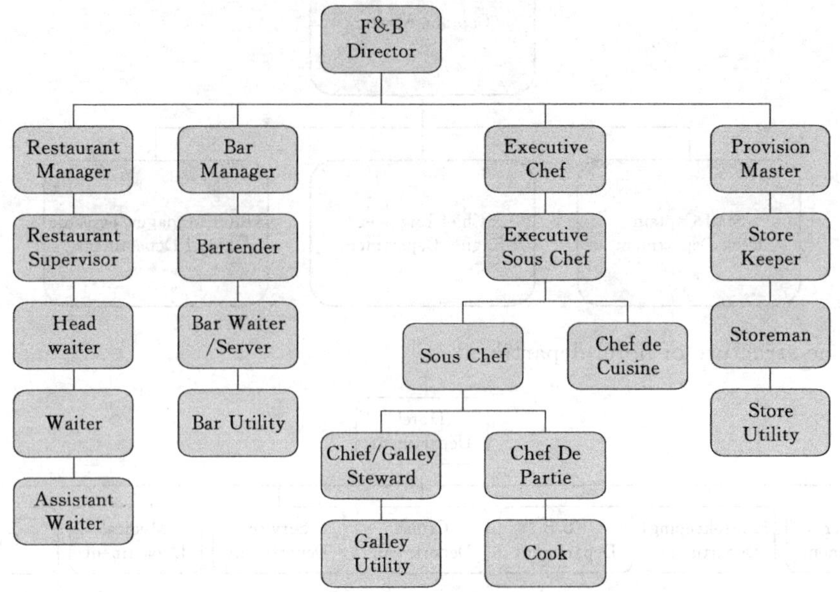

(6) The structure of cruise department

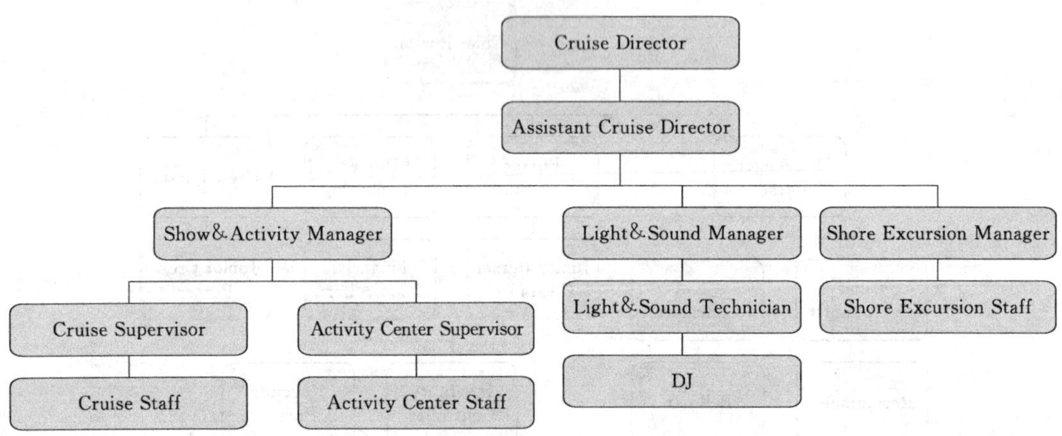

(7) The structure of service department

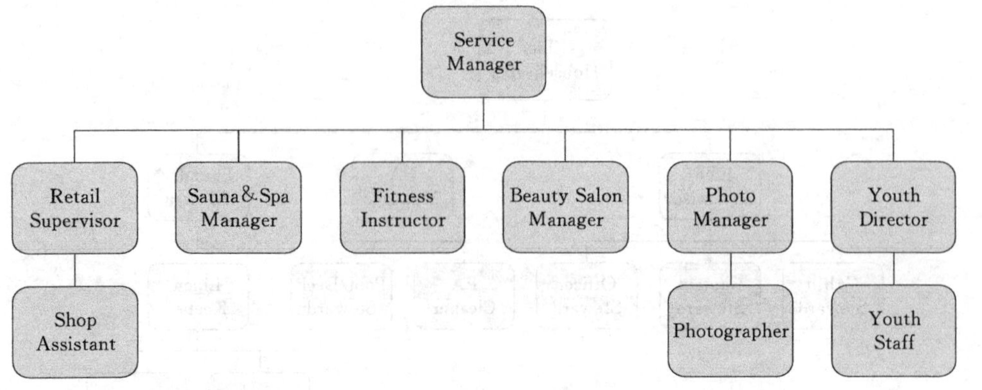

(8) The structure of casino (club)

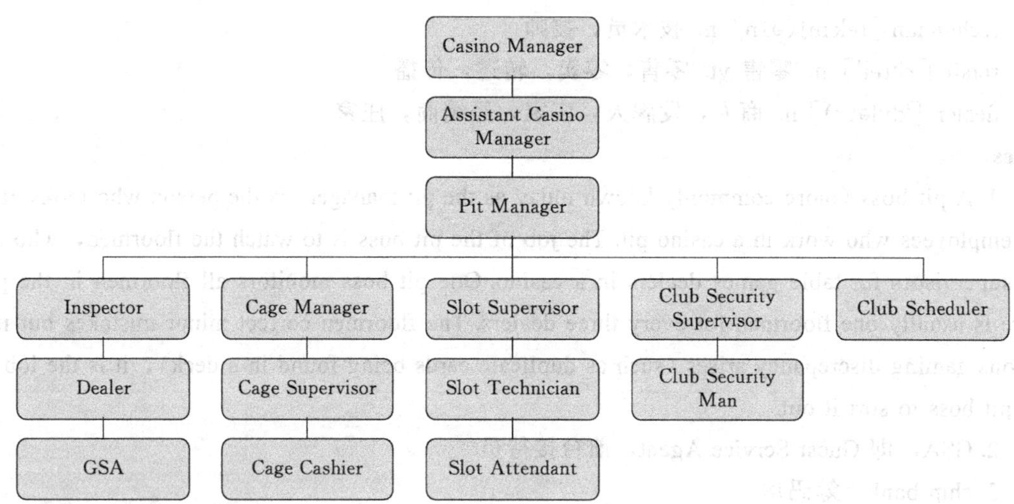

New words & expressions

master [ˈmɑːstə] n. 船长，主人，大师，硕士 adj. 主人的，熟练的，vt. 控制，精通

staff captain（大客轮上负责安全设施的）安全官，副船长

director [diˈrektə, daiˈrektə] n. 主任，主管，导演，（机关）首长，指挥仪，控制器

purser [ˈpəːsə] n. 事务长，主计官

financial controller 财务总监

inventory controller 库存控制总管

revenue purser 收益事务长

housekeeper [ˈhauskiːpə(r)] n. 主妇，女管家

supervisor [ˈsjuːpəvaizə] n. 监督人，管理人，检查员，督学，主管人，[计]（网络）超级用户

bellman [ˈbelmən] n. 敲钟人，传达员，行李员，更夫，礼宾员

junior [ˈdʒuːnjə] n. 年少者，晚辈，下级，大学三年级学生 adj. 年少的，下级的，后进的

supervise [ˈsjuːpəvaiz] v. 监督，管理，指导

linen [ˈlinin] n. 亚麻布，亚麻纤维制成的优质纸 adj. 亚麻布制的，亚麻的

laundry [ˈlɔːndri] n. 洗衣店，要洗的衣服，洗熨

bartender [ˈbɑːtendə(r)] n. 酒吧间销售酒精饮料的人，酒吧间 男招待

steward [ˈstjuəd] n. （轮船，飞机等）乘务员，干事

controller [kənˈtrəulə] n. 管理员，控制器

executive [igˈzekjutiv] adj. 实行的，执行的，行政的 n. 执行者，经理主管人员

chef [ʃef] n. 厨师

executive sous chef 行政副总厨

sous chef 副厨师长

Chef de Cuisine 厨师烹饪，烹饪大师傅

Chef de Partie 厨师领班

provision [prəˈviʒn] 供应，供应品，生活物质，储备物资

DJ abbr. （广播电台）流行音乐播音员，流行音乐节目主持人（disc jockey）

technician [tek'niʃ(ə)n] n. 技术员，技师
retail ['riːteil] n. 零售 vt. 零售，零卖，转述，传播
dealer ['diːlə(r)] n. 商人，发牌人，庄家，经销商，庄家

Notes

1. A pit boss (more commonly known today as the pit manager) is the person who looks after the employees who work in a casino pit. The job of the pit boss is to watch the floormen, who are the supervisors for table games dealers in a casino. One pit boss monitors all floormen in the pit; there is usually one floorman for every three dealers. The floormen correct minor mistakes but if a serious gaming discrepancy arises (such as duplicate cards being found in a deck), it is the job of the pit boss to sort it out.
2. GSA，即 Guest Service Agent，前台接待员
3. chip bank 筹码房
4. cage operation 筹码管理
5. soft count 纸币账房
6. hard count 硬币账房
7. Slot supervisor 老虎机主管
8. club scheduler 俱乐部排程员

Exercises

1. What's the shipboard structure?
2. What's the structure of hotel department?
3. What is the hotel director responsible for?
4. What is the food & beverage manager responsible for?
5. What is the chief housekeeper responsible for?
6. What is the cruise director responsible for?
7. Who are under the direct charge of F&B director?
8. What's the structure of purser department?
9. What are the lines of authority in the bar department?
10. What are the lines of authority in the restaurant department?
11. Who are under the direct charge of chief purser?
12. What's the main duty of crew purser?
13. Who are under the direct charge of chief housekeeper?
14. What is the PA manager responsible for?
15. What is the laundry master responsible for?
16. Who are under the direct charge of service manager?
17. What are the main duties of youth staff?
18. What does GSA of casino mean?

3.2.3 The General Lines of Authority & Identification Stripes of Officers Onboard

(1) The general lines of authority onboard

The hierarchy onboard is very rigid, different persons have different authorities and responsibilities, so the crew must comply with the related regulations made by the ship's management. The lines of authority onboard are as follows:

① Senior officers. For example: master, staff captain, chief engineer, staff chief engineer, hotel manager (director).

② Hotel officers. For example: chief purser, chief housekeeper, F&B manger, executive chef, cruise director, service manager.

③ Officers. For example: deck officers, engine officers, pursers, doctor, radio officer, head waiter, chef, sous chef, nurse, shore excursion manager, chef de cuisine, F&B trainer, stock controller.

④ Staff. For example: cruise ship company's staff, entertainment staff, shop personnel, photographers, casino staff.

⑤ Crew. All members of the ship's complement not mentioned above.

(2) The general identification stripes of officers onboard

The different officers onboard wears different identification stripes as follows:

① Deck department

Captain—4 yellow stripes with black;

Staff captain—3.5 yellow stripes with black;

Chief officer—3 yellow stripes with black.

② Engine department

Chief engineer—4 yellow stripes with purple;

Staff engineer—3.5 yellow stripes with purple;

First engineer—3 yellow stripes with purple.

③ Hotel department

Hotel director—4 yellow stripes with white;

Chief purser—3 yellow stripes with white;

F&B manager—3 yellow stripes with white;

Chief housekeeper—3 yellow stripes with white.

④ Infirmary (medical) department

Doctor—3 yellow stripes with red;

Assistant doctor—2 yellow stripes with red;

Nurse—2 yellow stripes with red.

Notes

The cruise director and his department's staff onboard wear no formal uniform and identification stripes, the main reasons are as follows:

1. Entertainment is relatively a new program onboard;

2. The cruise director and his department's staff should make passengers relax and feel at home, if their clothes are too formal, they will make passengers reserved and can't create light atmosphere.

New words & expressions

authority [ɔ:'θɔriti] n. 权威，威信，权威人士，权力，职权，著作权威

hierarchy ['haiərɑ:ki] n. 层次，层级，等级

radio [ˈreidiəu] n. 〈美〉无线电通信，无线电接收装置，无线电广播设备 v. 用无线电发送

cuisine [kwi(ː)ˈziːn] n. 厨房烹调法，烹饪，烹调风格

excursion [iksˈkəːʃən] n. 远足，游览，短程旅行，远足队，离题，[物] 偏移，漂移

trainer [ˈtreinə] n. 训练者，驯服者，驯马师，软运动鞋

stock [stɔk] n. 树干，库存，股票，股份 vt. 装把手于，进货，备有，放牧 vi. 出新芽，采购

controller [kənˈtrəulə] n. 管理员，控制器

personnel [ˌpəːsəˈnel] n. 人员，职员

photographer [fəˈtɔgrəfə] 摄影师 n. 摄影师

complement [ˈkɔmplimənt] n. 补足物，船上的定员 vt. 补助，补足

identification [aiˌdentifiˈkeiʃən] n. 辨认，鉴定，证明，视为同一

stripe [straip] n. 斑纹，条纹

uniform [ˈjuːnifɔːm] adj. 统一的，相同的，一致的 均衡的 n. 制服 vt. 使成一样，使穿制服

Exercises

1. What are the general lines of authority on board?
2. What's the captain's identification?
3. What's the chief engineer's identification?
4. What's the hotel director's identification?
5. What's the doctor's identification?
6. Why does the cruise director wear no stripes?

3.3 Job Description Onboard

3.3.1 Deck Department

Employees in this department are responsible for the running and maintenance of the cruise ship. Positions in the deck department include captain, staff captain, safety officer, security officer, first officers, second officers, third officers, chief radio officer, radio officers, etc.. Their duties include ensuring that the vessel meets strict safety requirements and international maritime regulations.

(1) Captain The captain is the highest rank on the cruise ship, responsible for the entire operation of the vessel, navigation and crew, must have a good knowledge of international maritime laws and company policies. Captain's licenses and all applicable certifications by a recognized maritime government body are required. Extensive experience with minimum five to eight years in subordinate positions on board ships and solid experience in all navigational electronic and computerized equipment are required. Diploma from an accredited maritime training school or facility and fluent English language skills are required.

(2) Staff Captain The staff captain is second in command, just after the ship captain, oversees daily operations and management as directed by the captain. Captain's licenses and all applicable certifications by a recognized maritime government body are required. Extensive experience with minimum five to eight years in subordinate positions on board ships and solid experience in all navigational electronic and computerized equipment are required. Diploma from an accredited maritime training school or facility and fluent English language skills are required.

(3) Chief/First Officer The first officer is the designated navigation officer and supervises the bridge operations and navigation equipment maintenance. Other responsibilities include maintenance of lifeboats, rescue boats and tenders. All applicable certifications by a recognized maritime government body are required. Extensive experience with minimum three to five years in subordinate positions on board ships and solid experience in all navigational electronic and computerized equipment are required. Diploma from an accredited maritime training school or facility and fluent English language skills are required.

(4) Second Officer The second officer is the designated navigation officer. All applicable certifications by a recognized maritime government body are required. Extensive experience with minimum two to three years in subordinate positions on board ships and solid experience in all navigational electronic and computerized equipment are required. Diploma from an accredited maritime training school or facility and fluent English language skills are required.

(5) Third Officer The third officer is the designated navigation officer. All applicable certifications by a recognized maritime government body are required. Extensive experience with minimum two to three years in subordinate positions on board ships and solid experience in all navigational electronic and computerized equipment are required. Diploma from an accredited maritime training school or facility and fluent English language skills are required.

(6) Junior Third Officer The junior third officer is the designated navigation officer in training. All applicable certifications by a recognized maritime government body are required. Extensive experience with minimum one to two years on board ships and solid experience in all navigational electronic and computerized equipment are required. Diploma from an accredited maritime training school or facility and fluent English language skills are required.

(7) Chief Radio Officer The chief radio officer is responsible for the entire communication center of the ship regarding weather, traffic, safety, etc., skilled electronics and telegraph repairs and operations of satellite hookups, faxes, Marisat communications. Other responsibilities include

maintaining the radio logbook, emergency radio communication devices and lifeboats. He/she is also responsible for delivering personal correspondence of crew members and passengers to and from the ship. All applicable certifications by a recognized maritime government body are nrequired. Extensive experience with minimum one to two years in subordinate positions on board ships and solid experience in all communication, electronic and satellite equipment are required. Diploma from an accredited maritime training school or facility and fluent English language skills are required.

(8) Radio Officer The radio officer maintains radio communications between ship and ship, ship and shore, skilled electronics and telegraph repairs and operations of satellite hook-ups, faxes, Marisat communications as directed by the Chief Radio Officer. All applicable certifications by a recognized maritime government body are required. Extensive experience with minimum one to two years in subordinate positions on board ships and solid experience in all communication, electronic and satellite equipment are required. Diploma from an accredited maritime training school or facility and fluent English language skills are required.

(9) Security Officer The security officer is responsible for ensuring security on the cruise ship including handling drugs interdiction, suspicious luggage, passengers and crew members, carrying out regular checks, enforcing safety regulations, etc.. All applicable certifications by a recognized maritime government body are required. Extensive experience in security and firearms handling are required. Military background is preferred. Fluent English language skills are required.

(10) Security Personnel The security personnel handles all shipboard security for the vessel as directed by the Security Officer. Extensive experience in security and firearms handling are required. Military background preferred. Good English language skills are required.

(11) Safety Officer The safety officer is responsible for passenger and crew safety drills, abandon ship procedures, crew safety training, supervision of ship's tenders. Extensive experience with minimum one to two years in subordinate positions on board ships is required. Diploma from an accredited maritime training school or facility and fluent English language skills are required.

(12) Bosun/First Mate The bosun is responsible for supervising general maintenance of assigned stations, assist in tender operations as directed by the safety officer. Experience with minimum one to two years on board ships is required. Tender captain's license and good English language skills are required.

(13) Carpenter The carpenter is responsible for all carpentry and woodwork on board. Skilled carpenter experienced in related background field is required. Basic English Language skills are required.

(14) Seaman The seaman is responsible for cleaning, painting, general maintenance of the vessel. Very basic knowledge of English language is required.

(15) Deck Attendant/Deckhand The deckhand is a handyman on a cruise ship, he does a wide variety of jobs, from painting to docking the ship, including general maintenance jobs, keeping the open decks in order-lounge chairs, etc.. No previous experience is required. However, general technical skills are a must. Very basic knowledge of Eng-

lish Language is required.

Notes

1. the running and maintenance of the cruise ship 邮轮的运行与维护

2. Captain's licenses and all applicable certifications by a recognized maritime government body are required. 要求船长具备公认的政府海事机构颁发的船长执照和所有适任证书。

3. an accredited maritime training school or facility 合格的海事培训学校或机构

4. second in command 副指挥

5. Other responsibilities include maintenance of lifeboats，rescue boats and tenders. 其他职责包括维护救生艇、救助艇及供应船（联络船）。

6. satellite hook-ups，faxes，Marisat communications 卫星连接、传真、海事卫星通信

7. drugs interdiction 禁毒

8. firearms handling 枪械处理

9. passenger and crew safety drills，abandon ship procedures 旅客和船员安全演习及弃船程序

10. Tender captain's license 供应船的船长证书

New words and expressions

licence [ˈlaisəns] n. 执照，许可证，特许 vt. 许可，特许，认可，发给执照

applicable [ˈæplikəbl] adj. 可适用的，可应用的

certification [ˌsəːtifiˈkeiʃən] n. 证明，证明书

minimum [ˈminiməm] adj. 最小的，最低的 n. 最小值，最小化

subordinate [səˈbɔːdinit] adj. 次要的，从属的，下级的 n. 下属 v. 服从

computerize [kəmˈpjuːtəraiz] vt. 用计算机处理，使计算机化

diploma [diˈpləumə] n. 文凭，毕业证书，证明权力、特权、荣誉等的证书，奖状

accredited [əˈkreditid] adj. 可接受的，可信任的，公认的，质量合格的

fluent [ˈflu(ː)ənt] adj. 流利的，流畅的

supervise [ˈsjuːpəvaiz] v. 监督，管理，指导

rescue [sreskjuː] vt. 援救，营救 n. 援救，营救

tender [ˈtendə] n. 交通船，补给船，小艇 adj. 嫩的，温柔的，软弱的

junior [ˈdʒuːnjə] n. 下级，（年龄、职位等）较低者 adj. 年少的，低级的，后进的

electronics [ilekˈtrɔniks] n. 电子学

telegraph [steligrɑːf] n. 电报机，电报 v. 打电报，发电报，打电报说

hookup [ˈhukʌp] n. 连接，转播，接线图

Marisat [ˈmærisæt] n. （为美国海军通信、商业海运及海上工业服务的）海洋卫星

logbook [ˈlɔgbuk] n. 航海日志，飞行日志，飞机航程表

device [diˈvais] n. 装置，设计，图案，策略，发明物，设备

correspondence [ˌkɔrisˈpɔndəns] n. 相应，通信，信件

drug [drʌg] n. 药，麻药，麻醉药，滞销货 vi. 〈俗〉吸毒 vt. 使服毒品，毒化

interdiction [ˌintə(ː)ˈdikʃən] n. 禁止

suspicious [səsˈpiʃəs] adj. （～of）可疑的，怀疑的

firearm [ˈfaiərɑːm] n. 火器，枪炮

preferred [priˈfɔːd] adj. 首选的

drill [dril] n. 钻孔机，军事训练，操练，（反复）练习，条播机 v. 训练，钻孔

abandon [əˈbændən] vt. 放弃，遗弃 n. 放任，狂热

carpenter [ˈkɑːpintə] n. 木匠

carpentry [ˈkɑːpintri] n. 木工工作

woodwork [ˈwudwəːk] 木制品，木造部分，木工手艺

handyman [ˈhændimæn] n. 受雇做杂事的人，做零活的人

Exercises

1. What are the main duties of staff captain?
2. What are the main duties of chief officer?
3. What are the main duties of chief radio officer?
4. What are the main duties of security officer?
5. What are the main duties of safety officer?
6. What are the main duties of bosun?
7. What are the main duties of seaman?
8. What are the main duties of deck attendant?

3.3.2 Engine Deparment

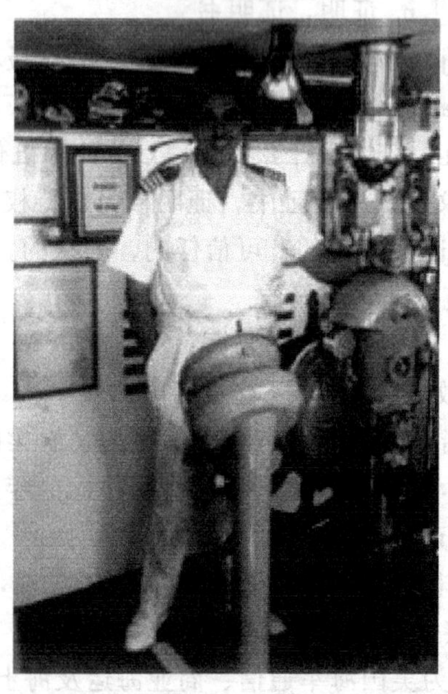

The engine department is responsible for the ship's engines, water supplies and maintenance. This department offers the cruise ships jobs like engine officers, chief engineer, first, second and third engineers, chief electrician, motorman, fitter, wiper, plumber, etc.

(1) Chief Engineer The chief engineer is responsible for the entire technical operations of the vessel including engineering, electrical, and mechanical divisions. Extensive experience with minimum five to eight years in subordinate positions on board ships is required. Diploma from accredited maritime training school or facility and fluent English lan-

guage skills are required.

(2) First Engineer The first engineer is responsible for the daily maintenance and operations of the engineering and technical aspects of the vessel as directed by the chief engineer. Extensive experience with minimum four to six years in subordinate positions on board ships is required. Diploma from accredited maritime training school or facility and fluent English language skills are required.

(3) Second Engineer The second engineer is responsible for the daily maintenance and operations of the engineering and technical aspects of the vessel as directed by the chief engineer. Extensive experience with minimum three to five years in subordinate positions on board ships is required. Diploma from accredited maritime training school or facility and fluent English language skills are required.

(4) Third Engineer The third engineer is responsible for the daily maintenance and operations of the engineering and technical aspects of the vessel as directed by the chief engineer. Extensive experience with minimum two to four years in subordinate positions on board ships is required. Diploma from accredited maritime training school or facility and fluent English language skills are required.

(5) Motorman The motorman is responsible for the daily maintenance and cleaning of specific engine parts as directed by the chief engineer. Experience with minimum one to two years on board ships is required. Diploma from accredited maritime training school or facility and good English language skills are required.

(6) Fitter The fitter is responsible for the daily maintenance and cleaning of engines and mechanical equipment as directed by the chief engineer. Experience with minimum one to two years on board ships is required. Diploma from accredited maritime training school or facility and basic English language skills are required.

(7) Wiper The wiper is responsible for trash pickup in engine room, tool pickup, general cleaning and painting of engine room. Basic English Language skills are required.

(8) Chief Electrician The chief electrician is responsible for the entire electrical system on board the ship. Extensive experience with minimum two to five years in subordinate positions on board ships is required. Diploma from accredited maritime training school or facility and fluent English Language skills are required.

(9) Electrician The electrician is responsible for the proper maintenance and repairs of the electrical system on board as directed by the chief electrician. Extensive experience with minimum one to three years on board ships is required. Diploma from accredited maritime training school or facility and good English language skills are required.

(10) Chief Air Conditioning Technician The chief air conditioning technician is responsible for the maintenance, repairs and supervision of all air conditioning and refrigeration systems as directed by the chief engineer. Extensive experience with minimum two to four years in subordinate positions on board ships is required. Diploma from accredited maritime training school or facility and fluent English language skills are required.

(11) Air Conditioning Technician The air conditioning technician is responsible for the

maintenance, repairs and supervision of all air conditioning and refrigeration systems as directed by the chief air conditioning Technician. Extensive experience with minimum two to four years in subordinate positions on board ships is required. Diploma from accredited maritime training school or facility and good English language skills are required.

(12) Plumber The plumber is responsible for the maintenance and repair of all plumbing. Experience with minimum one to two years on board ships is required. Basic English language skills are required.

(13) Upholsterer The upholsterer is responsible for re-upholstering of all furniture as required. Basic English language skills are required.

(14) Fireman The fireman is responsible for safety and firefighting on board the ship. Fire fighting certificate and basic English language skills are required.

Notes

1. the entire technical operations of the vessel including engineering, electrical, and mechanical divisions 整个船舶的技术操作，包括工程、电气和机械部门

2. trash pickup 垃圾收集

3. the proper maintenance and repairs of the electrical system on board 船上电气系统的正确维护和维修

4. the maintenance, repairs and supervision of all air conditioning and refrigeration systems 所有空调及制冷系统的保养、维修及监督

5. the maintenance and repair of all plumbing 所有管道的维护和维修

6. Fire fighting certificate 消防证书

New words and expressions

technical [ˈteknikəl] adj. 技术的，技术上的，技巧方面的

engineering [ˌendʒiˈniəriŋ] n. 工程（学），操纵，管理

mechanical [miˈkænikl] adj. 机械的，机械制的，机械似的，呆板的

motorman [ˈməutəmæn] n. 司机，电动机操作者

fitter [ˈfitə] n. 装配工，钳工 adj. 适当的，胜任的

wiper [ˈwaipə] n. 擦拭者，手帕

electrician [ilekˈtriʃ(ə)n] n. 电工，电学家

technician [tekˈniʃ(ə)n] n. 技术员，技师

supervision [ˌsjuːpəˈviʒən] n. 监督，管理

refrigeration [riˌfridʒəˈreiʃən] n. 冷藏，致冷，冷却

plumber [ˈplʌmbə] n. 水管工人

plumbing [ˈplʌmiŋ] n. 管子工作，铅工业，铅管品制造

upholsterer [ʌpˈhəulstərə] n. 装饰业者，家具商

furniture [ˈfəːnitʃə] n. 家具，设备，储藏物

fireman [ˈfaiəmən] n. 救火队员，消防队员

firefighting [ˈfaiəfait] n. 灭火，[军] 交火，火战，炮战

Exercises

1. What are the main duties of chief engineer?

2. What are the main duties of first engineer?
3. What are the main duties of motorman?
4. What are the main duties of fitter?
5. What are the main duties of wiper?
6. What are the main duties of chief electrician?
7. What are the main duties of chief air conditioning technician?
8. What are the main duties of plumber?

3.3.3 Purser Department

All departments unrelated to navigation and engine, fall under the hotel division. Jobs in the hotel department on a cruise ship are very similar to jobs you will find in a five-star hotel or resort. The hotel manager (director) oversees all shipboard services and is responsible for supervising all staff and crew in these departments. Department heads in turn report to the hotel manager and are accountable for the running of their individual departments. In general the hotel operations department is offering the following jobs: Hotel Manager (Director), Deputy Manager/Assistant Hotel Manager, Chief (Administration) Purser, etc.

(1) Hotel Manager The hotel manager supervises all other departments on board with the exception of deck and engine departments, extensive hotel experience of no less than five years as a hotel manager, a degree in hotel management and/or prior cruise ship experience are required. Fluent English language skills is required.

(2) Deputy Manager/Assistant Hotel Manager The assistant hotel manager supervises all other departments on board with the exception of deck and engine departments, extensive hotel experience of no less than five years as a hotel manager, a degree in hotel management and/or prior cruise ship experience required. Fluent English language skills are required.

In general the purser department is offering the following jobs: Chief (Administration) Purser, Purser, Assistant Purser, Junior Assistant Purser, Crew Purser, Shore Excursion Manager, Assistant Shore Excursion Manager, Cost Accountant, Revenue Accountant.

(1) Chief (Administration) Purser The administration purser supervises daily operations

of the pursers office/front desk as directed by the hotel manager. He/she is responsible for ensuring that all Immigration and Customs regulations are followed and that all documentation required by various port authorities/agencies is in proper order, coordinating the ship clearance in the various ports of call. He/she participates in the embarkation process by collecting immigration documentation to determine validity of documents and refers unusual documentation to the hotel director and/or port agent for final approval or denial. He/she meets ports agents and customs and immigration officials at the gangway at all ports to deliver documentation to clear the cruise ship and maintains a professional working relationship with port agents and customs and immigration officials. He/she must maintain current working knowledge of customs and immigration regulations and procedures. Previous hotel experience is preferable, a degree in hotel management and/or prior cruise ship experience is required. Fluent English language skills required. He/she has the possibilities for promotion to deputy manager.

(2) Assistant Purser The assistant purser is responsible for the reception desk, his/her duties are similar to duties at the front desk of a fine hotel, he/she provides guest services, information and shipboard announcements, exchanges traveller's checks and foreign currency, posts mail, provides safety deposit box service, provides banking services for passengers, assists with resolving guest complaints and any additional duties that may be assigned by the chief purser. Previous hotel experience and/or university degree are preferable. Fluent English language skills are required and speaking other languages (German, French or Spanish, etc.) is a plus. He/she has the possibilities for promotion to purser.

(3) Junior Assistant Purser (hotel receptionist) The receptionist works at the front desk as directed by the assistant purser. The Receptionist checks passengers in and out of their quarters. He/She is also responsible for answering passengers'queries, assisting with problems and complaints, taking payments for passenger accounts, accurately maintaining cash received and making announcements over the PA system. Various side duties, as assigned by the guest relations manager may include assisting with embarkation, manifest preparation, etc.. Previous hotel experience and/or university degree are preferable. Fluent English language skills are required and speaking other languages (German, French or Spanish) is a plus. He/She has the possibilities for promotion to Assistant Purser.

(4) The Guest Relations Manager (GRM) He/She is responsible for all aspects of passenger satisfaction onboard the ship, and for ensuring that all passenger requests, inquiries, and complaints are handled appropriately. Personally meets with any passengers who make complaints which cannot be resolved by the reception team, and tries to ensure a resolution which is satisfactory to the passenger and the company. Oversees the Guest Relations desk team, ensuring adequate scheduling at all times. Oversees the embarkation process. Attends social events onboard, often acting as host/hostess for travel agent or incentive groups. This position carries a high level of responsibility, and is a key position for ensuring passengers'satisfaction. Previous ship experience as guest relations manager is preferred, however experience in a similar shoreside position may be acceptable. Must be multi-

lingual, with fluent English, and other languages will be a benefit. Must have excellent social skills, and a clear speaking voice. The ability to manage a diverse team of people is needed, leading by example, maintaining company standards in a friendly but firm manner. Good communication skills are required, with the ability to interact at all levels.

(5) Crew Purser The purser handles the administration of the crew: sign-on and sign-off, cabin assignments, crew identification cards, etc.. Previous hotel experience and/or university degree are preferable. Accounting background is helpful. Fluent English language skills are required.

(6) Shore Excursion Manager The shore excursion manager is responsible for the presentation, promotion, supervision and arrangement of the shore excursions offered in the various ports of call. Experience in tourism, previous travel-related experience and/or minimum 1 year on board starting from an entry-level Cruise Staff are required. Fluent English language skills required.

(7) Assistant Shore Excursion Manager The assistant shore excursion manager is responsible for the promotion, selling and arrangements of the shore excursions offered in the various ports of call as directed by the shore excursion manager. Experience in tourism, previous travel-related experience and/or minimum 1 year on board starting from an entry-level cruise staff position are required. Fluent English language skills required.

(8) Cost Accountant His/her main responsibility is inventory control and managerial reporting, including generating daily food and supply cost, also weekly receiving and inventorying of all items in food, bar and photo departments. A major part of the work expected of the cost accountant is carried out on personal computers. English language skills are required for employment in this job.

(9) Revenue Accountant His main responsibility is the operation of cashless cabin charge system and NCR or MICROS register system. The duties include early morning closing of registers, running reports, balancing daily revenue and generating passenger statements. Fluent English skills are required for this job.

(10) PA (personal assistant)/Secretary All senior officers require Secretaries/PAs. Excellent secretarial skills and computer literate are needed for this job on a cruise ship.

There are many other administration jobs on board, these are just a part of available jobs.

Notes

1. Immigration and Customs regulations 移民和海关条例
2. are accountable for the running of their individual departments 负责各部门的运营
3. coordinating the ship clearance in the various ports of call 协调各停靠港口的船舶清关
4. He/she participates in the embarkation process by collecting immigration documentation to determine validity of documents. 他/她参加（旅客）登船过程，收集移民文件并确定其有效性。
5. to clear the cruise ship 为邮轮结关
6. manifest preparation 准备旅客名单

7. attends social events onboard 参加邮轮上的社交活动

8. must be multilingual 必须会使用多种语言

9. sign-on 办理上船手续（When you return from your vacation or join as a new crew，you will be met upon arrival and brought to the ship after which you will be welcome by a representative from the Crew Office/Personnel Department.）

10. sign-off 办理离船手续（When you are due for leave or finishing your contract，you are required to fill out a sign-off form and clearance form which can be obtained from the Crew Office/Personnel Department. On the day of your departure，your passport and airline ticket will be returned to you after having been processed by Immigration.）

11. inventory control and managerial reporting 库存控制和管理报告

12. NCR or MICROS register system NCR or MICROS 登记系统

13. running reports，balancing daily revenue and generating passenger statements 运营报告、日收入平衡和旅客生成报表

New words and expressions

exception [ik'sepʃən] n. 除外，例外，反对，异议

prior ['praiə] adj. 优先的，在前的 n. 预先 adv. 在

deputy ['depjuti] n. 代理人，代表

preferable ['prefərəbl] adj. 更可取的，更好的，更优越的

possibility [ˌpɔsi'biliti] n. 可能性，可能发生的事物

promotion [prə'məuʃən] n. 促销，促进，发扬，提升，提拔，晋升

ensure [in'ʃuə] vt. 保证，担保 v. 确保，确保，保证

immigration [ˌimi'greiʃen] n. 外来的移民，移居入境

regulation [reg ju'leiʃən] n. 规则，规章，调节，校准

documentation [ˌdɔkjumen'teiʃən] n. 文件

coordinate [kəu'ɔːdinit] n. 同等者，同等物 vt. 协调，调整，整理

clearance ['kliərəns] n. （船只的）结关，通过，出（入）港证（clearance papers），清除

participate [pɑː'tisipeit] vi. 参与，参加，分享，分担

embarkation [ˌembɑː'keiʃən] n. 乘坐，装载，从事

validity [və'liditi] n. 有效性，合法性，正确性

denial [di'naiəl] n. 否认，否定，谢绝，拒绝

currency ['kʌrənsi] n. 货币，流通

announcement [ə'naunsmənt] n. 宣告，发表，一项公告，一项私人告示

deposit [di'pɔzit] n. 保证金，存放物 vt. 存放，堆积 vi. 沉淀

assist [ə'sist] v. 援助，帮助

query ['kwiəri] n. 质问，询问，怀疑，疑问 v. 询问，表示怀疑

inquiry [in'kwaiəri] n. 质询，调查

satisfaction [ˌsætis'fækʃən] n. 满意，满足，令人满意的事物

appropriate [ə'prəuprieit] adj. 适当的

oversee ['əuvə'siː] v. 俯瞰，监视，检查，视察

adequate ['ædikwit] adj. 适当的，足够的

scheduling [ˈʃedjuːliŋ] n. 行程安排，时序安排
incentive [inˈsentiv] n. 动机 adj. 激励的
shoreside [ˈʃɔːsaid] adj. 岸的，岸上的，沿岸的，近岸的
diverse [daiˈvəːs] adj. 不同的，变化多的
interact [ˌintərˈækt] vi. 互相作用，互相影响
quarter [ˈkwɔːtə] n. 四分之一，地区，区间，方面，季
additional [əˈdiʃənl] adj. 另外的，附加的，额外的
accounting [əˈkauntiŋ] n. 会计学，清算帐目
excursion [iksˈkəːʃən] n. 远足，游览，短程旅行，远足队，离题，[物] 偏移，漂移
assignment [əˈsainmənt] n. 分配，委派，任务，(课外) 作业
accountant [əˈkauntənt] n. 会计 (员)，会计师
inventory [ˈinvəntri] n. 详细目录，存货，财产清册，总量
managerial [ˌmænəˈdʒiəriəl] adj. 管理的
reporting [riˈpɔːtiŋ] n. 报告
generate [ˈdʒenəˌreit] vt. 产生，发生
revenue [ˈrevinjuː] n. 收入，国家的收入，税收
cashless [ˈkæʃlis] adj. 无现款的，无现金的，无钱的
statement [ˈsteitmənt] n. 声明，陈述，综述
secretarial [ˌsekrəˈtɛəriəl] adj. 秘书的，书记的
literate [ˈlitərit] n. 善于写作的人，学者 adj. 有文化的，有阅读和写作能力的

Exercises

1. What are the main duties of hotel manager?
2. What are the main duties of administration purser?
3. What are the main duties of assistant purser?
4. What are the main duties of shore excursion manager?
5. What are the main duties of crew purser?
6. What are the main duties of cost accountant?
7. What are the main duties of revenue accountant?
8. What are the main duties of PA secretary in the hotel operations department?

3.3.4 Housekeeping Department

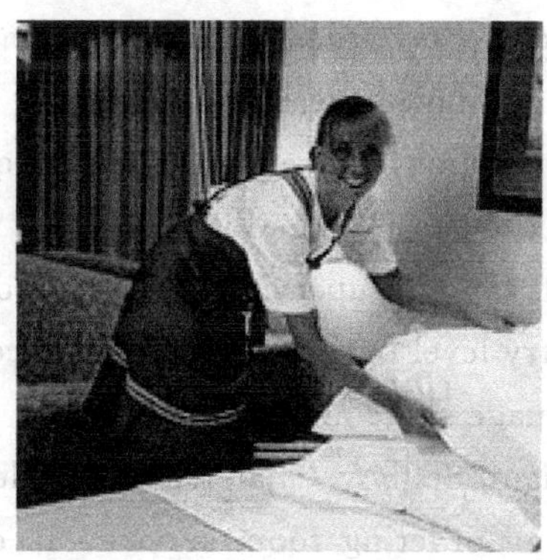

This department is responsible for making passengers comfortable while they are in their rooms. Its main duties include the care of the cabins, room and messenger service, and laundry pickup and delivery. Jobs of this department are very similar to the jobs you will find in a five-star hotel or resort: chief housekeeper, floor supervisor, head room steward/stewardess, cabin steward/stewardess, bell captain, bell boy, etc.. The housekeeping department is always behind the scenes but makes the entire ship worth living or staying on. The crew members of this department are also known as accommodation staff.

(1) Chief Housekeeper The chief housekeeper is directly responsible for the administrative function of the housekeeping department and the general cleanliness of the ship as a whole (cabin services, room services, bell services, passenger baggage handling and distribution), excluding the galley and bars. Maintains and ensures hygienic rules and regulations within the housekeeping department. High school education or higher, a minimum of five years related experience in the hospitality trade as an executive housekeeper in a first class hotel or prior ship experience in related position are required. Very good English language skills are required.

(2) Assistant Chief Housekeeper The assistant chief housekeeper supervises day to day operations of the department as directed by the chief housekeeper. Professional experience in hotels or prior ship experience in related position is required. Very good English language skills are required. He/She has the possibilities for promotion to chief housekeeper.

(3) Floor Supervisor The floor superviser supervises assigned floor of cabins and cabin stewards as directed by the chief housekeeper. Professional experience in hotels or prior ship experience in related position is required. Very good English language skills required. He/She has the possibilities for promotion to assistant chief housekeeper.

(4) Head Room Steward/Stewardess The head room steward/stewardess supervises assigned station of cabins and cabin stewards as directed by floor supervisor. Experience in hotels or prior cruise ship experience is required. Good English language skills are required. He/She has the possibilities for promotion to floor supervisor.

(5) Cabin Steward/Stewardess/Cabin Attendant The cabin steward/stewardess is responsible for daily cleaning of passenger cabins. No experience is required, some experience is preferred. Basic English language skills are required. He/She has the possibilities for promotion to Head Room Steward/stewardess.

(6) Assistant Cabin Steward/Stewardess The assistant cabin steward/stewardess is responsible for daily cleaning of assigned areas and passenger cabins, passenger laundry requests. This is an entry level position, no experience is required. Basic English language skills are required. He/She has the possibilities for promotion to Cabin Steward/Stewardess.

(7) Bell Captain The bell captain supervises bellboys, delivery of room service meals, gifts and flowers. This is an entry level position, no experience is required, some experience is preferred. Basic English language skills are required.

(8) Room Service Attendant/Bellboy (males and females) Their general duty is to provide guests with the option of ordering room service, to ensure that passengers receive

the service & the same comfort inside their cabins like they have in 5-stars dining room. Also they have to assist cabin stewards in the cabins cleaning after each disembarkation. It is recommended to have some previous restaurant or bar experience at least on the land. Ability to speak, read & write in English is an advantage.

(9) Cleaner/Utility Cleaner The cleaner is responsible for doing daily cleaning of all public areas. This is an entry level position, no experience is required. Very basic English language skills are required. He/She has the possibilities for promotion to cabin steward.

(10) Laundry Supervisor The laundry supervisor supervises and inspects the work of laundry staff to ensure a high level of quality and productivity. Cleans and stores hotel linens/uniforms in a timely, organized manner to ensure that hotel laundry and linen needs are met. He/she is responsible for cleaning of all the officers, management, staff and crew garments. Some experience in hotels or prior ship experience in related position are required. Basic English language skills are required.

(11) Assistant Laundry Supervisor The assistant laundry supervisor supervises and inspects the work of laundry staff to ensure a high level of quality and productivity as directed by laundry supervisor. Cleans and stores hotel linens/uniforms in a timely, organized manner to ensure that hotel laundry and linen needs are met. He/she is responsible for cleaning of all the officers, management, staff and crew garments. Some experience in hotels or prior ship experience in related position is required. Basic English language skills required. He/She has the possibilities for promotion to laundry supervisor.

(12) Laundry Man They wash, dry and iron all linen for cabins and dining rooms. Clean and press all officers'and crew's uniforms and do crew's personal laundry. Also provide dry cleaning and laundry service for passengers. They are also responsible for laundry facilities. They also have a number of assistant laundry men and utility laundry men. Very basic English language skills are required. He/she has the possibilities for promotion to assistant laundry supervisor.

(13) The Chief Linen Keeper The chief linen keeper supervises and coordinates activities of staff engaged in storing linens and wearing apparel. Assigns duties to staff. Inventory articles in stock such as table linens, towels, bed sheets, and uniforms. Confers with superintendent to request replacement of articles in short supply. Counts articles to ensure agreement with quantity specified on load sheet. Resolves customer complaints and modifies orders according to size, color, and type of articles specified. May supervise staff engaged in attaching labels and emblems, repairing, and altering linens and wearing apparel. May purchase linen supplies. Some experience in hotels or prior ship experience in related position are required. Basic English language skills are required.

(14) Pool Attendant He is responsible for doing cleaning and maintenance of all pool areas. No experience is required, This is an entry level position. Very basic English language skills are required.

Notes

1. the care of the cabins, room and messenger service, and laundry pickup and delivery 客

舱的保养、送餐服务和信使服务、换洗衣物的收集和交还

2. behind the scenes 在后台，在幕后

3. Cleans and stores hotel linens/uniforms in a timely，organized manner to ensure that hotel laundry and linen needs are met. 及时有条理地清洗和储存酒店布草和制服，以确保酒店对换洗的衣物和布草的需求得到满足。

4. wearing apparel 衣服，服装

5. inventory articles in stock 库存物品

6. to request replacement of articles in short supply 请求短缺物品的补充

7. Counts articles to ensure agreement with quantity specified on load sheet. 清点物品，以确保与货运单中记载的数量一致。

8. attaching labels and emblems 贴标签和标志

New words and expressions

resort [riˈzɔːt] vi. 求助，诉诸 n. 凭借，常去之地，胜地

stewardess [stjuːəˈdes，ˈstjuːədis] n. （轮船，飞机等）女乘务员

accommodation [əˌkɔməˈdeiʃən] n. 住处，膳宿，（车，船，飞机等的）预定铺位

administrative [ədˈministrətiv] adj. 管理的，行政的

distribution [ˌdistriˈbjuːʃən] n. 分配，分发，配给物，销售，分类，发送，发行

hospitality [ˌhɔspiˈtæliti] n. 好客，宜人，盛情

preferred [priˈfəːd] adj. 首选的

bellboy [ˈbelbɔi] n. 侍者

option [ˈɔpʃən] n. 选项，选择权，[经] 买卖的特权

comfort [ˈkʌmfət] n. 安慰，舒适，安慰者 vt. 安慰，使（痛苦等）缓和

room service 送餐服务

disembarkation [ˈdisembɑːˈkeiʃən] n. 起岸，登陆

recommend [rekəˈmend] vt. 推荐，介绍，劝告，使受欢迎

advantage [ədˈvɑːntidʒ] n. 优势，有利条件，利益

laundry [ˈlɔːndri] n. 洗衣店，要洗的衣服，洗熨

productivity [ˌprɔdʌkˈtiviti] n. 生产力

garment [ˈgɑːmənt] n. 衣服，外衣，外表

linen [ˈlinin] n. 亚麻布，亚麻制品 adj. 亚麻布制的，亚麻的

linen keeper 布草管理员

launder [ˈlɔːndə，ˈlɑːndə] n. 流水槽，槽洗机 v. 洗涤，清洗

press [pres] n. 压，按，印刷 vt. 压，熨 vi. 压，逼迫

apparel [əˈpærəl] n. 衣服，装饰

inventory [ˈinvəntri] n. 详细目录，存货，财产清册 vt. 为…开列存货清单

superintendent [ˌsjuːpərinˈtendənt] n. 主管，负责人，指挥者，管理者

replacement [riˈpleismənt] n. 归还，复位，交换，代替者，补充兵员

specify [ˈspesifai] vt. 指定，详细说明，列入清单

modify [ˈmɔdifai] vt. 更改，修改 v. 修改

label [ˈleibl] n. 标签，签条，商标，标志 vt. 贴标签于，指……为，分类

emblem ['embləm] n. 象征，徽章，符号 vt. 用象征表示

purchase ['pəːtʃəs] vt. 买，购买 n. 买，购买

Exercises

1. What are the main duties of chief housekeeper?
2. What are the main duties of floor supervisor?
3. What are the main duties of head room steward/stewardess?
4. What are the main duties of cabin steward/stewardess?
5. What are the main duties of bell captain?
6. What are the main duties of cleaner?
7. What are the main duties of laundry man?
8. What are the main duties of the chief linen keeper?

3.3.5 Food and Beverage Department

The food and beverage department is responsible for all of the dining rooms, restaurant-bars, bars, the galleys (kitchens), cleanup and provisions. The Food and Beverage Director (Manager) runs this department. Depending on the size of the cruise ship, there may be a number of restaurants, bars and galleys.

The Food and Beverage Manager is in charge of the management and supervision of all areas of the ship that serve food and beverages (the restaurants, bar, galley and related areas) . His/her responsibilities include food costing budgeting, calculating expenditures, training, maintaining a high standard of food quality, service, safe handling of food supplies, maintaining and ensuring that the hygienic standards are followed at all times. etc. . The Food and Beverages Manager is also in charge of food orders in bulk. Must have three/five years'food and beverage experience in a hotel or restaurant, or prior ship experience in related position. Culinary background and education are preferable. Must be certified by the USPH (United States Public Health) or CIEH (Chartered Institute of Environmental Health) .

(1) The restaurants (dining room) department

The Food and Beverage Department on a cruise ship offers the following restaurant jobs: Maitre D'Hotel/Restaurant Manager, Dining Room Head Waiter/Waitress, Dining Room Waiter/Waitress, Dining Room Assistant Waiter/Waitress, Dining Room Junior Waiter/Waitress, Cocktail Waitress/Waiter, Bartender, Buffet Steward/Stewardess.

① Restaurant Manager/Maitre D'Hotel. The restaurant manager, or maitre d'hotel, is responsible for the guests'satisfaction with food service in all restaurants and food outlets under his supervision. Responsible for the day to day operations and supervision of the restaurants including seating arrangements, maintaining a high standard of food quality and service, cleanliness of the restaurant, assigning work schedules, days off and side duties to all dining room and food outlets service personnel. Responsible for the training program of all food service personnel. Ensures all restaurants and food outlets is up to the hygienic standards. Reports directly to the Food and Beverage Manager. Must have a minimum of two to three years food and beverage experience with a hotel or restaurant or prior ship experience in related position. Must be fully knowledgeable of food operations, menus knowledge and cooking methods applied, menu cycles and service standards and grasp the knowledge of hygienic standards and procedures. Fluent English and additional languages-German, French, Italian or Spanish are highly desirable.

② Head Waiter/Waitress. He/She is responsible for a certain serving station in the dining room, supervises all waiters of his/her station. Creates an overall pleasant dining atmosphere and experience by providing guests with good quality food and beverage service. Supervises, guides and trains staff under his supervision on a daily basis. Coordinates special orders. Ensures that all guests'requests, inquiries and complaints are responded to promptly. Supervises general cleaning of his area of supervision according to company and hygienic standards. Lots of restaurant and prior cruise ship experience in related position are required. Fluent English language skills are required. Excellent knowledge of food, beverage and international cuisine and knowledge of legal hygienic standards and procedures are also required.

③ Waiter/Waitress. He/She is responsible for serving passengers, explaining the dishes, making recommendations, supervising assistant waiters assigned to their tables. Lots of experience and fluent English language skills are required. He/She has the possibilities for promotion to head waiter.

④ Assistant Waiter/Waitress. He/She is responsible for assisting dining room waiters/waitresses in the food and beverage service, serve passengers as directed by the waiter/waitress. Good English language skills are required. He/she has the possibilities for promotion to waiter/waitress.

⑤ Junior Waiter/Waitress. He/She is responsible for assisting dining room assistant waiters/waitresses in serving meals and drinks, clearing tables and delivering food and drinks. Some related experience is required. Fair English language skills are required. He/She has the possibilities for promotion to assistant waiter.

⑥ Buffet Steward/Stewardess. He/She is responsible for setting up the buffet, serving meals, drinks, cleaning tables, restocks the buffet line with food when necessary at the cruise lines buffets. No experience is required although some experience is preferable. Basic English language knowledge is required. He/She has strong possibilities for promotion to bar steward, junior waiter, assistant waiter and waiter.

(2) The bar department

The bar department is responsible for serving alcoholic beverages in areas such as night clubs, discos, decks, restaurants, room service, private parties and all bar areas on board cruise ships. With all the new ships being put into service there are many bar jobs for all nationalities.

① Bar Manager. The bar manager carries out supervisory responsibilities in accordance with the company policies, rules and regulations. Responsible for the operation and supervision of all public bars, lounges, crew bar and beverage service in the restaurants and decks. He/she has to consistently exceed guests'expectations and provide the highest level of product and services. Responsible for ensuring that the beverage sales forecasted for bars, lounges and restaurants on the ship are met and exceeded. Responsibilities include familiarizing and training employees; planning, assigning and directing work; appraising performance; rewarding and disciplining employees; addressing complaints and resolving problems. Additional duties and responsibilities may be assigned as needed. Must have full knowledge of current hygienic rules and regulations and maintains hygienic standards throughout the bar operations at all times. Minimum of 5 years of beverage-related management experience and fluent English are required.

② Assistant Bar Manager. The assistant bar manager assists the bar manager in the supervision and operation of the bars and lounges. Responsible for the bar staff and cleanliness of the bars and lounges. Ensures that designated areas are well covered with enough personnel. Helps the bar servers in busy hours. Participates in the on-the-job training process. Ensures that bar par-levels are maintained. Has full knowledge of current hygienic rules and regulations and maintains hygienic standards throughout the bar operations at all times. Generates new ideas and methods to increase bar revenue and improve bar service. Must have a minimum of three year's food and beverage experience and be trained in the entire bar department operations. Fluent English is required. Has the possibilities for promotion to bar manager.

③ Bar Accountant. The bar accountant is responsible for accounting procedures of the bar department. Accounting background and/or education are required. Must be able to speak and write English.

④ Bartender. The bartender is responsible for serving alcoholic beverages to passengers in lounges and on decks. The bartender should be knowledgeable in the art of making drinks. The bartender must provide fast, professional and courteous service to all guests. As a member of the beverage staff, he/she will be required to serve several passengers at their station at one time. In addition to mixing drinks most people have adopted the stereotype that bartenders are there to listen, therefore it is imperative for bartenders to have good social skills to converse with passengers. The bartender manages liquor and supply and provides general maintenance of the bar and lounge areas. He/she must comply with the necessary sanitary rules. Very importantly，he/she must know the cocktail/bar mixes and know the proper glass and garnish for each drink. He should learn the procedures for ordering supplies and beverages maintaining the indicated stock.. Some related experience is required. Good English Language skills are required.

⑤ Bar Waiter/Waitress（Cocktail Waitress/Waiter）. The bar waiter/waitresses is responsible for serving alcoholic beverages to passengers in all bar and lounge areas，set up bar stations，assist in re-stocking and cleaning. Must have experience in working in bars，restaurants or hotels. Good English language skills required. He/she has the possibilities for promotion to bartender.

⑥ Bar Boy/Bar Utility. He is responsible for cleanliness of lounges and re-stocking bar supplies. No experience is required，this is an entry level position. Very basic English Language skills is required. He has the possibilities for promotion to bar steward.

⑦ Wine Steward/Stewardess（Sommelier）. The wine steward/stewardess is vastly knowledgeable about wine and wine culture. The wine steward/stewardess makes suggestions on the menu or by request about which wine would enhance what meal. He/She will work in a station assigned by the head wine steward/stewardess and follow the daily schedule. Must be familiar with company service standards. Must use salesmanship techniques in order to achieve maximum sales. Accomplish tasks related to inventory，equipment control and maintenance. Must have comprehensive knowledge of the legal hygienic rules and regulations，and participate in training and re-enforcement. Minimum 3 years wine service experience in a 5-star restaurant or hotel is required. Must be knowledgeable of the wine list and able to discuss wines with guests who ask for advice. Knowledge how to pair wine with food is imperative. Must be able to read and speak clearly in English. Other languages are a plus.

Notes

1. food costing budgeting，calculating expenditures 食品成本预算，计算支出
2. USPH（United States Public Health） 美国公共卫生福利部
3. CIEH（Chartered Institute of Environmental Health） 英国环境卫生协会
4. food outlets 食品店
5. up to the hygienic standards 符合卫生标准
6. menu cycles 菜单周期
7. making recommendations 推荐，决策建议
8. setting up the buffet 设置自助餐
9. rewarding and disciplining employees 奖励和惩罚员工
10. addressing complaints 解决投诉
11. on-the-job training 在职培训
12. mixing drinks 调酒
13. general maintenance 一般保养

14. maintaining the indicated stock 维持预定的库存
15. participate in training and re-enforcement 参加培训和提升

New words and expressions

budget [ˈbʌdʒit] n. 预算 vi. 做预算，编入预算
calculate [ˈkælkjuleit] v. 计算，考虑，计划，打算
expenditure [iksˈpenditʃə，eks-] n. 支出，花费
culinary [ˈkʌlinəri] adj. 厨房的，烹调用的，厨房用的
certify [ˈsəːtifai] v. 证明，保证
maitre d'hotel [ˈmeitrədəuˈtel] n. 餐厅侍者总管，旅馆经理
outlet [ˈautlet，-lit] n. 出口，出路
knowledgeable [ˈnɔlidʒəbl] adj. 知识渊博的，有见识的
menu [ˈmenjuː] n. 菜单
cycle [ˈsaikl] n. 周期，循环，自行车 vi. 循环，轮转，骑自行车 vt. 使循环
desirable [diˈzaiərəbl] adj. 值得要的，合意的，令人想要的，悦人心意的
quality [ˈkwɔliti] n. 质量，品质，性质
recommendation [ˌrekəmenˈdeiʃən] n. 推荐，介绍（信），劝告，建议
restock [ˈriːˈstɔk] vt. 重新进货，再储存
nationality [ˌnæʃəˈnæliti] n. 国籍，国家，部落，民族，民族性
supervisory [ˌsjuːpəˈvaizəri] adj. 管理的，监督的
in accordance with 与…一致，按照，依据
consistent [kənˈsistənt] adj. 一致的，调和的，坚固的，[数、统] 相容的
exceed [ikˈsiːd] vt. 超越，胜过 vi. 超过其他
forecast [ˈfɔːkɑːst] n. 先见，预测，预报 vt. 预想，预测，预报，预兆
familiarize [fəˈmiljəraiz] v. 熟悉
appraise [əˈpreiz] v. 评价
discipline [ˈdisiplin] n. 纪律，学科 v. 训练
address [əˈdres] n. 致辞，演讲，说话的技巧 vt. 向……致辞，演说，忙于
generate [ˈdʒenəˌreit] vt. 产生，发生
lounge [laundʒ] n. 闲逛，休闲室 vi. 闲荡，懒洋洋地躺卧 vt. 虚度光阴
stereotype [ˈstiəriəutaip] n. 陈腔滥调，老套 vt. 使用铅版，套用老套，使一成不变
imperative [imˈperətiv] n. 命令，诫命，需要 adj. 紧急的，必要的，势在必行的
liquor [ˈlikə] n. 液体，汁，酒精饮料 vt. 浸水 vi. 喝酒
converse [kənˈvəːs] vi. 谈话，交谈，认识 n. 相反的事物，倒 adj. 相反的
comply with 照做，遵守
sanitary [ˈsænitəri] adj. （有关）卫生的，（保持）清洁的，清洁卫生的 n. 公共厕所
garnish [ˈgɑːniʃ] v. 装饰
enhance [inˈhɑːns] vt. 提高，增强 v. 提高
salesmanship [ˈseilzmənʃip] n. 推销术，说服力，销售，推销
technique [tekˈniːk] n. 技术，技巧，方法，表演法，手法
maximum [ˈmæksiməm] n. 最大量，最大限度，极大 adj. 最高的，最多的，最大极

限的

accomplish [ə'kɔmpliʃ] vt. 完成，达到，实现

comprehensive [ˌkɔmpri'hensiv] adj. 全面的，广泛的，能充分理解的，包容的

sommelier [ˌsɔmə'ljei] n. 〈法语〉斟酒服务员，管酒的侍者

participate [pɑː 'tisipeit] vi. 参与，参加，分享，分担

enforcement [in'fɔːsmənt] n. 执行，强制

Exercises

1. What are the main duties of food and beverage manager?
2. What are the main duties of restaurant manager?
3. What are the main duties of head waiter?
4. What are the main duties of waiter?
5. What are the main duties of buffet steward?
6. What are the main duties of bar manager?
7. What are the main duties of bar accountant?
8. What are the main duties of bartender?
9. What are the main duties of bar waiter?
10. What are the main duties of wine steward?

3.3.6 Galley/Kitchen Department

There are dozens of jobs in the galley (kitchen), many of which require extensive prior restaurant or cruise ship experience. The galley is usually divided into the hot galley and cold galley. The hot galley positions include all types of cooking-vegetables, fish, soup, and grill. The cold galley positions include baking, pastry, and buffets. With all of this food preparation and dining, there has to be a team responsible for cleaning up after the passengers and cooks. A cleaning crew (utility division) washes all of the dishes and tableware (including the pots and pans), changes the table cloths, vacuums the floors, and cleans the windows and bar areas. In general the galley department offers the following cruise ship jobs: Executive Chef, Assistant Executive Chef/Sous Chef, Chef De Partie, First Cook, Second Cook/Third Cook, Cook Trainee, Crew Cook/Crew Cook Assistant/Crew Cook Trainee, Crew Cook Utility/Crew Messman, Provision Master/Storekeeper, Assistant Provision

Master/Storekeeper, Pastry Chef Supervisor, Assistant Pastry Chef Supervisor, Pastry Man, Pastry Trainee, Baker Supervisor, Baker Trainee, Galley Cleaner, Dishwasher/Pot washer.

(1) Executive Chef (Chef de Cuisine is often synonymous with the title of executive chef) The executive chef is in charge of everything related to the kitchen, including food planning, quality control, menu creation, staff management, cleanliness, safe food handling and business aspects. Ensures the efficient operation of all food production areas: constantly analyzing cost and quality of food production, knowing to manage within set budgets. Responsible for implementing and maintaining all standards set by the corporate office: establishes the manner and means to train personnel in his/her area of responsibility according to standard operating procedures. Must possess strong leadership skills. Accomplish tasks related to inventory, equipment control and maintenance, must have comprehensive knowledge of the legal rules and regulations, and participate in training and re-enforcement. While the position requires extensive cooking experience and often involves actively cooking, it also involves a high level of management and business aspects of the kitchen. He/She can also be referred to as the "chef" or "head chef" . Although "head chef " may seem redundant, the word "chef " has come to be applied to any cook, kitchen helper or a fast food operator, making the distinction necessary. Eight to ten years in subordinate position on board and/or hotel and restaurant experience are required. Good English language skills required. Culinary school education is required. Must be able to read and speak clearly in English. Other languages are a plus.

(2) Sous chef The Sous Chef is the direct assistant of the executive chef and is second in command. They may be responsible for scheduling, the day to day operations of the galley staff, assisting the executive chef with the food planning, preparation and quality control and filling in for him/her when the executive chef is off-duty. Produces and maintains the highest food quality and control for all food products served in all areas, according to company standards. Supervises and checks all food outlets, buffets, action stations, and food displays for creativity, quality, cleanliness and food safety. Helps organize and train subordinates. Participates in galley crew on-board training program. Accomplishes tasks related to inventory, equipment control and maintenance. Must have comprehensive knowledge of United States Public Health rules and regulations, and participate in training and re-enforcement. Four to five years in subordinate position on board and/or hotel and restaurant experience are required. Good English language skills are required. Culinary school education is required. Must be able to read and speak clearly in English. Other languages a plus. He/She has the possibilities for promotion to executive chef.

(3) Chef De Partie The chef de partie is responsible for the confection of various menu items according to the provided recipes and photos. Responsible for the production of food, as indicated, in his specific work station. Ensures that production in his station is efficient and that no waste occurs. Ensures that his team reports for work on time, and maintains his area of supervision in accordance with legal hygienic rules and regulations. His/Her duties al-

so include the cleaning and sanitizing of his/her working area and working utensils following related legal hygienic rules and regulations at all times. A chef de partie, also known as a "station chef " or "line cook", is in charge of a particular area of production. In large kitchens, each station chef might have several cooks and/or assistants. In most kitchens, however, the station chef is the only worker in that department. Line cooks are often divided into a hierarchy of their own, starting with "First Cook", then "Second Cook", and so on as needed. Four to five years in subordinate position on board and/or hotel and restaurant experience are required. Must have comprehensive knowledge of the legal hygenic rules and regulations. Good English Language skills are required, Other languages are a plus. Culinary school education is required. He/She has the possibilities for promotion to the executive chef.

(4) First Cook The first cook supervises second and third cooks, bakers, pastry cooks and provisions. Responsible for food preparation and cooking as directed by the executive chef. Two to three years in subordinate position on board and/or hotel and restaurant experience are required. Good English language skills required. Culinary school education is required. He/She has the possibilities for promotion to the assistant executive chef.

(5) Second Cook/Third Cook They are responsible for food preparation and cooking as directed by the first cook, supervises bakers, pastry cooks, cleaners and provisions. One or two years in subordinate position on board and/or hotel and restaurant experience are required. Fair English language skills are required. Culinary school education is required. They have the possibilities for promotion to First Cook.

(6) Cook Trainee The cook trainee is responsible for food preparation and cooking as directed by the first cook. Prior hotel/restaurant experience is required. Culinary school education is required. Basic English language skills are required. He/She has strong possibilities for promotion to third cook.

(7) Crew Cook/Crew Cook Assistant/Crew Cook Trainee They are responsible for food preparation and cooking of the crew as directed by the first cook. Prior hotel/restaurant experience is required. Culinary school education is required. Basic English language skills are required. He/She has strong possibilities for promotion to third cook.

(8) Crew Cook Utility/Crew Messman They are responsible for cleaning, general maintenance as directed by the first cook. This is an entry level position, no experience is required. Very basic English language skills are required. They have the possibilities for promotion to buffet steward.

(9) Provision Master/Storekeeper The provision master is responsible for the entire storage, ordering and distribution of all food supplies as directed by the executive chef. Food and beverage background is essential, knowledge of accounting is required. Good English language skills are required.

(10) Assistant Provision Master/Storekeeper The assistant provision master is responsible for the storage, ordering and distribution of all food supplies as directed by the provision master/storekeeper. Food and beverage background is essential, knowledge of accounting is required. Good

English language skills are required.

(11) Pastry Chef Supervisor The pastry chef supervisor is responsible for the supervision of the pastry staff, oversees the developing and preparation of all pastries. Culinary background of no less than three years restaurant/hotel experience or prior experience in subordinate position on board is required. Good English language skills are required.

(12) Assistant Pastry Chef Supervisor He/She is responsible for the supervision of the pastry staff as directed by the pastry chef supervisor, oversees the developing and preparation of all pastries. Culinary background of no less than three years restaurant/hotel experience or prior experience in subordinate position on board is required. Good English language skills are required. He/She has the possibilities for promotion to pastry chef supervisor.

(13) Pastry Man (Pastry Staff) The pastry staff are responsible for creating and preparing of all pastries as directed by the pastry chef supervisor. Culinary background of no less than two years restaurant/hotel experience or prior experience in subordinate position on board is required. Fair English language skills are required. He/She has the possibilities for promotion to assistant pastry chef supervisor.

(14) Pastry Trainee (pastry support staff) The pastry trainee is responsible for assisting in the preparation and cooking of all pastries as directed by the pastry chef supervisor, cleaning and maintenance of pastry stations. Culinary background of no less than one year restaurant/hotel experience or prior experience in subordinate position on board is required. Basic English language skills are required. He/She has the possibilities for promotion to pastry man.

(15) Baker Supervisor The baker supervisor is responsible for the supervision of the baker staff. Controls the preparation and cooking of all bakery products. Culinary background of no less than three years restaurant/hotel experience or prior experience in subordinate position on board is required. Good English language skills are required.

(16) Assistant Baker Supervisor He/She is responsible for the supervision of the baker staff as directed by the baker supervisor. Assists in the preparation and cooking of all bakery products. Culinary background of no less than three years restaurant/hotel experience or prior experience in subordinate position on board is required. Good English language skills are required. He/She has the possibilities for promotion to baker supervisor.

(17) Baker (bakery staff) He/She is responsible for preparation and cooking of all bakery products as directed by the baker supervisor. Culinary background of no less than two years restaurant/hotel experience or prior experience in subordinate position on board is required. Fair English language skills are required. He/She has the possibilities for promotion to assistant baker supervisor.

(18) Baker Trainee (bakery support staff) He/She is responsible for assisting in the preparation and cooking of all bakery products as directed by the baker supervisor. Culinary background of no less than one year restaurant/hotel experience or prior experience in subordinate position on board is required. Basic English language skills are required. He/She has

the possibilities for promotion to baker.

(19) Galley Cleaner He/She is responsible for cleaning and maintenance of assigned galley stations. This is an entry level position, no experience is required. Minimum English language skills are required. He/She has the possibilities for promotion to assistant cabin steward.

(20) Dishwasher/Pot washer He/She is responsible for cleaning and stacking of all galley and passengers dishes, pots, pans, etc.. This is an entry level position, no experience is required. Minimum English language skills are required. He/She has the possibilities for promotion to assistant cabin steward.

Notes

1. The galley is usually divided into the hot galley and cold galley. 厨房通常分为热厨房与冷厨房。
2. vacuums the floors 用吸尘器打扫地板
3. to manage within set budgets 在预算内经营管理
4. off-duty 不值班，不在岗
5. train subordinates 培训下属
6. culinary school 烹饪学校
7. the confection of various menu items 各菜单项的甜点
8. baker trainee 面包师实习生

New words and expressions

executive [igˈzekjutiv] adj. 实行的，执行的，行政的 n. 执行者，经理主管人员
grill [gril] n. 烤架，铁格子，烤肉 v. 烧，烤，严加盘问
bakin [ˈbeikiŋ] n. 烘焙，一次烘焙的量
pastry [ˈpeistri] n. 面粉糕饼，馅饼皮
implement [ˈimplimənt] n. 工具，器具 vt. 贯彻，实现 v. 执行
corporate [ˈkɔːpərit] adj. 社团的，法人的，共同的，全体的
vacuum [ˈvækjuəm] n. 真空，空间，真空吸尘 adj. 真空的 vt. 用真空吸尘器打扫
trainee [treiˈniː] n. 实习生，练习生，新兵
messman [ˋmesmən] n. (海军) 食堂值勤兵
synonymous [siˈnɔniməs] adj. 同义的
aspect [ˈæspekt] n. 样子，外表，面貌，(问题等的) 方面
redundant [riˈdʌndənt] adj. 多余的
distinction [disˈtiŋkʃən] n. 区别，差别，级别，特性，声望，显赫
confection [kənˈfekʃən] n. 糖果，蜜饯，调制，[药] 糖膏 (剂)，精制工艺品
recipe [ˈresipi] n. 处方
baker [ˈbeikə] n. 面包师，面包工人，〈美〉(便携式) 烘炉
provision [prəˈviʒən] n. 供应，(一批) 供应品，预备，防备，规定
essential [iˈsenʃəl] adj. 本质的，实质的，基本的 n. 本质，实质，要素，要点
bakery [ˈbeikəri] n. 面包店
stack [stæk] n. 堆，一堆，堆栈 v. 堆叠

Exercises

1. What are the main duties of executive chef?
2. What are the main duties of sous chef?
3. What are the main duties of chef de partie?
4. What are the main duties of first cook?
5. What are the main duties of cook trainee?
6. What are the main duties of provision master?
7. What are the main duties of pastry chef supervisor?
8. What are the main duties of baker supervisor?
9. What are the main duties of baker?
10. What are the main duties of galley cleaner?

3.3.7 Cruise Staff Department

The cruise staff department is responsible for all of the activities and entertainment on board and ashore. The cruise director is in charge of the cruise staff. The size of this staff, like all of the other departments, is dependent on the size of the cruise ship. Entertainers such as singers, dancers, and musicians are needed on ships along with shore excursion leaders/coordinators, dive masters, and lecturers. Most of the cruise staff have a lot of interaction with the passengers, and must be able to focus on providing an enjoyable time for the cruisers. This demands that all cruise staff have to be almost like cheerleaders-upbeat, happy, and courteous to everyone. The cruise staff department offers the following cruise ship jobs: Cruise Director, Assistant Cruise Director, Social Hostess, Cruise Staff, Disc Jockey/DJ, Fitness Instructor/Trainer, Youth Activities Coordinator/Youth Counsellor, Scuba Diving/Water Sports Instructor, Golf Instructor.

(1) Cruise Director The cruise director is in charge of all onboard entertainment, creates, coordinates, and implements all the daily activities, acting master of ceremonies at social activities and evening shows. The cruise director is in charge of all onboard entertainment. Most cruise directors have worked their way up from cruise staff positions and have had some kind of career in entertainment themselves. Each cruise line looks for different qualities in a cruise director. The best way to learn how to become a cruise director is to work

for one as an assistant cruise director or staff member. Generally, the cruise director is an entertainer and usually performs a couple of times a voyage. Originally the cruise director was the lead entertainer but now this role is more administrative and acts as a supervisor to the rest of the cruise staff department. The cruise director is the most visible crew member to the passengers. Professional entertainment background or 2-5 years on board working experience is preferred. Public speaking, delegate responsibilities and strong organizational abilities are required. Fluent English language skills are required.

(2) Assistant Cruise Director The assistant cruise director coordinates the cruise staff personnel activity schedules, supervise and act as master of ceremonies at specific passenger activities as directed by the cruise director, and assists in creating the daily programs. This position supports the cruise Director with managing and supervising the cruise staff. Similar to the cruise Director, the Assistant Cruise Director is consistently visible to the passengers onboard. The Assistant Cruise Director assists with the routine passenger's activities and helps coordinate the evening's activities. This position dedicates a large amount of time to socialization with the guests and participation in shipboard activities. Entertainment, recreation, hotel or resort experience or 1-2 years onboard working experience is preferred. Public speaking, delegate responsibilities and strong organizational abilities are required. Fluent English Language skills are required. He/She has the possibilities for promotion to cruise director.

(3) Social Hosts and Hostess Social Hosts and Hostesses, As a member of the cruise staff, hosts and hostesses are constantly in the public eye and often serve as the mouthpiece for the ship. Duties can include greeting passengers as they board and disembark, assisting shore excursions staff, giving port talks, arranging parties and dinners, acting as master of ceremonies at selected events and introducing the captain to passengers at the captain's cocktail party. Occasionally, the host/hostess will assist in the library. When applying for these positions, applicants should stress public relations experience or education in public relations. An outgoing personality is extremely important for this position as you are required to socialize with the passengers on a regular basis. This position reports to the cruise director or assistant cruise director. Public speaking, delegate responsibilities and strong organizational abilities are required. Fluent English Language skills are required. She has the possibilities for promotion to cruise director.

(4) Cruise Staff The cruise staff positions are often entry-level social positions. This job is for the enthusiastic and extroverted only. They may be requested to organize passenger's activities golf, quizzes, and bingo, etc.. Some experience in a similar type environment is preferred. Fluent English language skills are required. They have the possibilities for promotion to assistant cruise director.

(5) Disc Jockey/DJ He/She should have a diverse music foundation to span the generations of the passengers. Experience in a hospitality position will increase a disc jockey's marketability because of the necessity to socialize gracefully with passengers. Experience with lighting and sound is a big asset as well. Some disc jockeys work closely with the stage man-

ager in assisting with show production. Hotel, resort or night club experience are preferred. Fluent English language skills required.

(6) Fitness Instructor/Trainer The fitness instructor is responsible for passengers'exercise activities, sports. Must have some related qualifications and certificates such as aerobic qualification. At least three months experience in teaching is required. Instructors are required to take a variety of aerobic classes, supervise the gymnasium and also offer personal training to guests. Fluent English Language skills are required.

(7) Youth Activities Coordinator/Youth Counsellor (Youth Staff) The youth activities coordinator is responsible for organizing children's activities and taking care of children onboard. Some experience with children is preferred. Fluent English language skills are required.

(8) Scuba Diving/Water Sports Instructor The water sports instructor conducts daily diving and snorkeling programs, maintains related equipments. Diving instructor's certificate and CPR/first aid certificate are required. Fluent English language skills are required.

(9) Golf Instructor The golf instructor is responsible for operating golf simulator, playing golf with passengers, other cruise staff duties. This position call for very independent individuals who have the capacity and patience to teach at all levels and the ability to interact in social situations with the cruise line guests, staff and port personnel. He/she must also possess the motivation and business acumen to operate the onboard operation in its entirety, from self-promotion, instruction and conducting shore excursions. Fluent English language skills required.

Notes

1. dive masters 潜水教练

2. Most of the cruise staff have a lot of interaction with the passengers, and must be able to focus on providing an enjoyable time for the cruisers. 大多数邮轮员工与乘客有许多互动，并且必须能够致力于为邮轮游客提供一段令人愉快的时光。

3. Cheerleaders 拉拉队队长

4. upbeat 积极乐观的

5. youth counsellor 青少年辅导员

6. scuba diving 戴水肺潜水

7. the most visible crew member to the passengers 游客最能看得见的乘务员

8. the enthusiastic and extroverted 最热情外向的人

9. serve as the mouthpiece for the ship 充当邮轮的代言人

10. aerobic qualification 有氧健身的资格

11. snorkeling program 用通气管潜水项目

12. CPR/first aid certificate 心肺复苏术/急救证书

13. in its entirety 作为一个整体

New words and expressions

ceremony [ˈserimәni] n. 典礼，仪式，礼节，报幕员

master of ceremony 节目主持人，司仪

career [kə'riə] n. （原意：道路，轨道）事业，生涯，速度
visible ['vizəbl] adj. 看得见的，明显的，显著的 n. 可见物
delegate ['deligit] n. 代表 vt. 委派……为代表
organizational [ˌɔgənai'zeiʃənəl] adj. 组织的
dedicate ['dedikeit] vt. 献（身），致力，题献（一部著作给某人）
outgoing ['autgəuiŋ] n. 外出，开支，流出 adj. 对人友好的，喜欢外出的
mouthpiece ['mauθpiːs] n. 话筒，代言人，乐器的吹口
occasionally [ə'keiʒənəli] adv. 有时候，偶尔
socialization [ˌsəuʃəlai'zeiʃ(ə)n] n. 社会化，社会主义化
participation [pɑːˌtisi'peiʃən] n. 分享，参与
disc [disk] n. （= disk）圆盘，唱片 vt. 灌唱片
jockey ['dʒɔki] n. 职业赛马骑师，（机器的）操作员
DJ 唱片节目报告员，唱片音乐节目广播员
enthusiastic [inˌθjuːzi'æstik] adj. 热心的，热情的
extroverted ['ekstrəvəːtid] adj. 外向性的，喜社交的
golf [gɔlf] n. 高尔夫球 vi. 打高尔夫球
quiz [kwiz] n. 测验，提问，恶作剧 v. 对……进行测验，盘问，挖苦
bingo ['biŋgəu] n. 一种赌博游戏，烈酒
diverse [dai'vəːs] adj. 不同的，变化多的
foundation [faun'deiʃən] n. 基础，根本，建立，创立，地基，基金，基金会
span [spæn] n. 跨度，跨距，范围 v. 横越
marketability [ˌmɑːkitə'biliti] n. 可销售性，适合市场性
necessity [ni'sesiti] n. 必要性，需要，必需品
socialize ['səuʃəlaiz] vi. 参加社交活动，发生社交往来 vt. 使社会化，使社会主义化
stage [steidʒ] n. 舞台，戏剧，活动场所 vt. 上演，筹备，举行
fitness ['fitnis] n. 健身，健康，适当，适切性
aerobic [ˌεə'rəubik] adj. 依靠氧气的，与需氧菌有关的，增氧健身法的
gymnasium [dʒim'neiziəm，gim'nɑːziəm] n. 健身房，体育馆
coordinator [kəu'ɔːdineitə] n. 协调者，同等的人或物
counsellor ['kaunsələ] n. 顾问，律师，辅导员
scuba ['skuːbə] n. 水中呼吸器
diving ['daiviŋ] n. 潜水，跳水
snorkel ['snɔːkl] vi. 用通气管潜游 n. （潜水艇或潜水者的）通气管
first aid 急救
patience ['peiʃəns] n. 耐性，忍耐
interact [ˌintər'ækt] vi. 互相作用，互相影响
acumen [ə'kjuːmən] n. 敏锐，聪明
entirety [in'taiəti] n. 全部，完全

Exercises

1. What are the main duties of cruise director?

2. What are the main duties of assistant cruise director?
3. What are the main duties of social hostess?
4. What are the main duties of cruise staff?
5. What are the main duties of DJ?
6. What are the main duties of fitness instructor?
7. What are the main duties of youth counsellor?
8. What are the main duties of water sports instructor?
9. What are the main duties of golf instructor?

3.3.8 Entertainment Department

No other industry has been growing so rapidly in the past seven years as the cruise industry. Just for the recent years all leading cruise lines have doubled their fleets and number of employees. Full scale Broadway and Las Vegas style production shows are performed aboard most of the cruise ships. More and more entertainers are joining the the entertainment department of the cruise ships. The entertainment department is responsible for all onboard entertainment, including shows and cabarets. The cruise director is also in charge of all entertainers. The Entertainment Department on a cruise ship consists of the following positions: Cruise Director, Guest Entertainer, Lounge Performer, Dancer, Singer, Musician, Production Manager, Assistant Production Manager, Sound & Light Technician, Disc Jockey/DJ, Fitness Instructor, Youth Activities Coordinator, Arts & Crafts Instructor, etc..

(1) Guest Entertainer The guest entertainer provides entertainment that caters to people of all ages, usually offers a complete and strong 40-50 minutes self-contained show catering to a wide diversity of ages.

(2) Lounge Performer The lounge performer is responsible for entertaining in certain locations on board: piano bar, night club, etc. and providing their own music and materials. Solid experience and ability to play a wide diversity of musical styles are required. Fluent English language skills are required.

(3) Dancer & Singer They are responsible for main production shows, cabarets, etc.. Extensive experience in production shows is required.

(4) Musician The musician is responsible for the performance of show band including

piano, saxophone/reeds, trumpet, trombone, bass, guitar, drums. Extensive professional experience is required. Fair English language skills are required.

(5) Production Manager The production manager is responsible for running the production shows and managing the technical staff. Extensive technical and practical education and/or hands-on experience are required.

(6) Assistant Production Manager The assistant production manager assists in running the production shows and any activities that require technical assistance. Extensive technical and practical education and/or hands-on experience are required. He/She has the possibilities for promotion to production manager.

(7) Sound & Light Technician He/She is responsible for assisting in running the production shows and any activities that require technical assistance. Technical and practical education and/or hands-on experience are required. He/She has the possibilities for promotion to assistant production manager.

(8) Arts & Crafts Instructor He/She must be a friendly, patient and creative individual who enjoys teaching craft projects to the guests while the ship is at sea or on select port days. The instructor will be responsible for providing the supplies needed to make the crafts and must prepare an original project for each class.

(9) Caricature Artist During a cruise assignment, a caricature's responsibility is to provide quick and fun caricature drawings which are offered at no charge to passengers. Usually the Caricaturist is situated in popular, high traffic areas of the ship sketching individuals, as well as groups of family and friends travelling together. Generally less than five minutes should be spent with each individual drawing. Caricaturists must be friendly, creative and have excellent social skills.

(10) Dance Instructors Most of dance instructors commonly travel as a duo. The couple must be proficient in all dance styles from the classics to the current fads and offer lessons to passengers of all ages and abilities. Dance Instructors must be outgoing, friendly and prepared for anything.

(11) Guest Lecturers This can be a fun job. There is not usually a salary for this position. However, He/she get a cruise for himself/herself and companion in return for just a few hours of your time. There is no age limit and he/she can be asked to join another ship in the fleet several times per year. The most common subjects of lectures are: Arts and Crafts, Bridge, Numerology, Fortune-telling, Handwriting Analysis, Golf Instruction, Antiques and Self-improvement, etc.. Typical benefits would be-return air ticket, short-term cruise, free single or shared stateroom, a drinks allowance, all services of the ship provided to paying passengers, shore excursions, dining with passengers and/or officer's mess.

Notes

1. Full scale Broadway and Las Vegas style production shows 全规模的百老汇和拉斯维加斯风格的制作节目

2. self-contained show 独立表演

3. hands-on experience 实际动手操作的经验
4. caricature drawings 漫画绘画
5. high traffic areas 高流量交通区域
6. Most of dance instructors commonly travel as a duo. 大多数的舞蹈教师通常两人同行。
7. from the classics to the current fads 从经典到时尚
8. numerology 数字命理学，数字占卦术
9. fortune-telling 算命，占卜

New words and expressions

scale [skeil] n. 刻度，衡量，比例，比例尺 vt. 依比例决定，测量 vi. 剥落，攀登，衡量

Broadway ['brɔːdwei] n. 纵贯纽约市的大街道，百老汇

performer [pə'fɔːmə(r)] n. 表演者

contain [kən'tein] vt. 包含，容纳，容忍 vi. 自制 v. [数] 可被……除尽

cater ['keitə] vi. 备办食物，满足（需要），投合

diversity [dai'vəːsiti] n. 差异，多样性

saxophone ['sæksəfəun] n. [音] 萨克斯管（铜管类乐器）

reed [riːd] n. 芦苇，芦笛，簧片，管乐器

trumpet ['trʌmpit] n. 喇叭

trombone ['trɔmbəun] n. 长号

bass [beis] n. 低音部，男低音，低音乐器 adj. 低音的

guitar [gi'tɑː] n. 吉他，六弦琴 vi. 弹吉他

patient ['peiʃənt] n. 病人，患者 adj. 忍耐的，耐心的

original [ə'ridʒənəl] adj. 最初的，原始的，独创的，新颖的 n. 原物，原作

select [si'lekt] vt. 选择，挑选 adj. 精选的

craft [krɑːft] n. 工艺，手艺

caricature [ˌkærikə'tjuə] n. 讽刺画，漫画，讽刺描述法 vt. 画成漫画讽刺

duo ['dju(ː)əu] n. 〈意〉二重唱，艺人的一对

proficient [prə'fiʃənt] n. 精通

fad [fæd] n. 时尚，一时流行的狂热，一时的爱好

companion [kəm'pænjən] n. 同伴，共事者

numerology [ˌnjuːmə'rɔlədʒi, nuː-] n. 数字命理学

fortune ['fɔːtʃən] n. 财富，运气，好运，命运 vt. 给……以大宗财富

antique [æn'tiːk] n. 古物，古董 adj. 古时的，过时的

allowance [ə'lauəns] n. 津贴，补助，宽容，允许 vt. 定量供应

mess [mes] n. 混乱，脏乱 v. 弄乱

Exercises

1. What are the main duties of guest entertainer?
2. What are the main duties of lounge performer?
3. What are the main duties of dancer and singer?
4. What are the main duties of musician?

5. What are thc main duties of production manager?
6. What are the main duties of sound and light technician?
7. What are the main duties of arts and crafts instructor?
8. What are the main duties of caricature artist?
9. What are the main duties of guest lecturer?

3.3.9 Medical Department (Infirmary Onboard)

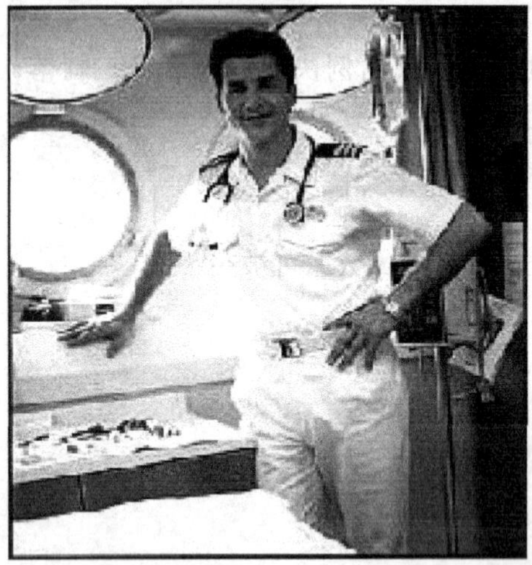

The medical department offers the following job positions: Chief Doctor/Physician, Doctor/Physician and Registered Nurse. The department usually consists of one or two doctors and one to four nurses depending on the onboard facilities. Aboard cruise ships doing world cruises or remote itineraries, the need for a full surgical staff and a dentist may be more common. Medical staff is either hired directly by cruise line medical departments or through concessionaire companies servicing their line.

(1) Chief Doctor/Physician. The chief doctor oversees the entire shipboard medical facilities, treatment mostly to passengers and sometimes crew, if required. Current license, extensive experience with cardiac and primary care, trauma, internal, and emergency medicine are required. Two to three years in subordinate positions on board ships are required. Diploma from an accredited medical school and fluent English language skills are required.

(2) Doctor/Physician. The doctor is responsible for treatment mostly to crew members and sometimes passengers, if required. Current license, extensive experience with cardiac and primary care, trauma, internal, and emergency medicine are required. Diploma from an accredited medical school and fluent English language skills are required. He/She has the possibilities for promotion to chief doctor.

(3) Registered Nurse. The registered nurse is responsible for treatment to passengers and crew. Diploma from accredited nursing school with a minimum of two years'recent hospital experience is required. Experience with cardiac care, trauma, internal medicine and fluent English language skills are required.

Notes

extensive experience with cardiac and primary care, trauma, internal, and emergency medicine are required. 具有广泛的心脏和基本保健、创伤、内科和急诊医学的经验。

New words and expressions

physician [fi'ziʃən] n. 医师，内科医师

register ['redʒistə] n. 记录，登记，注册 vt. 记录，登记，注册 vi. 登记，注册

aboard [ə'bɔːd] adv. 上船（飞机、车）prep. 在（船、飞机、车）上，上（船、飞机、车）

remote [ri'məut] adj. 遥远的，偏僻的，细微

itinerary [ai'tinərəri，i't-] n. 路线

surgical ['səːdʒikəl] adj. 外科的，外科医生的，手术上的 n. 外科病房，外科手术

dentist ['dentist] n. 牙科医生

cardiac ['kɑːdiæk] n. 强心剂，强胃剂 adj. 心脏的，（胃的）贲门的

trauma [ə'trɔːmə] n. [医] 外伤，损伤

internal [in'təːnl] adj. 内在的，国内的

emergency [i'məːdʒnsi] n. 紧急情况，突然事件，非常时刻，紧急事件

Exercises

1. What are the main duties of chief doctor?
2. What are the main duties of doctor?
3. What are the main duties of registered nurse?

3.3.10 Beauty Salon/Spa

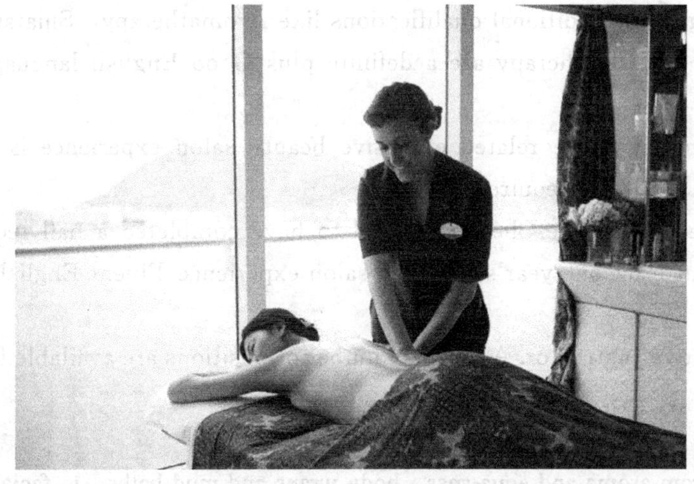

The salons and spas department on board most of the luxury cruise ships offer passengers full service treatments ranging from aroma and aqua-spas, body wraps and mud baths, to facials, massages and hairdos. Even the smaller and older ship are now paying more attention to fitness on board, resulting in an ever growing need for beauty and skin care professionals. Onboard salons and spas are either run in-house or by a concessionaire company who are responsible for hiring of the following cruise ship job positions: hair stylist/hairdresser, beauty therapist/beautician, cosmetologist, nail technician, physiotherapist, massage therapist, and aerobic & fitness instructor. The salons are equipped with the latest in beauty technology and it is the responsibility of the staff to put it to good use promoting treatments and satisfying passengers. Working hours can sometimes be long, especially on formal nights, which usually fall on a sea day.

(1) Beauty Salon Manager. The beauty salon manager oversees entire operations of the beauty salon, accounting and management of the salon staff. Extensive beauty salon and managerial experience are required.

(2) Assistant Beauty Salon Manager. The assistant beauty salon manager manages the day to day operations of the beauty salon as directed by the salon manager. Beauty salon and managerial experience are required. He/She has the possibilities for promotion to salon manager.

(3) Beautician. He/She must have some related qualifications. For applicants applying outside Europe, an International equivalent will be accepted. Note that a qualification in facial and body electrotherapeutics is essential.

(4) Hair Stylist/Hairdresser. The beauty salon experience is required. Generally, must have completed a three-year hairdressing apprenticeship or full time training course at a certified college. In addition, applicants must be fully qualified in both ladies and men's hairdressing. It is also important that hairdressers can cope with both a busy column and a demanding clientele. Fluent English language skills required. He/She has the possibilities for promotion to assistant salon manager.

(5) Massage Therapist. The related extensive experience is required. Must be qualified in related massage. Any additional qualifications like Aromatherapy, Shiatsu, Reflexology, Reiki Healing or Sports Therapy are a definite plus. Good English language skills are required.

(6) Cosmetologist. The related extensive beauty salon experience is required. Fluent English language skills are required.

(7) Nail Technician. He/She is required to have completed a nail technician training course and have at least one year's full time salon experience. Fluent English language skills required.

(8) Alternative Instructor. A limited number of positions are available for Yoga and Tai Chi instructors.

Notes

1. ranging from aroma and aqua-spas, body wraps and mud baths, to facials, massages and hairdos （服务范围）从芳香疗法和水疗、身体裹敷和泥巴浴到美容、按摩和做发型

2. beauty and skin care professionals 美容及皮肤护理专业人员

3. hair stylist/hairdresser, beauty therapist/beautician, cosmetologist, nail technician, physiotherapist, massage therapist, and aerobic & fitness instructor. 发型师/美容师，美容治疗师/美容师，美容师，美甲师，理疗师，按摩治疗师和有氧健身教练。

4. either run in-house or by a concessionaire company 要么由自己内部经营，要么由特许公司经营

5. to put it to good use promoting treatments and satisfying passengers 充分利用（新技术）以促进治疗并让游客满意。

6. facial and body electrotherapeutics 面部和身体电疗

7. cope with both a busy column and a demanding clientele 应付众多苛刻的客户

8. Any additional qualifications like Aromatherapy，Shiatsu，Reflexology，Reiki Healing or Sports Therapy are a definite plus. 任何有额外的像芳香疗法、按摩、足疗、灵气治疗或运动疗法合格证的人肯定受到优先考虑。

New words and expressions

in-house [inhaus] 起源于机构内部的，机构内部的

stylist ['stailist] n. 自成流派者，文体家，设计师

hairdresser ['hɛədresə(r)] n. （为女子做发的）理发师，美容师

therapist ['θerəpist] n. 临床医学家

beautician [bjuː'tiʃən] n. 美容师

cosmetologist [ˌkɔzmə'tɔlədʒist] n. 美容品业者，美容师

physiotherapist ['fiziəu'θerəpist] n. 理疗家，物理疗法家

satisfy ['sætisfai] vt. 满足，使满意，说服，使相信 v. 满意，确保

equivalent [i'kwivələnt] adj. 相等的，相当的，同意义的 n. 等价物，相等物

apprenticeship [ə'prentisˌʃip] n. 学徒的身份，学徒的年限

certified ['səːtifaid] adj. 被鉴定的

demanding [di'mɑːndiŋ; (US)di'mændiŋ] adj. 过分要求的，苛求的

clientele [ˌkliːɑːn'teil] n. 诉讼委托人，客户

aromatherapy [ərəumə'θerəpist] n. 用香料按摩

shiatsu [ʃi'ætsuː] n. (Jap.)〈医〉指压，指压按摩疗法

reflexology [ˌriːflek'sɔlədʒi] n. 反射论

healing ['hiːliŋ] n. 康复，复原 adj. 有治疗功用的

therapy ['θerəpi] n. 治疗

yoga ['jəugə] n. 瑜伽，瑜伽术

alternative [ɔːl'təːnətiv] n. 二中择一 adj. 选择性的，二中择一的

Exercises

1. What are the main duties of beauty salon manager?
2. What are the main duties of assistant beauty salon manager?
3. What are the main duties of beautician?
4. What are the main duties of hair stylist?
5. What are the main duties of hairdresser?
6. What are the main duties of massage therapist?
7. What are the main duties of cosmetologist?
8. What are the main duties of nail technician?
9. What are the main duties of alternative instructor?

3.3.11 Photo Department

The photo department is responsible for taking photos for both the passengers and crew. The skillful photographers can take various pictures for everyone, and they can also use advanced equipments to develop the films in time. Some cruise lines run their own photo department operations, some cruise lines tender out the department to some concessionaire companies. The department on a cruise ship offers the following cruise ship jobs: photo manager, assistant photo manager, photographer. Seen everywhere on board and ashore, the photographers are constantly entertaining both the passengers and crew while creating instant memories for everyone around them. Most photographers are employed through concessionaire companies.

(1) Photo Manager. The photo manager oversees entire operations of the photo department. Photography and related managerial experience are required. Fluent English Language skills are required.

(2) Assistant Photo Manager. The assistant photo manager oversees day to day operations of the photo department. Photography and related managerial experience are required. Fluent English language skills are required. He/She has the possibilities for promotion to photo manager.

(3) Photographer. The photographer is responsible for passengers' portraits, photo processing. Some experience is required. Whilst generally either formal qualifications or photo experience are required. Good English language skills are required. He/She has the possibilities for promotion to assistant photo manager.

Notes

1. to develop the films in time 及时冲洗胶卷（照片）

2. tender out the department to some concessionaire companies 通过招标出租给一些特许经营公司

3. instant memories 瞬间记忆

New words and expressions

photographer [fətɔgrəfə] n. 摄影师

instant ['instənt] adj. 立即的，直接的，方便的，即时的

portrait ['pɔːtrit] n. 肖像，人像

whilst [waiist] conj. 时时，同时

processing [prəu'sesiŋ] n. 处理

Exercises

1. What are the main duties of photo manager?
2. What are the main duties of assistant photo manager?
3. What are the main duties of photographer?

3. 3. 12 Gift Shops Department

The gift shop department on a cruise ship offers the following jobs: gift shop manager, assistant gift shop manager, shop assistant / gift shop sales associate. The gift shop personnel are responsible for the running of the on board shops, which generally consist of a boutique, a cosmetic and fragrance counter, and a souvenir and gift shop. Concessionaire companies who hire applicants with experience in retail, sales, and customer service run most of the shops. Some cruise lines operate their gift shop departments themselves and some cruise lines tender out the department to some concessionaire companies.

(1) Gift Shop Manager The gift shop manager oversees entire gift shop operations, accounting and manages retail staff. Retail and managerial experience are required.

(2) Assistant Gift Shop Manager The assistant gift shop manager oversees the day to day operations and assists in managing the retail staff. Retail and managerial experience are required. He/ She has the possibilities for promotion to gift shop manager.

(3) Shop Assistant/Gift Shop Sales Associate The shop assistant is responsible for selling souvenir items, local products, fashion clothing and T-shirts, camera film, etc.. Some retail experience is preferred. Fluent English language is required. He/She has the

possibilities for promotion to assistant gift shop manager.

Notes

1. a boutique, a cosmetic and fragrance counter 一个精品店，一个化妆品和香水柜台
2. retail staff 零售人员
3. fashion clothing 时装

New words and expressions

gift [gift] n. 赠品, 礼物, 天赋, 才能

associate [əˈsəuʃieit] vt. 使发生联系 vi. 交往 n. 合作人, 同事 adj. 副的

personnel [ˌpəːsəˈnel] n. 人员, 职员

boutique [buːˈtiːk] n. 专卖流行衣服的小商店

cosmetic [kɔzˈmetik] n. 化妆品 adj. 化妆用的

fragrance [ˈfreigrəns] n. 芬芳, 香气, 香味

retail [ˈriːteil] n. 零售 adj. 零售的 vt. 零售, 转述 vi. 零售 adv. 以零售方式

souvenir [ˈsuːvəniə] n. 纪念品

Exercises

1. What are the main duties of gift shop manager?
2. What are the main duties of assistant gift shop manager?
3. What are the main duties of shop assistant?

3.3.13 Casino Department

Some cruise lines operate the department themselves and some cruise lines tender out the department to some concessionaire companies. The casino department consists of the following cruise ship positions: casino manager, casino dealer/croupier, cashier and slot technician. In compliance with international custom laws, the casino is only allowed to open while in international waters; usually three miles out to sea. Subsequently the staff only work while at sea and have port days off.

(1) Casino Manager The casino manager oversees entire operations of the casino, accounting, manages casino staff. Casino and managerial experience is required. Fluent

English language skills are required.

(2) Assistant Casino Manager The assistant casino manager oversees operations of the casino as directed by the casino manager, accounting procedures. Casino experience is required, usually begin on board as a croupier. Good English language skills are required. Has the possibilities for promotion to casino manager.

(3) Casino Dealer/Croupier The casino dealer is responsible for the operations of roulette, blackjack, baccarat. Experience is required. Good English language skills are required. Has the possibilities for promotion to assistant casino manager.

(4) Slot Technician The slot technician is responsible for the maintenance and repairs of all casino devices and machines. Extensive mechanical and electrical background and/or education are required.

(5) Cashier The cashier is responsible for the accounting of revenue as directed by the casino manager. This is an entry-level position. Accounting experience is preferable.

Notes

1. casino dealer 赌场发牌人
2. casino croupier 赌场上的总管理人，副主持人
3. slot technician 赌博机技术员
4. in compliance with international custom laws 遵守国际惯例法
5. have port days off 港口日放假

New words and expressions

dealer [ˈdiːlə] n. 经销商, 商人

croupier [ˈkruːpiə] n. 赌场上的总管理人, 副主持人

cashier [kəˈʃiə] n. （商店等的）出纳员,（银行或公司的）司库

slot [slɔt] n. 缝, 狭槽, 细长的孔, 硬币投币口, 狭通道

subsequently [ˈsʌbsikwəntli] adv. 后来, 随后

operation [ˌɔpəˈreiʃən] n. 运转, 操作, 实施, 作用, 业务, 工作

roulette [ru(ː)ˈlet] n. 轮盘赌, 点线机, 轮迹线, 刻骑缝孔的齿轮

blackjack [ˈblækdʒæk] v. 以棒打, 胁迫 n. 扑克牌的二十一点

baccarat [ˈbækərɑː] n. 一种纸牌赌博

mechanical [miˈkænikl] adj. 机械的, 机械制的, 机械似的, 呆板的

Exercises

1. What are the main duties of casino manager?
2. What are the main duties of assistant casino manager?
3. What are the main duties of casino dealer?
4. What are the main duties of slot technician?
5. What are the main duties of the cashier of casino?

3.3.14 Other Individual Jobs

(1) Art Auctioneer Art galleries around the world make their art available for sale through various cruise lines. The art auctioneer makes art available for bid and sale to pas-

sengers of ships. More cruise lines are opting to add auctions to their ongoing list of entertainment and services offered aboard cruise vessels. There are several concession companies who run auctions on board of most cruise ships. Auctions are among the most profitable activities aboard the big cruise ships after the casino, bars and giftshops. The auctions are run in a similar way to land based auctions, with the auctioneer giving a brief talk on each piece prior to starting the bidding. The auctioneer must be smart, responsible, money motivated and sales driven. Art knowledge is a plus. Good clear English is a must, as they must speak and communicate in front of groups of people.

(2) Information Technology (IT) Positions The operation and maintenance of all areas of the cruise ship's on board computer systems, both hardware and software is the responsibility of the information technology department. Candidates are required to have experience of the major software applications and an in-depth knowledge of network operating systems management, techniques, configuration and topologies as the entire hotel department is operated by an internal computer system. Internet cafes and computer centers are available on board cruise ships worldwide. The way in which they operate varies according to the cruise company or concessionaire running the facilities. The computer labs are overseen by a computer officer or internet cafe manager. Internet service onboard a cruise

ship is transmitted via satellite, resulting in a much higher cost involved in collecting regular e-mail. Candidates must have an in-depth knowledge of computers, computer & Internet services and major software applications.

① Shipboard Systems Manager. The shipboard systems manager is responsible for the day to day operations of AS/400/Windows NT/POS platforms. Must be required to have 1-2 years AS/400 and Win/NT experience. POS knowledge is an advantage. Must speak fluent English.

② Computer Systems Hardware Technician. The computer systems hardware technician is responsible for installations, maintenance, troubleshooting and upgrading of computer hardware, software, personal computer networks, peripheral equipment and electronic mail systems; assesses user training needs and trains users in effective use of applications. Must have completed two years of college-level course in computer science, information technology or a related field and two years of general computer installation, maintenance and repair experience. Must speak fluent English.

③ Internet Manager. Almost all cruise ships have internet cafe now, and the responsibilities of this position include running and managing it effectively. Duties also include troubleshooting and passenger assistance. The internet manager must possess basic computer knowledge, proficiency in Microsoft Office, sales and managerial experience and excellent customer service skills. Must be creative, self motivated, multi-task oriented and possess excellent written and oral communication and presentation skills. Energetic and outgoing personality is a plus. Must speak fluent English.

(3) Clergyman The clergymen generally provide the passengers with on board church services when cruise ships are at sea or in a foreign port on a Sunday. This is especially true for religious holidays such as Christmas and Easter. If the need arises, rabbis are also employed for the Jewish holidays. This is not normally a paid position, but rather a working vacation in which the clergymen render their services for the opportunity to cruise.

Notes

1. art auctioneer 艺术拍卖
2. The art auctioneer makes art available for bid and sale to passengers of ships. 艺术品拍卖

师为船上乘客提供艺术品的买卖。

3. More cruise lines are opting to add auctions to their ongoing list of entertainment and services offered aboard cruise vessels. 更多的邮轮公司选择将拍卖添加在他们正在进行的娱乐和服务的列表中。

4. to starting the bidding 开始招标

5. internet cafes and computer centers 网吧和电脑中心

6. troubleshooting 发现并修理故障

7. peripheral equipment 外围设备

8. assesses user training needs and trains users in effective use of applications 评估用户培训需求，培训用户有效应用

9. must be creative, self motivated, multi-task oriented 必须具有创造性，自我激励，适应多重任务的

10. church services 教会服务

11. Christmas and Easter 圣诞节和复活节

New words and expressions

auctioneer [ˌɔːkʃəˈniə] n. 拍卖人 vt. 拍卖

gallery [ˈgæləri] n. 走廊、戏院、美术陈列室, 画廊, 图库

opt [ɔpt] vi. 选择

ongoing [ˈɔngəuiŋ] adj. 正在进行的

auction [ˈɔːkʃən] n. 拍卖 vt. 拍卖

hardware [ˈhɑːdwə] n. 五金器具,（电脑的）硬件,（电子仪器的）部件

software [ˈsɔftwə] n. 软件

candidate [ˈkændidit] n. 候选人, 投考者

application [ˌæpliˈkeiʃən] n. 请求, 申请, 申请表, 应用, 应用程序, 应用软件

network [ˈnetwəːk] n. 网络, 网状物, 广播网

configuration [kənˌfig juˈreiʃən] n. 构造, 结构, 配置, 外形

topology [təˈpɔlədʒi] n. 拓扑, 布局拓扑学

worldwide [ˈwəːldwaid] adj. 全世界的

transmit [trænzˈmit] vt. 传输, 转送, 传达, 传导, 传播 vi. 发射信号, 发报

via [ˈvaiə, ˈviːə] prep. 经, 通过, 经由

POS abbr. n. [计] Point Of Sells , 电子收款机系统

installation [ˌinstəˈleiʃən] n. [计] 安装, 装置, 就职

troubleshooting [ˈtrʌblˈʃuːtiŋ] n. 发现并修理故障, 解决纷争

peripheral [pəˈrifərəl] adj. 外围的 n. 外围设备

assess [əˈses] vt. 估定, 评定

oriented [ˈɔːrientid, ˈəʊ-] adj. 导向的

presentation [ˌprezenˈteiʃən] n. 介绍, 陈述, 赠送, 表达

energetic [ˌenəˈdʒetik] adj. 精力充沛的, 积极的

Exercises

1. What are the main duties of auctioneer onboard?

2. What are the main duties of shipboard systems manager?
3. What are the main duties of computer systems hardware technician onboard?
4. What are the main duties of internet manager onboard?
5. What are the main duties of clergymen onboard?

3.4 Language & Communication

3.4.1 Shipboard Language

(1) What is the common language spoken aboard cruise ships?

The cruise ship is an international community, English is very important because it is the common language on board.

(2) Why is it important to have a single language?

It is very important to have a simple language (English) onboard, because it is:

① the requirement of safety (safety drill, fire, man overboard, etc.);

② the requirement of politeness/courtesy (manner) to passengers and colleagues;

③ the requirement of communication with passengers and colleagues.

3.4.2 Shipboard Communication

(1) Communication is a two-way progress, it is a course of sending & receiving signals. Communication is especially important onboard because:

① it is impossible not to communicate onboard;

② communication is the exchange of information, news, ideas or opinions among people;

③ communication can help crew and passengers understand each other, and make happy and polite atmosphere onboard.

(2) Verbal, vocal & visual language

What are they?

① verbal language

The words that we say. It is spoken language, not written language.

② vocal language

It is the tone & projection of the voice. It is connected with the voice and used in speaking. e.g. the tongue is one of the vocal organs.

③ visual language

It is what people see: body language and appearance. It is connected with the sense of sight.

(3) What is good communication?

Psychologist Albert Mehrabian researched three elements of communication: words, tone of voice and body language. More interestingly, Mehrabian studied how people communicate feelings and attitudes. If your body language and tone of voice disagree with your words, listeners tend to believe your body and voice. Look at this conversation. Mary (smiling) "John, how are you today?" John (with a sad face and voice) "I'm great, thanks." Here, Mary will believe John's voice and face more than his words. Thus, for good communication, the body, the voice, and the words must match each other. If the body, voice and words disagree, listeners will be confused. Moreover, if we like a speaker, 55% of our feelings come from his/her body language, 38% of our feelings come from his/her voice, and only 7% of our feelings come from his/her words. These numbers are about feelings and attitudes, not about the message in the words. But Mehrabian's research reveals that your tone of voice, your body language, and not just your words, are essential for good communication.

I Albert Mehrabian was born 1939, currently Professor Emeritus of Psychology, UCLA (abbr. University of California at Los Angeles). He has become known best by his publications on the relative importance of verbal and nonverbal messages. His findings on inconsistent messages of feelings and attitudes have been quoted throughout human communication seminars worldwide, and have also become known as the *7%-38%-55%* Rule.]

(4) Three elements of communication and the "7%-38%-55% Rule"

In his studies, *Mehrabian* (1971) comes to two conclusions. Firstly, that there are basically three elements in any face-to-face communication: words, tone of voice, body language. secondly, the nonverbal elements are particularly important for communicating feelings and attitude, especially when they are incongruent: if words and body language disagree, one tends to believe the body language. It is emphatically not the case that nonverbal elements in all senses convey the bulk of the message, though this is how his conclusions are frequently quoted. When delivering a lecture or presentation, for instance, the textual content of the lecture is delivered entirely verbally, but nonverbal cues are very important in conveying the speaker's attitude towards their words, notably their belief or conviction.

(5) Attitudes and congruence

According to Mehrabian, these three elements account differently for our liking for the person who puts forward a message concerning their feelings: words account for 7%, tone of voice accounts for 38%, and body language accounts for 55% of the liking. They are often abbreviated as the "3Vs" for verbal, vocal & visual. For effective and meaningful communication about emotions, these three parts of the message need to support each other, they have to be "congruent". In case of any "incongruence", the receiver of the message might be irritated by two messages coming from two different channels, giving cues in two different directions.

It becomes more likely that the receiver will trust the predominant form of communication, which to Mehrabian's findings is nonverbal (38% + 55 %), rather than the literal meaning of the words (7 %). It is important to say that in the respective study, Mehrabian conducted experiments dealing with communications of feelings and attitudes (i. e., like-dislike), and that the above, disproportionate influence of tone of voice and body language becomes effective only when the situation is ambiguous. Such ambiguity appears mostly when the words spoken are inconsistent with the tone of voice or body language of the speaker (sender).

(6) Misinterpretation of Mehrabian's Rule

This "*7%-38%-55%* Rule" has been overly interpreted in such way, that some people claim that in any communication situation, the meaning of a message was being transported mostly by nonverbal cues, not by the meaning of words. This generalization, from the initially very specific conditions in his experiments, is the basic mistake around "Mehrabian's rule", and on his webpage Mehrabian clearly states this: Total Liking = 7% Verbal Liking + 38% Vocal Liking + 55% Facial Liking. Please note that this and other equations regarding relative importance of verbal and nonverbal messages were derived from experiments dealing with communications of feelings and attitudes (i. e., like-dislike). Unless a communicator is talking about their feelings or attitudes, these equations are not applicable.

(7) Body language triangle

The following body language triangle shows what are positive and what are negative in the communication, it can help us how to communication with passengers efficiently.

Positive (open)

co-operative

smiles

interested

proper eye contact

body language & voice support

open-minded

Negative submissive	aggressive
(closed)	(closed)
weak voice	hard voice
slow speech	fast speech
looks down	too much eye contact
mouth covered	space invasion
scared of new information	thinks himself perfect
defensive	defensive
narrow-minded	intimidates people
	narrow-minded

(If we are cooperative, opportunity will come to you, we can change everything around.)

(8) First impressions

① The first impression is the most important.

"First time, every time."

In fostering your favorable image the first impression is very important. It can be decisive. Once it is formed, it is difficult to change. In fact, its importance can never be underestimated.

How do you impress your guests at first sight? Here are some major methods:

a. Make careful preparation before the arrival of the passengers. e. g. Get to know the nature, composition and interests of passengers, better still get to know something of each individual; Predict individual needs and possible problems.

b. You must look nice and smart. Pay attention to your clothes, hair-do and makeup.

c. Make yourself easy to identify. Wear a name card or a badge

d. Make your self-introduction brief, interesting and easy to remember.

e. Show your efficiency. Settle passengers onboard as quickly as possible.

f. Show your good manners. Use respectable titles in greeting your guests. Do not hold out your hand to ladies or the elderly or VIPs first. Wait for their initiative. Handshake should not be perfunctory, long or forceful. Do not avoid eye contact in handshake.

g. Remember the name of your guests as soon as possible. Better to ask each what he or she would like to be called.

② Good impressions

The 90—90 rule

According to research, you have 90 seconds to create 90% of your overall first impression. or

People make up 90% of their mind about you during their first 90 seconds of contact with you.

In short, 90 seconds to create 90% of the first impression, if the first impression is bad, very difficult to change (turn around).

(9) How to read passengers?

The following are the main personality types among passengers, they can help you to offer individual services to passengers.

Personality Types

Controller: easy to reach an agreement; (loud) pay attention to facts and results	Thinker: logic; in order; (quite) understanding
Sentimentalist: thought or judgement arising (quite) from feeling; not social.	Entertainer: need attention; (loud) like to be noticed; full of energy.

In short, we should communicate with passengers according to their different characteristics.

(10) How to start conversation?

Generally speaking, if we want to open conversation, use special questions, if we want to close conversation, use general questions or disjunctive questions. e. g.

Open	Close
how, where, when, what, why, who, etc.	isn't it, did he, are you, will you, have you, can you, etc.

("open" question means " need more information, be more friendly and interested", we should use more "open" questions to start conversation to communicate with passengers.)

(11) Listening skills

Listening is very difficult, it's an art. Everybody loves a good listener, as the old saying goes, listening is the greater part of learning. The Bible says, "Be swift to hear, slow to speak." in other words, ease off. Let the other person have his turn at bat. One of great British statesmen, Winston Churchill ever said, "Speech is silver while silence is gold." There is great value in silence when communicating with passengers.

So we should:

① Listen with an open mind. We should be attentive and go back to empathy when we listen to passengers.

② Listen all the way through. We should be patient from beginning to end when we listen to passengers.

③ Watch for verbal/visual signals. We should pay attention to passengers' verbal/visual clues when we listen to passengers.

④ Become an careful observer. We should see and notice the passengers carefully when we listen to passengers.

(12) How to be an excellent communicator?

Communication is a top priority when working onboard a cruise ship. The behavioral characteristics of an excellent communicator are as follows.

① Positive body language.

② Warm, friendly and enthusiastic.

③ Clear, concise, straight to the point.

④ Quality voice tone.

⑤ Good listener.

⑥ Sincere, patient and empathetic.

⑦ Good questioning skills.

⑧ Open and approachable.

⑨ Good eye contact.

⑩ Good interpersonal skills.

⑪ Sober and balanced.

Poor communicators are generally the opposite of the above.

(13) What are the benefits of excellent communication skills ?

Excellent communication skills will bring the following values to the workplace:

① Improved efficiency.

② Greater empathy and respect.

③ Sharing of knowledge.

④ Confidence and enthusiasm grows.

⑤ More responsibility, trust and loyalty.

⑥ Quality company image.

⑦ Enhanced environment.

⑧ Optimized energy and time.

⑨ Crew will feel part of something special.

⑩ Collaboration leading to synergy.

⑪ More productive and smoother operation.

⑫ Cooperation and motivation rises.

Notes

1. an international community 一个国际社会
2. safety drill 安全演习
3. man overboard 人员落水
4. verbal, vocal & visual language 字面语言、声音语言和身体语言
5. the tone & projection of the voice 声音的语调和发射、发出
6. the sense of sight 视觉
7. match each other 相配
8. UCLA（abbr. University of California at Los Angeles）〈美〉加利福尼亚大学洛杉矶分校
9. verbal and nonverbal messages 语言和非语言信息
10. inconsistent messages of feelings and attitudes 情绪和态度的不一致的信息
11. in all senses 在任何意义上来说
12. nonverbal cues 非语言暗示
13. literal meaning 字面意义
14. fostering your favorable image 培养你的良好形象
15. hair-do and makeup 发型和化妆
16. Do not avoid eye contact in handshake. 在握手时不要避免目光接触。
17. personality types 人格类型, 性格类型
18. disjunctive questions 反意问句
19. Be swift to hear, slow to speak. 要迅速地听，慢慢地说。
20. ease off 不要着急
21. Let the other person have his turn at bat. 让别人有击球的机会
22. go back to empathy 换位思考
23. interpersonal skills 人际交往技能，人际关系技巧
24. sober and balanced 冷静与平衡
25. greater empathy and respect 更大的共鸣和尊重
26. enhanced environment 改善环境，提高环境的价值
27. optimized energy and time 优化精力和时间
28. Crew will feel part of something special. 船员会感觉到一部分特别的东西。
29. Collaboration leading to synergy. 协同合作。
30. smoother operation 平稳运转

New words and expressions

aboard [ə'bɔːd] adv. 在船上, 上船 prep. 在（船、飞机、车）上, 上（船、飞机、车）

overboard ['əuvəbɔːd] adv. 自船上落下, 在船外

courtesy ['kəːtisi, 'kɔː-] n. 谦恭, 允许, 礼貌

manner ['mænə] n. 礼貌, 风格, 方式, 样式, 习惯

impossible [im'pɔsəbl] adj. 不可能的, 不会发生的, 难以忍受的

verbal ['vəː bəl] adj. 口头的

vocal [ˈvəukl] adj. 发嗓音的, 声音的, 有声的, 歌唱的 n. 元音, 声乐作品
visual [ˈvizjuəl] adj. 看的, 视觉的, 形象的, 栩栩如生的
tone [təun] n. 音调，语调
projection [prəˈdʒekʃən] n. 发射
tongue [tʌŋ] n. 舌头, 舌状物, 语言, 说话方式, 口语 vt. 舔, 闲谈, 斥责 vi. 吹管乐器
psychologist [psaiˈkələdʒist] n. 心理学者
disagree [ˌdisəˈgriː] vi. 不一致, 不适宜
match [mætʃ] n. 火柴, 比赛, 竞赛, 匹配 v. 相配, 相称, 比赛, 相比, 匹配
reveal [riˈviːl] vt. 展现, 显示, 揭示, 暴露
publication [ˌpʌbliˈkeiʃən] n. 出版物, 出版, 发行, 公布, 发表
nonverbal [ˈnɔnˈvəːbəl] adj. 不用动词的, 不用语言的
inconsistent [ˌinkənˈsistant] adj. 不一致的, 不协调的, 矛盾的
quote [kwəut] vt. 引用, 引证, 提供, 提出, 报（价）
seminar [ˈseminɑː] n. 研究会, 讨论发表会
incongruent [inˈkɔŋgruənt] adj. 不一致的
emphatically [imˈfætˈkəli] adv. 强调地, 用力地
sense [sens] n. 官能, 感觉, 判断力, 见识 vt. 感到, 理解, 认识
presentation [ˌprezenˈteiʃən] n. 介绍, 陈述, 赠送, 表达
textual [ˈtekstjuəl] adj. 本文的, 原文的
cue [kjuː] n. 暗示, 提示, 球杆
congruence [ˈkɔŋgruəns] n. 适合, 一致, 叠合, 全等, 相合性
liking [ˈlaikiŋ] n. 爱好, 嗜好
account for（指数量等）占
abbreviate [əˈbriːvieit] v. 缩写, 缩短, 简化, 简写成, 缩写为
receiver [riˈsiːvə] n. 接受者, 接收器, 收信机
irritate [ˈiriteit] vt. 激怒, 使急躁 v. 刺激
predominant [priˈdɔminənt] adj. 卓越的, 支配的, 主要的, 突出的, 有影响的
finding [ˈfaindiŋ] n. 发现, 发现物, 决定, [律] 裁决
literal [ˈlitərəl] adj. 文字的, 照字面上的, 无夸张的
disproportionate [ˌdisprəˈpɔːʃənit] adj. 不成比例
ambiguous [ˌæmˈbig juəs] adj. 暧昧的, 不明确的
ambiguity [ˌæmbiˈg juːiti] n. 含糊, 不明确
misinterpretation [ˈmisinˌtəːpriˈteiʃən] n. 误译, 曲解
overly [ˈəuvəli] adv. 过度地, 极度地
generalization [ˌdʒenərəlaiˈzeiʃən] n. 一般化, 普遍化, 概括, 广义性
communicator [kəˈmjuːnikeitə] n. 交流者, 发报机, 列车内通报器
equation [iˈkweiʃən] n. 相等, 平衡, 综合体, 因素, 方程式, 等式
triangle [ˈtraiæŋgl] n. [数] 三角形, 三人一组, 三角关系
positive [ˈpɔzətiv] adj. 肯定的, 实际的, 积极的, 绝对的 adj. [数] 正的，[电] 阳的 .
cooperative [kəuˈɔpərətiv] adj. 合作的, 协力的

opportunity [ˌɔpəˈtjuːniti] n. 机会, 时机
change around 使---变得正确，使信服
negative [ˈnegətiv] n. 否定, 负数, 底片 adj. 否定的, 消极的, 负的, 阴性的 vt. 否定, 拒绝 .
submissive [səbˈmisiv] adj. 顺从的
defensive [diˈfensiv] adj. 防御用的, 自卫的 n. 防御
narrow-minded 心胸狭隘的
aggressive [əˈgresiv] adj. 好斗的, 敢作敢为的, 有闯劲的, 侵略性的
intimidate [inˈtimideit] v. 胁迫，威吓
impression [imˈpreʃən] n. 印象, 感想, 盖印, 压痕
foster [ˈfɔstə] vt. 养育, 抚育, 培养, 鼓励, 抱（希望）n. 养育者, 鼓励者
decisive [diˈsaisiv] adj. 决定性的
underestimate [ˈʌndərˈestimeit] vt. 低估, 看轻 n. 低估
at bat 轮到击球
badge [bædʒ] n. 徽章, 证章
identify [aiˈdentifai] vt. 识别, 鉴别, 把 . . . 和 . . . 看成一样 v. 确定
efficiency [iˈfiʃənsi] n. 效率, 功效
manner [ˈmænə] n. 礼貌, 风格, 方式, 样式, 习惯
perfunctory [pəˈfʌŋktəri] adj. 马马虎虎的
initiative [iˈniʃiətiv] n. 主动
handshake [ˈhændʃeik] n. 握手
controller [kənˈtrəulə] n. 管理员, 控制器
disjunctive [disˈdʒʌŋktiv] adj. 分离性的
ease off v. 放松, 缓和, 减轻 减轻某人之
logical [ˈlɔdʒikəl] adj. 合乎逻辑的, 合理的
realistic [riəˈlistik] adj. 现实（主义）的, 实际的
priority [praiˈɒriti] n. 优先, 优先权, [数] 优先次序, 优先考虑的事
enthusiastic [inˌθjuːziˈæstik] adj. 热心的, 热情的, 热烈的, 狂热的
concise [kənˈsɑis] adj. 简明的，简洁的, 简约, 精炼
empathetic [empəˈθetik] adj. 移情作用的, 同感的（等于 empathic）
approachable [əˈprəutʃəb(ə)l] adj. 亲切的, 可接近的
interpersonal [ɪntəˈpəːs(ə)n(ə)l] adj. 人际的, 人与人之间的
sober [ˈsəubə] adj. 冷静的，清醒的, 未醉的 vt. 使严肃, 使醒酒，使清醒
workplace [ˈwəːkpleis] n. 工作场所，车间, 工厂
optimize [ˈɔptimaiz] vt. 使最优化，使尽可能有效
collaboration [kəˌlæbəˈreiʃn] n. 合作，协作, 通敌，勾结
synergy [ˈsinədʒi] n. 协同，配合，企业合并后的协力优势或协合作用

Exercises

1. What is the common language spoken aboard cruise ships?
2. Why is it important to have a single language?
3. What is communication?

4. How many types of languages are there in the communication? What are they? Would you please explain them?
5. What's good communication?
6. What does the three elements of communication mean?
7. What's the misinterpretation of Mehrabian's Rule?
8. What are the values of verbal, vocal and visual in the communication?
9. What are the characteristics of an "open" person?
10. What are the characteristics of a "submissive" person?
11. What are the characteristics of an "aggressive" person?
12. Why is the first impression the most important?
13. What is the 90—90 Rule?
14. What is the "open" conversation?
15. What is the "close" conversation?
16. How to listen to passengers?
17. How to be an excellent communicator?
18. What are the benefits of excellent communication skills ?

3.5 Team Work & Disciplinary Procedure Onboard

3.5.1 Team Work

There is an old saying which goes, one swallow does not make a summer. On the cruise ships, we have to work with all ranks of colleagues with different backgrounds, we should cooperate with them well, none of them is dispensable, we must respect them, value their contribution, there is no reason for us to get proud. In order for a team to function effectively it takes all kinds of positive players, and each play style is equally as important as the other. A healthy blend of all player role types will bond the team together faster and produce best results.

So teamwork is very important in our service work, good teamwork can make our job easy. In order to do teamwork well, we should do as follows.

① Often communicate with colleagues and understand each other.

② Be cooperative with colleagues.

③ Be flexible to get along with colleagues and seek common ground while reserving differences.

④ Be aware of colleagues' needs and help each other.

3.5.2 Disciplinary Procedure Onboard

Generally speaking, if you work as a crew member onboard, the disciplinary procedure for you is made up of the following steps.

Step1. Informal discussion

This means your superior discusses your mistake with you informally.

Step2. Verbal warning

This means your superior warns you for your mistakes verbally.

Step3. Formal warning

This means your superior warns you for your mistakes formally.

Step4. Written reprimand

This means your superior gives you a severe written scolding because of your severe mistakes.

Step5. Dismissal from the ship

This means you are discharged from the ship because of your offence.

Step6. Dismissal from the company.

This means you are discharged from the ship's company because of your offence.

Notes

1. teamwork 团队精神，团队合作
2. There is an old saying which goes, one swallow does not make a summer. 常言说，独木不成林。
3. all ranks of colleagues 各个级别的同事
4. value their contribution 重视他们的贡献
5. positive players 积极的成员
6. bond the team together 将整个团队团结在一起
7. seek common ground while reserving differences 求同存异
8. disciplinary procedure 纪律程序
9. formal warning 正式警告
10. written reprimand 书面训诫

New words and expressions

teamwork [ˈtiːmwəːk] n. 联合作业, 协力

swallow [ˈswɔləu] n. [鸟] 燕子, 吞咽, 喉 vt. 咽, 淹没, 吞没, 取消

dispensable [disˈpensəbl] adj. 不是必要的, 可有可无的

contribution [ˌkɔntriˈbjuːʃən] n. 捐献, 贡献, 投稿

flexible [ˈfleksəbl] adj. 柔韧性, 易曲的, 灵活的, 柔软的, 可通融的

aware [əˈwεə] adj. 知道的, 明白的, 意识到的

procedure [prəˈsiːdʒə] n. 程序, 手续

informal [inˈfɔːməl] adj. 不正式的, 不拘礼节的

verbal [ˈvəːbəl] adj. 口头的

formal [ˈfɔːməl] adj. 正式的, 合礼仪的, 整齐匀称的 n. 正式的社交活动

reprimand [ˈreprimɑːnd] n. 申斥

dismissal [disˈmisəl] n. 免职, 解雇, 不予考虑

Exercises

1. How to do teamwork well?
2. What is disciplinary procedure onboard?
3. What does “written reprimand” mean?

Part 4

Customer Service

4.1 What Is Customer Service

Customer service is the perceived value of the manner in which our customers are treated. It is the greatest quality we sell as a cruise line.

4.2 Why Are Our Customers Important

① Our customers pay for us to be employed in the first instance.

② Our customers determine the success of our company.

③ Our customers determine the success of the cruise industry.

If everyone onboard works towards the same goal of delivering on our promises and becomes customer minded, by providing excellent service first time, every time, we will achieve our overall goal to everyone's mutual benefit. It takes just one person to ruin a cruise by not being committed to the company's goals and objectives.

4.3 Why Is Good Customer Service Important

Good customer service is very important, because:

① Satisfied customers take us less time, cause less stress & are more pleasant to deal with, and also can give us more fun!

② Bad news travels fast-only tell us 5% if customers are unhappy-tell the other 95% to their friends, family and colleagues.

③ Customers can have a lifetime value if they get good customer service. They come back again and again and do good propaganda for your company.

④ Finding new passengers costs 5 times as much as encouraging existing ones to return. Finding new passengers must do a lot of promotions. e. g. for TOPAZ, 78% passengers come back.

In short, if we offer good customer service, we can get more money (both company and us), lifetime value, more fun (enjoy yourself) and good reputation.

4. 4 Two Types of Customers-external & Internal Customers

(1) Internal customers Internal customers mean work colleagues who treat customers each other.

Please remember: Think of our work colleagues as our customers, and treat them in the same manner in which we would treat passengers.

(2) External customers External customers mean passengers who pay us for the service given.

Note: Please maintain a positive outlook towards passengers, colleagues, superiors and our company.

4. 5 Positive Attitude & Negative Attitude Towards Passengers, Colleagues, Supervisors

(1) Positive Attitude

① Always greet passengers in a friendly way.

② Remember behavior breeds behavior.

③ Remember to smile.

④ Always be positive in front of passengers, colleagues or supervisors.

⑤ Always be positive about the ship, your work and the company.

⑥ Remember that your attitude in life always determines your altitude.

⑦ Always be polite to passengers, colleagues and supervisors.

⑧ Follow the rules of complaint handling (serving excellence).

⑨ Always demonstrate positive body language (eye contact, correct posture, open).

⑩ Show willingness at all times towards passengers, colleagues and supervisors.

(2) Negative Attitude

① Do not walk past passengers without acknowledging them.

② Do not swear, shout or show negative emotions.

③ Do not walk around with a grumpy, angry or depressed face.

④ Do not show negativity in front of passengers, colleagues or supervisors.

⑤ Do not gossip or complain about the ship, your work or the company.

⑥ Do not go around in gangs of friends onboard.

⑦ Do not chew gum in public or smoke over and around non smokers.

⑧ Do not use your mobile phone in public areas.

⑨ Do not think that you know best, without carefully listening to your colleagues and supervisors.

⑩ Do not forget that your personal image, uniform and grooming standards must be in line with the company standards at all times.

4.6 What Is Good Customer Service

Generally speaking, good customer service demands us to:

① Make customer happy;

② Own high quality behaviour;

③ Own high service standards;

④ Smile;

⑤ Be friendly;

⑥ Be helpful (be quick, show interests, etc.).

In the service areas, the most important is people (service staff), if not good, everything is wasted.

Note: At present, global wealth (money) spreads evenly, more and more people have money to travel on the cruise ships, in addition, exposures and competitions are increased, so improved standards are needed.

4.7 What Is Bad Customer Service

Generally speaking, bad customer service refers to the follows:

① Waiting;

② No smiling;

③ Not interested;

④ Not my problem (evade responsibility);

⑤ Be impatient;

⑥ Be arrogant.

Notes

1. Customer service is the perceived value of the manner in which our customers are treated. 客户服务是我们的客户对所接受的服务态度的感知价值。

2. become customer minded 有顾客意识的

3. providing excellent service first time, every time 每次都提供优质的服务
4. mutual benefit 互惠互利
5. It takes just one person to ruin a cruise by not being committed to the company's goals and objectives. 只要有一个人不履行公司承诺的目标和任务，他就会毁掉这次游程。
6. cause less stress 带来更少的压力
7. lifetime value 终生价值
8. maintain a positive outlook 保持积极乐观的精神面貌
9. Remember behavior breeds behavior. 记住行为举止
10. determine your altitude 决定你的高度
11. serving excellence 卓越的服务
12. correct posture 正确姿势
13. without acknowledging them 没有与他们打招呼
14. Do not go around in gangs of friends onboard. 在船上不要拉帮结对四处走动。
15. smoke over and around non smokers 不要对着或围着非吸烟者吸烟
16. know best 最了解
17. your personal image, uniform and grooming standards 你的个人形象、制服和整饰标准
18. global wealth（money）spreads evenly 全球财富均匀分布
19. evade responsibility 逃避责任

New words and expressions

perceive［pə'siːv］v. 意识到，察觉，发觉，理解
in the first instance 首先，最初
deliver on 履行，实行
take up　v. 拿起, 开始从事, 继续, 吸收, 责备, 拘留, 占据, 认购
stress［stres］n. 重压, 逼迫, 压力, 重点, 着重, 强调, 重音 vt. 着重, 强调, 重读
satisfy［'sætisfai］vt. 满足, 使满意, 说服, 使相信 v. 满意, 确保
deal with v. 安排, 处理, 涉及, 做生意
colleague［'kɔliːg］n. 同事, 同僚
customer［'kʌstəmə］n. 消费者，顾客
lifetime［'laiftaim］n. 一生, 终生, 寿命
reputation［ˌrepju(ː)'teiʃən］n. 名誉, 名声
external［eks'təːnl］adj. 外部的, 客观的,［医］外用的, 外国的, 表面的 n. 外部, 外面
internal［in'təːnl］adj. 内在的, 国内的
acknowledge［ək'nɔlidʒ］vt. 承认，鸣谢，对……打招呼，告知已收到
Grumpy［'grʌmpi］adj. 脾气坏的，性情粗暴的，脾气暴躁的，性情乖戾的
depressed［di'prest］adj. 情绪低落的，沮丧的，萧条的
negativity［ˌnegə'tivəti］n. 否定性，消极性，负性
gossip［'gɔsip］n. 流言蜚语，谣言，爱讲闲话的人 vi. 传播流言，说长道短
mobile［'məubail］adj. 移动的，可移动的；变化的 n. 风铃，（可随风摆动的）悬挂饰物
quality［'kwɔliti］n. 质量, 品质, 性质
behaviour［bi'heivjə］n. 行为, 举止, 习性

waste [weist] n. 废物, 浪费, 损耗, 消耗 adj. 废弃的 vt. 浪费, 消耗

global ['gləubəl] adj. 球形的, 全球的, 全世界的

wealth [welθ] n. 财富, 财产, 大量

evenly ['iːvənli] adv. 均匀地, 平坦地

exposure [iks'pəuʒə] n. 暴露, 揭露, 曝光, 揭发, 揭露, 方向, 陈列

competition [kɔmpi'tiʃən] n. 竞争, 竞赛

superior [sjuː'piəriə] n. 长者, 高手, 上级 adj. 较高的, 上级的, 上好的, 出众的, 高傲的

evade [i'veid] v. 规避, 逃避, 躲避

Exercises

1. What is customer service?
2. Why are our customers important?
3. Why is good customer service important?
4. How many types of customers are there on board? what are they respectively?
5. What attitude should we keep towards passengers, colleagues and supervisors?
6. What attitude should we avoid towards passengers, colleagues and supervisors?
7. What is good customer service?
8. What is bad customer service?
9. Would you please tell one of your bad service experiences?

4.8 Why Do Business Lose Customers

The reasons for business to lose customers are various, the following are the rates of the different influences on the customers market.

1%—die;

3%—move away;

4%—float (move from one company to another);

7%—recommend move (friend's recommendation);

8%—natural complaints;

9%—cost (more expensive);

68%—bad service.

4.9 The 4 Basic Needs of Customers

The customers have 4 fundamental needs learned through time and experience onboard, they are as follows.

(1) The need to be understood Paraphrase back what is being said. Listen for feelings communicated as well as the content of the message.

(2) The need to feel welcome Provide a warm and friendly welcome. Use a vocabulary everyone will understand. Engage in friendly conversation.

(3) The need to feel important Learn to address others by name. Do something special. Tune into individual needs.

(4) The need for comfort Make customers at ease. Relieve anxiety. Explain in the service procedures carefully and calmly.

4. 10 State of Mind for Offering Services to Passengers

When we offer service to passengers, we should keep a good state of mind, this can be outlined as follows.

① We should see something from passengers' angle / point and anticipate what passengers expect.

② We should pay attention to details of matter and should not neglect small things, because all small things make a big thing.

③ Our service should exceed passengers' expectations.

4. 11 Passengers' Expectations

Generally passengers' expectations can be summarized as follows.

(1) Professional experience We should be skillful at our work, look smart, wear clean uniform and take our job seriously, etc..

(2) Friendliness and courtesy We should be courteous and friendly to passengers, smile, use an energetic tone of voice, speak politely, do not interrupt them and address them by name.

(3) Delivering high quality service We should read passenger and determine passenger's needs, and then offer service, finally check if the passenger is satisfied with the service, etc..

(4) Solving passenger's problem We should listen to passenger's problem carefully and express our apologies, and then take action to resolve the problem immediately, finally check if the passenger is content with the solution.

(5) Improving service quality We should report passenger's feedback and share our ideas with our colleagues in order to improve our service.

(6) Find opportunities to offer service We should try our best to find opportunities to offer more service to passengers.

(7) Empathy We should listen to guests attentively, put ourselves in their shoes.

4. 12 The 5 Ps

The 5Ps is short for "proud, professional, polite, prompt, personal".

(1) Proud We should be proud of ourselves and our work.

(2) Professional We should be smart, quick, clean, neat and skillful at our jobs.

(3) Polite We should be friendly and respect passengers.

(4) Prompt We should offer service quickly and efficiently, don't keep passengers waiting.

(5) Personal We should remember passengers' names, cabin numbers, etc. and offer individual service.

Notes

1. move away 离开，搬到别处去住
2. natural complaints 自然投诉
3. Paraphrase back what is being said. 解释所说的内容
4. Listen for feelings communicated as well as the content of the message. 倾听情感的传达以及信息的内容。
5. Engage in friendly conversation. 进行友好交谈
6. Tune into individual needs. 协调个性化需求
7. Relieve anxiety. 缓解焦虑
8. take our job seriously 认真对待我们的工作
9. use an energetic tone of voice 用一种充满活力的声音
10. report passenger's feedback 报告客人的反馈

New words and expressions

influence [ˈinfluəns] n. 影响, 感化, 势力 vt. 影响, 改变

market [ˈmɑːkit] n. 市场, 销路, 行情 vt. 在市场上交易 vi. 在市场上买卖

move away 离开

float [fləut] n. 漂流物, 浮舟, 漂浮, 浮萍, 彩车 vi. 浮动, 飘浮, 散播 .

recommend [rekəˈmend] vt. 推荐, 介绍, 劝告, 使受欢迎

mind [maind] n. 头脑, 智力 vi. 介意, 照顾 vt. 注意, 留意, 照看, 介意

detail [ˈdiːteil, diˈteil] n. 细节, 详情 vt. 详述, 细说

exceed [ikˈsiːd] vt. 超越, 胜过 vi. 超过其他

expectation [ˌekspekˈteiʃən] n. 期待, 预料, 指望, [数] 期望（值）

responsibility [risˌpɔnsəˈbiliti] n. 责任, 职责

flexibility [ˌfleksəˈbiliti] n. 弹性, 适应性, 机动性, 挠性

deliver [diˈlivə] vt. 递送, 陈述, 释放, 交付, 引渡, 瞄准

solution [səˈljuːʃən] n. 解答, 解决办法, 溶解, 溶液解决方案

apologize [əˈpɔlədʒaiz] vi. 道歉, 辩白

take action 采取行动, 提出诉讼

feedback [ˈfiːdbæk] n. [无] 回授, 反馈, 反应

opportunity [ˌɔpəˈtjuːniti] n. 机会, 时机

determine [diˈtəːmin] v. 决定, 确定, 测定, 使下定决心

courtesy [ˈkəːtisi, ˈkɔː-] n. 谦恭, 允许, 礼貌

professional [prəˈfeʃənl] n. 自由职业者, 专业人员 . adj. 专业的, 职业的

prompt [prɔmpt] vt. 促使 adj. 敏捷的, 迅速的, 即时的 adv. 准时地

efficiently [i'fiʃəntli] adv. 有效率地, 有效地

Exercises

1. What is the main reason for business to lose customers? What is the rate of this reason for business to lose customers?
2. What are the 4 fundamental needs of customers?
3. When you offer services to passengers, what state of mind should you keep?
4. What are guest's expectations?
5. What are the 5Ps? What does "personal" mean here?

4. 13 Anticipating the Customer's Needs

We should make a careful study of the passengers' basic conditions, predict individual needs and possible problems.

How do you view your passengers?

Each of them has his individual needs, this is true in any situation. No two individuals are alike, this is especially so with westerners.

(1) Equal service

Before we talk about individual needs and possible problems, we'd better get some information about equal service.

All passengers should enjoy equal service, there is no doubt about that. On the other hand, individual attention is necessary because no two passengers have the same needs, interests or difficulties.

Equality is a primary human right. There should be no discrimination against any guest on grounds of sex, age, profession, cultural background, skin color, financial status, religious belief. In terms of consumer rights there should be equal service for the same consumer status.

Discrimination is only very seldom practiced deliberately by people. What makes discrimination is often not deep-rooted prejudice, it is caused by negligence. It may arised out of your unconsciousness, it is easier to root out purposeful discrimination. It is not easier to uproot discrimination through ignorance and carelessness.

Do not just relate with female passengers if you are female; Do not just relate with male passengers if you are male.

Do not relate more to young people like you simply because you share more with your peers.

Do not relate more with people who happen to share your background or interests.

Do not sit or walk with the same tourists many times, change your neighbors and conversational partners, mix up well with everyone of your passengers.

(2) Individual attention

Equal service is not opposed to individual attention. The right to service is equal, but the need of individual attention is different. Young people need less attention than elderly people. They tend to be more independent. They show courtesy and respect to the latter, letting them have more attention. Some people get tired more easily, they need a word of care. Some are a bit shy, they need a word of encouragement. Some are a little too adventurous, they need a word of warning. Some may be physically handicapped, they need a helping hand.

At the beginning of the voyage, some passengers may be a little too excited. It is great to be on the deluxe cruise ship on the blue sea. Warning then should be given to them not to overspend their energy. Some may experience serious culture shock, care must be taken to relieve their physical tension and mental stress, and culture differences should be carefully explained. Towards the end of journey some may leave things behind, they should be reminded not to make haste.

Individuals vary in physical fitness, knowledge structure, intellectual abilities, spiritual pursuits, travel motivations, emotions, will power, tastes and interests, needs and desires, temperament and character, attitudes and manners, customs and habits, views and beliefs. It is not easy to relate to a world of individuals. It is a skill, an art. It is not enough just to learn psychology and public relations. It takes years of pains, patience, practice and experience. Many books are available on these subjects. Knowledge and science are possible to teach, experience and art are not, so we must learn from books, from veteran crew, and also from our own work experiences.

For examples:

① In the bar. In the morning, foreign tourists like to drink coffee; before lunch and dinner, they like to drink Bloody marry for stimulating the appetite (or whet) .

② At the reception. When tourists go out, if it rains outside, we should offer them umbrellas, when tourists come back with wet umbrellas, we should give them plastic bags to hold wet umbrellas.

③ In the dining room. When foreign tourists have breakfast, some need maple syrup; the vegetarians need to be served vegetarian food.

④ In the cabin department. If some tourists are ill, we should ask if they need to send breakfast to their rooms; if some tourists lose their way, we should take the initiative to help them.

⑤ In the shopping center. Different tourists like to buy different goods. e. g. Ladies like to buy jewellery articles, perfume; gentlemen like to buy tobacco and wine.

Notes

1. No two individuals are alike, this is especially so with westerners. 没有两个人是完全一样的，对西方人尤其如此。

2. financial status 财务状况

3. the same consumer status 相同消费的阶层

4. deep-rooted prejudice 根深蒂固的偏见

5. It may arised out of your unconsciousness. 它可能产生于你的潜意识

6. share more with your peers 多与你的同事分享
7. mix up well with everyone of your passengers 与你的每个客人打成一片
8. Equal service is not opposed to individual attention. 平等服务与个别关注并不矛盾。
9. a helping hand 帮助，支持；一臂之力
10. to overspend their energy 透支体力
11. culture shock 文化冲击
12. to relieve their physical tension and mental stress 缓解身体紧张和精神紧张
13. to make haste 急速，赶快
14. spiritual pursuits 精神追求
15. will power 意志力，自制力，毅力
16. temperament and character 气质和性格
17. veteran crew 经验丰富的乘务员
18. stimulating the appetite（or whet）开胃
19. maple syrup 枫蜜，枫浆
20. take the initiative to help them 主动帮助他们

New words and expressions

anticipate [æn'tisipeit] vt. 预期, 期望, 过早使用 v. 预订, 预见, 可以预料
view [vjuː] n. 景色, 风景, 观点, 见解 vt. 观察, 观看
predict [pri'dikt] v. 预知, 预言, 预报
attention [ə'tenʃən] n. 注意, 关心, 关注, 注意力,（口令）立正!
discrimination [disˌkrimi'neiʃən] n. 辨别, 区别, 歧视
ground [graund] n. 地面 adj. 土地面上的 vt. 把……放在地上, 打基础
background ['bækgraund] n. 背景, 后台, 不重要或不引人注目的地方或位置
financial [fai'nænʃəl, ˌfi-] adj. 财政的, 金融的
consumer [kən'sjuːmə] n. 消费者
religious [ri'lidʒəs] adj. 信奉宗教的, 虔诚的, 宗教上的, 修道的, 严谨的
deliberately [di'libəritli] adv. 故意地
deep-rooted 深深植根于
prejudice ['predʒudis] n. 偏见, 成见, 损害, 侵害 v. 损害
negligence ['neglidʒəns] n. 疏忽
unconsciousness n. 无意识, 意识不清
root out v. 用鼻拱出, 发现
purposeful ['pəːpəsful] adj. 有目的的
uproot [ʌp'ruːt] vt. 连根拔起, 根除
ignorance ['ignərəns] n. 无知, 不知
careless ['kεəlis] adj. 粗心的, 疏忽的
relate [ri'leit] vt. 叙述, 讲, 使联系, 发生关系
peer [piə] n. 同等的人, 贵族 vi. 凝视, 窥视 vt. 与……同等, 封为贵族
background ['bækgraund] n. 背景, 后台, 不重要或不引人注目的地方或位置

mix up n. 混和，混淆 v. 混淆，调好
oppose [ə'pəuz] vt. 反对，使对立，使对抗，抗争 vi. 反对
overspend [əuvə'spend] vt. 超支，花费超出 vi. 超支
shock [ʃɔk] n. 打击，震动，冲突，. vt. 使震动，使休克 vi. 震动，吓人 .
relieve [ri'liːv] vt. 减轻，解除，援救，救济，换班
tension ['tenʃən] n. 紧张（状态），不安，拉紧，压力 vt. 拉紧，使紧张
stress [stres] n. 重压，逼迫，压力，强调，重音 vt. 着重，强调
remind [ri'maind] vt. 提醒，使想起
haste [heist] n. 匆忙，急忙
fitness [fitnis] n. 适当，适切性
knowledge ['nɔlidʒ] n. 知识，学问，认识，知道，< 古> 学科
spiritual ['spiritjuəl] adj. 精神上的
pursuit [pə'sjuːt] n. 追击
motivation [ˌməuti'veiʃən] n. 动机
motion [i'məuʃən] n. 情绪，情感，感情
desire [di'zaiə] vt. 想望，期望，希望 n. 愿望，心愿，要求 v. 要求
temperament ['tempərəmənt] n. 气质，性情，易激动，急躁
attitude ['ætitjuːd] n. 姿势，态度，看法，意见
manner ['mænə] n. 礼貌，风格，方式，样式，习惯
psychology [sai'kɔlədʒi] n. 心理学，心理状态
patience ['peiʃəns] n. 耐性，忍耐
available [ə'veiləbl] adj. 可用到的，可利用的，有用的
veteran ['vetərən] n. 老兵，老手，富有经验的人 adj. 经验丰富的
belief [bi'liːf] n. 信任，信心，信仰
character ['kæriktə] n. （事物的）特性，性质，字符，性格，特征，人物 .
mental ['mentl] adj. 精神的，智力的

Exercises

1. What does "anticipating the customer's needs" mean?
2. What is "equal service"?
3. What does "individual attention" mean?
4. Would you please give an example about how to anticipate the customer's needs at the reception?
5. Would you please give an example about how to anticipate the customer's needs in the dining room?

4.14 How to Satisfy the Needs of Our Guests

(1) Need for attention/appreciation/recognition

① Greet them with a warm smile and say: "*Good morning/Good afternoon/Good evening, Mr. Tan. Welcome back! It's nice to see you on board again.*"

② Maintain eye contact with the guest when talking to him/her.

③ Mention his/her name and title if you know it. Get to know his/her name if he/she is a regular guest.

④ Do not discriminate.

⑤ Show appreciation rather than irritation when they air some comments/complaints to you. You can say: "*Thank you, sir, for calling my attention to this matter*" or "*We appreciate your concern, sir. Thank you so much.*"

⑥ Never criticize guests' look or mistakes. You will only hurt their ego.

⑦ Be very alert and prompt in satisfying their requests, lest they feel neglected.

⑧ Be very sensitive to the guest's feelings. Never embarrass them in front of others, attempt to correct their mistakes or talk to them in a loud or arrogant tone.

(2) Need for information

① Be familiar with the menu as well as the different cruise ship facilities and services to be able to answer guests' queries correctly.

② Give advance information which you consider important for the guests to know, like informing them of preparation time (let them know how long they have to wait), out-of-stock items, etc.

③ Never settle a question with "I DON'T KNOW" answer. Refer to the right person or the right department if the items asked for are not familiar to you. You can say: "*May I refer you to our Front Office Manager, Ms. Annie? She is in the best position to answer your queries.*"

(3) Need for belonging

① Be friendly; maintain gracious expressions and smile when talking to guests.

② Give him a warm welcome with a warm-hearted smile as you say, "*Good Morning/Afternoon/Evening!*" Have someone receive/welcome him.

③ Welcome him back if you see him the second time. You can say: "*We're glad to see you again, Mr. Tan.*" Or if he is the host, say: "*We're glad to have your party once again on our ship, Mr. Tan. Thank you for your continued patronage.*"

④ Make your guest feel very important by giving him your full attention and be alert to respond with a friendly gesture when he's lonely or bored. Give some extra favor if you have the opportunity.

⑤ Get to know your guest's preferences and favorites like his/her favorable table, drink, etc. And offer it to him/her before he asks for it. You can say:

"*May I get your favorite dry Martini on the rocks, Mr. Tan?*"

⑥ Be generous in expressing gracious remarks like, "*I hope you enjoy your dinner*".

(4) Need for safety and security

① Take note of items lost by the guest in the lounge, restaurant and function rooms. Surrender them to your supervisor to be stored in the lost-and-found section for the guest to claim therein.

Excuse me for reaching over you.

Will (Won't, Would, Wouldn't, Could, Couldn't, Can, Can't) you join us?

Join us, will (won't, would, wouldn't, could, couldn't, can, can't) you?

Go with us, if you like (please) .

Won't you stay a little longer?

Can I ask you to stay a little longer?

Don't let's go yet, OK?

Let's go, shall we (if you like, if you are ready) .

Would you mind my sitting here?

Would you mind if I sit here?

Can I take this seat?

What can I do for you?

What would you like me to get for you?

I'll be happy to be of help.

At your service, sir (madam) .

We'll go out of our way to make you happy.

It's a great pleasure to do what we can.

Would you do me a favor?

Can I ask a favor of you?

May I know your name?

May I be excused?

I should say so (think so) .

I should think not (say not) .

I would rather say no.

It is simply perfect, if you allow me to say so.

I'd like very much to join you, but sorry I really couldn't manage this time, thank you just the same.

Ladies and gentlemen, It's a great pleasure to work with you on this program. Allow me to extend a most warm welcome to you.

Ladies and gentlemen, It's been a great pleasure to work with you.

I'll cherish our wonderful memories. Come again. Nice journey home.

Notes

1. Your inner feeling should find expression in overt speech. 你的内心感情应该设法在公开谈话中表达。
2. live up to passengers' expectations 不辜负客人的期望
3. well-tailored 考究的
4. Much obliged. 非常感谢。
5. I can manage. 我自己能解决。
6. Excuse me for reaching over you. 对不起，我拿（放）一下东西。
7. at your service 听候吩咐，乐意帮助

New words and expressions

inner [ˈinə] adj. 内部的, 里面的, 内心的 n. 内部
expression [iksˈpreʃən] n. 表达, 表情, 脸色, 措辞 n. 表达式, 符号
sincere [sinˈsiə] adj. 诚挚的, 真实的, 真诚的
modest [ˈmɔdist] adj. 谦虚的, 谦让的, 适度的
refine [riˈfain] vt. 精炼, 精制, 使文雅高尚
humorous [ˈhjuːmərəs] adj. 富幽默感的, 滑稽的, 诙谐的, 异想天开的
well-tailored 干净利索的
courteous [ˈkəːtjəs] adj. 有礼貌的, 谦恭的
expressive [iksˈpresiv] adj. 表现的, 表达……的, 有表现力的, 富于表情的
oblige [əˈblaidʒ] vt. 迫使, 责成
awfully [ˈɔːfuli] adv. 非常, 很, 十分
interrupt [ˌintəˈrʌpt] vt. 打断, 中断, 妨碍, 插嘴 vi. 打断
reach [riːtʃ] n. 延伸, 区域 vt. 到达, 伸出 vi. 达到, 延伸, 伸出手
favor [ˈfeivə] n. 好感, 宠爱, 关切, 好意 vt. 支持, 喜欢, 证实, 赐予
cherish [ˈtʃeriʃ] vt. 珍爱, 怀抱（希望等）
memory [ˈmeməri] n. 记忆, 记忆力, 回忆, 存储（器）, 内存

Exercises

1. How to express your welcome to passengers? Please give some examples.
2. How to express your good will to passengers? Please give some examples.
3. How to express thanks to passengers? Please give some examples.
4. How to express apologies to passengers? Please give some examples.
5. What are the basic requirements of speaking?

4.16 The Culture Mistakes We Should Avoid

① Do not extend your hand to elderly visitors and ladies before they extend their hands. Do not pump the hands of people, hold them too long, use too much force or make the handshake perfunctory. In handshake, do not avoid eye contact.

When you give verbal greetings, guard against these:

You must be tired now.

You have had a hard time.

You have had a tiring journey.

Instead use these:

How was the trip? Did you have a pleasant trip?

Welcome, I have been expecting you.

I'm glad to work with you.

Hope that we will have a pleasant trip together.

If elderly tourists decline your help, do not insist. They may prefer independence. They do not like the idea of feeling old.

② Later on the trip, mind your daily greetings. Avoid Chinese culture habits. Do not use these:

Have you eaten?

Where are you going?

Where have you been?

Use these instead:

Hello! How are you? How are you doing this morning?

③ When you start a conversation, avoid personal topics, use impersonal topics. Do not say:

Are you married?

Do you have a family?

How many children have you got?

How old are you?

Where are you from?

What else will you do except travel in China?

What are you going to do when you return home?

Do you like China?

What are your impressions of China?

Always remember to begin a conversation with impersonal subjects. Personal subjects come only after friendship is made, and only when your conversational partner no longer minds revealing personal information.

Conversational openers can be:

Nice weather, isn't it?

I hope it will clear up soon.

It's a little rainy (dry, windy, snowy, cloudy, sunny), isn't it?

Is this typical spring weather?

What is autumn like here?

Did you hear the news that...?

Did you watch the program...?

There is no change in the program.

We will have a very nice (busy) day.

④ Private things are taboos. All taboos must be avoided at all times on all occasions. Examples of taboos are:

How old are you?

Are you married?

How many children do you have?

What does your husband (wife) do?

How much money did you spend on this dress?

What was the price of the book?

Other taboos are:

Peeping over somebody's shoulders, glancing at somebody's letter, playing with others' things, entering a room without permission....

⑤ When you make an appointment, avoid statements and commands. Do not use these:

Come down to the lobby at eight.

I'll come over to your place.

Come over to my room.

We will meet in the recreation room.

Instead you say:

Would you come down to the lobby... ?

Shall we meet in the recreation room?

Can I come over to your place?

Would you come over to my room?

⑥ Say a lot more thanks than you do when you speak Chinese. Remember to say "Thank you" in the following situations:

When you receive anything handed over to you, even if it is something of yours that is being returned to you.

When you hear a compliment, do not say "No, no, no, far from it".

Examples are:

A: Your English is very good.

B: Thank you, I'm glad to hear that.

A: What a beautiful dress! I love the color.

B: Thanks, I'm glad you like it.

When the host welcomes you at the door, do not just smile, you must express your thanks, you can say:

Thank you for asking me over.

Thank you for the invitation.

When drink or food is offered to you, say "Thank you", if you do not object, do not expect to be offered for more than once. If you do not care for it, do not just say "No", you must say "No, thank you."

⑦ Westerners use many more apologies than we do, so when you speak English, do not forget to express your apology in the following situations:

When you cough or sneeze or pass a person, be sure to say "Excuse me." When you interrupt, be sure to say "Sorry to interrupt you."

When you reach at dinner, remember to say "Excuse my reaching." When you are late, you must say "Sorry to be late."

On the other hand, you must not apologize in the following situation:

When you give a gift, do not say "It is nothing", or "It isn't much" or "It was not expensive" or "It is not very particular."

When you treat a friend to dinner, do not turn down his or her thanks. Do not say "It isn't special" or "It is very simple" or "I'm a very poor cook."

⑧ Another area of possible mistakes is gift-exchange.

When you receive a gift, do not just say "Thank you," You must say: "Oh, this is lovely, I like it very much. It's very kind of you."

When you give a gift, you must say that it is special and why it is special. You can say "I choose it especially for you" or "It suits you very well" or "It is unique" or "It is very Chinese. I hope it will remind you of me."

When your friend thank you for the gift, do not just smile, say: " I'm glad you like it."

⑨ Leaving-taking also presents difficulties to Chinese speakers of English.

Overstaying is one error. Abrupt leaving is another.

Apologies like these must be avoided:

I'm sorry to have troubled you. I'm sorry to have taken you so much time.

Instead you should say:

Thank you for this lovely evening.

Thank you for this lovely talk (dinner).

The other way round, when your guest thanks you for the visit, you should say:

I'm glad you could come. Please come again.

Notes

1. pump the hands of people 使劲握别人的手
2. make the handshake perfunctory 握手太敷衍
3. do not avoid eye contact 不要避免眼睛接触，要看着对方
4. give verbal greetings 口头问候
5. I'm glad to work with you. 我很高兴和你一起工作。
6. decline your help 拒绝你的帮助
7. They may prefer independence. 他们可能更喜欢独立。
8. avoid personal topics, use impersonal topics 避免个人话题，使用非个人话题
9. conversational openers 开场白
10. Private things are taboos. 私人的事情是禁忌。
11. at all times on all occasions 在任何时间任何场合
12. peeping over somebody's shoulders 从别人背后偷看
13. hear a compliment 听到赞美
14. leaving-taking 告别，道别
15. Overstaying is one error. Abrupt leaving is another. 停留过久是一个错误，突然离开也是一个错误。

New words and expressions

arrival [ə'raivəl] n. 到来, 到达, 到达者

avoid [ə'vɔid] vt. 避免, 消除

greeting ['griːtiŋ] n. 祝贺, 问候

extend [iks'tend] v. 扩充, 延伸, 伸展, 扩大 [军] 使散开

pump [pʌmp] n. 泵, 抽水机 vt. (用泵) 抽 (水), 抽吸

handshake ['hændʃeik] n. 握手

guard against 提防, 预防

decline [di'klain] vi. 下倾, 下降 v. 拒绝, 衰落 n. 下倾, 下降, 衰败, 衰落

independence [ˌindi'pendəns] n. 独立, 自主

impersonal [im'pəːsənl] adj. 非个人的

reveal [ri'viːl] vt. 展现, 显示, 揭示, 暴露

opener ['əupənə] n. 开启的人, 开始者

clear up v. 整理, 消除, 放晴

taboo [tə'buː] n. （宗教）禁忌、避讳 adj. 忌讳的 vt. 禁忌, 避讳

occasion [ə'keiʒən] n. 场合, 时机, 机会

peep [piːp] n. 窥视, 隐约看见 vi. 窥视, 偷看

glance [glɑːns] vi. 扫视, 匆匆一看 n. 一瞥, 眼光, 匆匆一看

statement ['steitmənt] n. 声明, 陈述, 综述

come over 过来, 过来, 抓住

hand over 移交

compliment ['kɔmplimənt] n. 称赞, 恭维, 致意 vt. 称赞, 恭维

object ['ɔbdʒikt] n. 物体, 目标, 宾语, 对象 vi. 反对 vt. 提出……来反对

apology [ə'pɔlədʒi] n. （为某种思想, 宗教, 哲学等）辩解, 道歉

particular [pə'tikjulə] n. 细节 adj. 特殊的, 特别的, 独特的, 详细的

remind [ri'maind] vt. 提醒, 使想起

unique [juː'niːk] adj. 唯一的, 独特的

overstay ['əuvə'stei] v. 逗留过久, 停留超过（时间）

Exercises

1. When you give greetings to foreigners, what should you guard against? What should you do instead?

2. When you give daily greetings to foreigners, which Chinese culture habits should you avoid?

3. When you start a conversation with foreigners, what should you avoid? What should you do instead? Would you please give some examples?

4. To western tourists, private things are taboos, would you please give some examples?

5. When you make an appointment, what should you avoid? Would you please give some examples? What should you do instead? Would please give some examples?

6. When you hear a compliment, what should you do? Would you please give some examples?

7. How to avoid gift-exchange mistakes? Please give some examples.

8. How to avoid leaving-taking mistakes? Please give some examples.

Part 5

Hygiene and Environmental Protection on the Cruise Ships

5.1 Why Should We Study Hygiene Onboard a Cruise Ship

Understanding and applying all of the hygiene standards and procedures is an absolute requirement for all crew members, particularly for those that handle food or are involved in food-related operations, contact with passengers or cleaning of any nature. Practicing bad sanitation and hygiene at work could harm us personally, our passengers and colleagues with severe potential consequences for the company. For example, in the United States alone, food borne diseases cause approximately 76 million diseases and 5000 deaths per year. This part will talk about the most important issues concerning hygiene onboard all cruise ships. Our undivided attention on this topic is essential to our role and responsibility onboard.

5.2 Public Health Challenges Onboard

For your own safety, health and welfare in addition to that of your colleagues and passengers, it is important to first understand the public health challenges faced in a unique shipboard environment. Generally speaking, there are 8 public health challenges onboard a cruise ship which are as follows.

5.2.1 Closed Micro Community

Passengers and crew alike live and work in a closed environment, therefore, the risk of illness is higher.

5.2.2 Dense Population

In addition to a close environment there are a large number of passengers and crew in a relatively small surface area.

5.2.3 International Passengers and Crew

Passengers and crew onboard come from different countries, therefore, the risk of carrying illnesses is greater.

5.2.4 Mobile and Interactive Population

Many of the population onboard is moving around and interaction levels are high.

5.2.5 Rapid Turnover

Passengers and crew alike change (embark or disembark) frequently.

5.2.6 Variable Quality and Safety of Provision

As food provisioning needs to arrive in very high volumes, it's nearly impossible to check if all food items consumed are of best quality all the time.

5.2.7 Potential for Explosive Disease Outbreaks

This is due to a close environment, whereby the risk for exposure concerning disease outbreaks may be high.

5.2.8 No Standardized Medical Care System

Even though there are hospitals onboard, their capabilities may be not adequate to treat certain diseases and incidents.

Notes

1. severe potential consequences 严重的潜在后果
2. food borne diseases 食源性疾病
3. undivided attention 一心一意
4. the public health challenges faced in a unique shipboard environment 一个独特的船舶环境中面临的公共卫生挑战
5. surface area 表面积
6. the risk for exposure 承担的风险
7. Their capabilities may be not adequate to treat certain diseases and incidents. 他们的能力可能不足以治疗某些疾病和应对某些事件。

New words & expressions

hygiene [ˈhaidʒiːn] n. 卫生，卫生学

be involved in [biː inˈvɔlvd in] 涉及，专心，卷入

sanitation [ˌsæniˈteiʃn] n. 卫生系统或设备

welfare [ˈwelfeə] n. 福利，幸福，繁荣，安宁

community [kəˈmjuːniti] n. 社区，社会团体，共同体，[生态]群落

dense [dens] adj. 密集的，稠密的，浓密的，浓厚的，愚钝的

mobile [ˈməubail] adj. 移动的，可移动的，变化的，易变的，交融的

interactive [ˈintərˈæktiv]adj. 互相作用的，相互影响的，[计]交互式的；互动的

turnover[ˈtəːnəʊvə(r)]n. 翻滚，周转，逆转，营业额，成交量 adj. 可翻下的

variable [ˈvɛəriəbl] adj. 变化的，可变的 n. 可变因素，变量

all the time [ɔːl ðə taim] 向来，一向，时时刻刻，每时每刻

potential [pəˈtenʃəl] adj. 潜在的，有可能的 n. 潜力，潜能

explosive [iksˈpləusiv] adj. 爆炸的，易爆炸的，突增的，暴躁的 n. 爆炸物，炸药

outbreak [ˈautbreik] n. （战争，怒气等的）爆发，突然发生

whereby [hwɛəˈbai] adv. 通过……，借以，与……一致

standardized [ˈstændədaizd] adj. 标准的，定型的 v. 使合乎规格，使标准化

Exercises

1. Why should we study hygiene onboard a cruise ship?
2. What are the 8 public health challenges onboard a cruise ship?

5.3 The Definition and Importance of Food Hygiene and Safety

5.3.1 What is Food Hygiene

Food hygiene means all practices, procedures and precautions which prevent food poisoning and food spoilage, includes:

① Preventing food contamination;

② Preventing bacterial growth;

③ Killing bacteria;

④ Care & cleanliness of premises and equipments;

⑤ Good food delivery, storage, display and sale;

⑥ Personal hygiene;

⑦ Good design of food premises;

⑧ Pest control;

⑨ Waste control.

5.3.2 What is Food Safety

Food safety is protecting food from anything that could cause harm.

So in order to keep food safety onboard, health officers and captain often do a big inspection on ship's food premises.

5.3.3 Costs of Bad Food Hygiene

Bad food hygiene may produce a lot of costs as follows.

① Food poisoning—possibly cause death;

② Food spoilage—waste a lot of money;

③ Food complaints;

④ Prosecution, fines and imprisonment;

⑤ Closure of company;

⑥ Causing pests;

⑦ Causing civil action;

⑧ Remedial costs.

Thousands of people throughout the world become ill every year because of the food and drinks they have. These illnesses are called food borne illnesses, it's very easy to stop them, but they especially transmit very quickly on ships if they are not controlled immediately. For example: On some cruise ship, one cook had bad hygiene, 800 people nearly died.

5.3.4 Bad Food Hygiene Impact on Business

Bad food hygiene results in a lot of negative influences on business as follows.

① Bad publicity;

② Loss of reputation;

③ Reduced business;

④ Lower profits;

⑤ Closure of company and job losses.

5.3.5 Benefits of Good Hygiene

Good hygiene may produce a lot of benefits as follows.

① Leading to satisfied customers;

② Leading to good reputation;

③ Leading to increased business;

④ Leading to higher profits;

⑤ Keeping within the law;

⑥ Lowering wastage costs;

⑦ Leading to better conditions to work;

⑧ Keeping staff happy (happier staff).

Obviously factors other than good hygiene also influence these benefits.

Notes

1. food poisoning and food spoilage 食物中毒和食物腐败
2. food premises 食肆
3. waste control 废物管理

4. remedial costs 治疗费用
5. negative influences 消极影响，负面影响
6. keeping within the law 遵纪守法
7. lowering wastage costs 降低损耗成本

New words & expressions

hygienic [haiˈdʒiːnik] adj. 卫生学的, 卫生的
hygiene [ˈhaidʒiːn] n. 卫生, 卫生学
procedure [prəˈsiːdʒə] n. 程序, 手续
precaution [priˈkɔːʃən] n. 预防, 警惕, 防范
poisoning [ˈpɔizniŋ] n. 中毒
spoilage [ˈspɔilidʒ] n. 损坏
contamination [kənˌtæmiˈneiʃən] n. 玷污, 污染, 污染物
bacterial [bækˈtˈiərˈiəl] adj. 细菌的
growth [grəuθ] n. 生长, 种植, 栽培, 发育, 等比级数
delivery [diˈlivəri] n. 递送, 交付, 分娩, 交货, 引渡
cleanliness [ˈklenlinis] n. 洁癖, 清洁
premise [ˈpremis] n. 房屋, 办公室，事务所
pest [pest] n. 有害物
waste [weist] n. 废物, 浪费, 损耗, 消耗, 地面风化物, 垃圾, 荒地
complaint [kəmˈpleint] n. 诉苦, 抱怨, 牢骚, 委屈, 疾病
prosecution [ˌprɔsiˈkjuːʃən] n. 进行, 经营, 检举, 起诉
fine [fain] n. 罚款, 罚金, 晴天, 精细 vt. 罚款, 精炼
imprisonment [imˈprɪzənmənt] n. 关押
closure [ˈkləuʒə] n. 关闭 vt. 使终止
civil [ˈsivl] adj. 全民的, 市民的, 公民的, 民间的．民事的, 根据民法的,
remedial [riˈmiːdjəl] adj. 治疗的, 补救的
throughout [θru(ː)ˈaut] prep. 遍及, 贯穿 adv. 到处, 始终, 全部
transmit [trænzˈmit] vt. 传输, 转送, 传达, 传导, 发射, 遗传, 传播
impact [ˈimpækt] n. 碰撞, 冲击, 冲突, 影响, 效果 vt. 对……发生影响
publicity [pʌbˈlisiti] n. 公开，宣传
reputation [ˌrepju(ː)ˈteiʃən] n. 名誉, 名声
profit [ˈprɔfit] n. 利润, 益处, 得益 vi. 得益, 利用 vt. 有益于, 有利于
loss [lɔs] n. 损失, 遗失, 失败, 输, 浪费, 错过, [军] 伤亡, 降低

Exercises

1. What is food hygiene?
2. What is food safety?
3. What are the costs of bad food hygiene?
4. What is the impact of bad food hygiene on business?
5. What are the benefits of good hygiene?

5.4 The Hygiene Supervising Organizations of Cruise Ships

5.4.1 CIEH

CIEH is short for "Chartered Institute of Environmental Health" . Now this structure covers over 100 countries, it is one of the strictest environmental health inspection structures in the world. It is a learned society whose constitution is in a Royal Charter. The original organization was founded in 1883 and was called the Association of Public Sanitary Inspectors. It is an independent professional body and registered charity representing those who work in environmental health and related disciplines. Its primary function is the promotion of knowledge and understanding of environmental health issues.

EHO is short for "Environmental Health Officers", usually they are employed by local authority environmental health department, they are very powerful people.

(1) Their duties involve:

① Investigation of food poisoning outbreaks;

② Inspection of all food premises registered with the authority;

③ Inspection of food;

④ Education and training of environmental health.

As well as these functions, they also act as advisors.

(2) Their powers include:

① Improvement. They have right to make food premises' hygiene better.

② Prohibition. They have right to forbid the making and sale of unqualified food.

③ Disqualification. They have right to disqualify the food premises which are not up to the required hygiene standard.

④ Prosecution. They have right to bring a criminal charge against the food premises which break the law.

5.4.2 USPH

USPH is short for "United States Public Health", it is an organization whose main role is to ensure that safe food handling and working practices are carried out on all ships, which include:

(1) Personal hygiene To ensure the highest levels of cleanliness. Emphasizing on clean uniforms, jewelry, hair and hand, etc..

(2) Hygienic practices Ensuring that the correct protective outfits are worn and that all rules and regulations are met.

(3) Food contamination Exercising and ensuring the correct rules is used to protect food during storage, transportation, preparation, holding and service.

(4) Equipment and utensils Ensuring all employees to learn the correct procedures for

usage.

(5) Storage and preparation Ensuring that all foods are stored in the correct manner and location.

(6) Display and service Ensuring all foods on display are protected from contamination.

(7) Equipment and ware washing Ensuring that all equipment is cleaned and maintained to USPH standards.

(8) Chemical training Ensuring all employees to learn the correct procedures for storing, measuring, and labeling chemicals.

(9) Waste disposal Ensuring all employees to learn garbage segregation and understand fully the environmental awareness.

Notes

1. It is a learned society whose constitution is in a Royal Charter. 它是依据皇家宪章建立的一个学会。
2. environmental health and related disciplines 环境卫生及相关学科
3. food poisoning outbreaks 食物中毒突发事件
4. all food premises registered with the authority 在行政机关登记的所有食品场所
5. to bring a criminal charge against the food premises which break the law 对违反法律的食品场所进行刑事指控
6. working practices 操作练习
7. protective outfits 保护装备
8. to learn garbage segregation and understand fully the environmental awareness 要学习垃圾分类，充分领会环境意识

New words & expressions

environmental [inˌvaiərənˈmentl] adj. 周围的, 环境的 n. 环境论
charter [ˈtʃɑːtə] vt. 租, 包（船、车等）n. 宪章
institute [ˈinstitjuːt] n. 学会, 学院, 协会 vt. 创立, 开始, 提起（诉讼）
authority [ɔːˈθɔriti] n. 权威, 威信, 权威人士, 权力, 职权, 著作权威
involve [inˈvɔlv] vt. 包括, 笼罩, 潜心于, 使陷于
investigation [inˌvestiˈgeiʃən] n. 调查, 研究
outbreak [ˈautbreik] n. （战争的）爆发,（疾病的）发作
register [ˈredʒistə] n. 记录, 登记簿 vt. 登记, 注册, 把……挂号 vi. 登记
advisor [ədˈvaizə(r)] n. 顾问,〈美〉（学生的）指导老师
improvement [imˈpruːvmənt] n. 改进, 进步
prohibit [prəˈhibit] vt. 禁止, 阻止
disqualification [disˌkwɔlifiˈkeiʃən] n. 剥夺资格, 不合格
prosecution [ˌprɔsiˈkjuːʃən] n. 进行, 经营, 检举, 起诉
criminal [ˈkriminl] n. 罪犯, 犯罪者 adj. 犯罪的, 犯法的, 罪恶的
charge [tʃɑːdʒ] n. 负荷, 电荷 v. 装满, 控诉, 责令, 告诫, 加罪于, 收费
break the law 违犯法律

emphasize [ˈemfəsaiz] vt. 强调, 着重 v. 强调

outfit [ˈautfit] n. 用具, 全套装配 vt. 配备, 装备 vi. 得到装备

label [ˈleibl] n. 标签, 签条, 商标 vt. 贴标签于, 指……为, 分类, 标注

garbage [ˈgɑːbidʒ] n. 垃圾, 废物

segregation [ˌsegriˈgeiʃən] n. 分离，分开，隔离

Exercises

1. What are CIEH and EHO?
2. What are the duties of EHO?
3. What are the powers of EHO?
4. What is USPH?
5. What are the main duties of USPH for supervising the cruise ships?

5.5 What Is Food Poisoning

5.5.1 What Is Food Poisoning

It's an acute inflammation of the digestive tract caused by the consumption of contaminated food. It results in abdominal pain, often with diarrhea and vomiting.

5.5.2 Coutaminated Food Will Cause Illnesses

Food is not harmful in itself, if contaminated, it will cause illnesses. The illnesses are caused by the follows.

(1) Micro-organisms ①bacteria;
② viruses.

(2) Chemicals ①pesticides;
②herbicides;
③cleaning agents;
④disinfectants.

(3) Metals.

(4) Plants. e. g. red beans, toadstools, some green potatoes, some green tomatoes.

Of all these, bacteria are by far the most common.

5.5.3 The Main Symptoms of Food Poisoning

① diarrhoea;

② abdominal pain;

③ nausea;

④ vomitting;

⑤ fever;

⑥ Headache.

Notes

1. an acute inflammation of the digestive tract 消化道急性炎症
2. contaminated food 被感染的食物
3. abdominal pain 腹痛
4. cleaning agents 清洁剂

New words & expressions

acute [ə'kjuːt] adj. 敏锐的, [医] 急性的, 剧烈
inflammation [ˌinflə'meiʃən] n. 怒火, 发火, 燃烧, [医] 炎症, 发炎
digestive [di'dʒestiv, dai-] adj. 消化的, 有助消化的
tract [trækt] n. 广阔的地面, 土地, 地方, 地域, (解剖) 管道, 小册子
consumption [kən'sʌmpʃən] n. 消费, 消费量, 肺病
contaminate [kən'tæmineit] v. 污染
result in 导致
toadstool ['təudstuː l] n. 毒菌
abdominal [æb'dɔminl] adj. 腹部的
diarrhoea [ˌdaiə'riə] n. 腹泻
vomit ['vɔmit] n. 呕吐, 呕吐物 vi. 呕吐, 大量喷出 vt. 吐出, 呕吐
harmful ['hɑːmful] adj. 有害的, 伤害的
microorganism [maikrəu'ɔːgəniz (ə) m] n. [微生] 微生物, 微小动植物
bacteria [bæk'tiəriə] n. 细菌
virus ['vaiərəs] n. [微] 病毒, 滤过性微生物, 毒害, 恶毒
chemical ['kemikəl] adj. 化学的 n. 化学制品, 化学药品
pesticide ['pestisaid] n. 杀虫剂
herbicide ['həːbisaid] n. 除草剂
disinfectant [disin'fekt (ə) nt] n. 消毒剂
metal ['metl] n. 金属
plant [plaːnt] n. 植物, 庄稼, 工厂 vt. 种植, 栽培, 培养, 安置 vi. 种植
symptom ['simptəm] n. [医] [植] 症状, 征兆
nausea ['nɔːsjə] n. 反胃, 晕船, 恶心, 作呕, 极度的不快
fever ['fiːvə] n. 发烧, 发热, 热病 v. (使) 发烧, (使) 患热病, (使) 狂热
headache ['hedeik] n. 头痛, 令人头痛之事

Exercises

1. What is food poisoning?
2. What conditions can make food harmful?
3. What do microorganisms mainly mean?
4. Which chemicals can contaminate food and make it harmful? Please list four kinds.

5.6 Food Borne Diseases

In addition to food poisoning there are also food borne illnesses.

5. 6. 1 What's Food Borne Disease

It's a disease that is carried or transmitted to people by food including water.

5. 6. 2 Food Poisoning and Food Borne Disease Are Different

(1) Food poisoning Caused by eating food contaminated with harmful substances, the microorganisms are living and growing in the food; Food poisoning is caused by a large number of bacteria; Bacteria need to grow in food.

(2) Food borne disease This is the disease that is caused by microorganisms which are carried in the food or water, they don't grow or multiply in the food or water, they need to get into our bodies to do that; Even a small number of microorganisms can also cause illness; Microorganisms do not need to grow in food; Food borne disease is often caused by water.

(3) The main symptoms of food borne diseases

① Campylobacter;

② E. coli;

③ Dysentery;

④ Typhoid;

⑤ Cholera;

⑥ Brucellosis;

⑦ Tuberculosis.

These cannot be controlled by stopping their growing, they must be kept out of food at all costs.

Notes

1. harmful substances 有害物质
2. They must be kept out of food at all costs. 必须不惜一切代价使他们远离食物。

New words & expressions

in addition to 除……之外

transmit [trænz'mit] vt. 传输, 转送, 发射, 遗传 vi. 发射信号, 发报

substance ['sʌbstəns] n. 物质, 实质, 主旨

reject [ri'dʒekt] n. 被拒之人, 被弃之物 vt. 拒绝, 抵制

multiply ['mʌltipli] v. 繁殖, 乘, 增加

campylobacter ['kæmpiləu ˌbæktə] n. 动物传播的一种疾病，弯曲菌

coli ['kəulai] [拉] 大肠（杆）菌的

dysentery ['disəntri] n. [医] 痢疾

typhoid ['taifɔid] n. [医] 伤寒症 adj. 伤寒的, 斑疹伤寒症的

cholera ['kɔlərə] n. [医] 霍乱

brucellosis [ˌbruːsə'ləusis] n. 普鲁氏菌病

tuberculosis [tjuˌbəːkju'ləusis] n. 肺结核

keep out of（使）置身于……之外

at all costs 不惜任何代价

Exercises

1. What are the main symptoms of food poisoning?
2. What's food borne disease?
3. What are the differences between food poisoning and food borne disease?
4. What are the main symptoms of food borne disease?

5.7 Microorganisms

Microorgmisms include: bacteria, viruses, parasites, mould and fungi. (some are good. e. g. yoghurt, cheese).

5.7.1 Bacteria

What are bacteria?

They are one of the family of microbes, they are single celled organisms and found everywhere. Most of them are harmless, harmful ones are called pathogens, some are useful, e. g. yoghurt, cheese.

Some cause spoilage—make food go "off ", they are easy to be found and don't usually cause illness.

Pathogens don't usually spoil the food—make them very hard to detect their presence in food, usually cause illness.

Most pathogens can not be seen, smelt, tasted or felt in food.

5.7.2 Characteristics of Bacteria

The characteristics of bacteria are as follows.

① They are very small, a pin head can be covered by millions of bacteria;

② They like to move in a moist condition;

③ They present different shapes;

④ They have millions of different types;

⑤ They are composed of a single cell.

5.7.3 Pathogenic Bacteria

(1) The bacteria that cause harm are called pathogenic bacteria ("pathogenic" means "disease-producing"). They can grow in the food without any sign, the food looks, tastes, smells the same.

(2) Sources of pathogenic bacteria The pathogenic bacteria mainly come from:

① Raw foods, e. g. poultry, meat, eggs, shellfish, vegetables, etc.;

② Pests, e. g. insects, rats, pets, birds, etc.;

③ People;

④ Air and dust, e. g. air conditioning, sneeze (if someone sneezes in the air, bacteria can travel 250km/per hour.) .

⑤ Dirt and waste food;

⑥ Water.

5.7.4 Spoilage Bacteria

Food spoilage bacteria make the food look, taste and smell off. This will be obvious to the customers and us and will not be eaten.

5.7.5 Useful (or Helpful) Bacteria

Useful bacteria have a lot of functions as follows.

① Grow crops;

② Make foods;

③ Digest the food we eat;

④ Treat the sewage to make it safe;

⑤ Develop new food;

⑥ Create medical drugs;

⑦ Create laundry and cleaning products.

5.7.6 Growth of Bacteria

Food poisoning bacteria don't usually get into food in large numbers. It is usually in low level contamination and then grows to poisoning level.

How do bacteria grow?

They grow very simply, they adopt the way of binary fission, if they are given right conditions, one bacterium can be divided into two every 10-20 minutes, so one bacterium can be divided into 100, 000, 000 in 9 hours! But they are still invisible.

On eating some bacteria cause illness by infection, the others release toxins (poisons) in the food.

5.7.7 Conditions for Bacterial Growth

All bacteria vary in their growth requirements to some extent, but we can say that they all need the following conditions: the right temperature, time, the right food, moisture.

(1) Temperature and bacteria

The effect of temperature on food poisoning pathogens can be split into three types:

① Cold. Bacteria are dormant below 5 Celsius degrees.

② Hot. Bacteria are destroyed above 63 Celsius degrees if given enough time.

③ Warm. Bacteria will grow between 5 and 60 Celsius degrees, this is the danger zone. For most bacteria, the ideal temperature is 37 Celsius degrees (human body temperature), when growth is the most rapid.

Bacteria's growth is much slower near the two extremes of the danger zone.

Foods are likely to be in the danger zone when:

They are left in a warm room;

They are slowly warming up;

They are cooked after cooked;

They are left in sunny windows;

Hot gravy/sauce is poured on cold food;

They are in vehicles in hot weather.

Notes

1. Some noticeable temperatures are as follows:

Water boils at the temperature of 100℃ (212 ℉);

Minimum cooking temperature above 74℃ (165 ℉);

Hot hold temperature 60℃ (140 ℉);

Danger zone: 5℃-60℃ (41 ℉-140 ℉);

Body temperature 37℃ (98.6 ℉) —The best temperature for bacteria;

Cold hold temperature below 5℃ (41 ℉);

Refrigeration temperature 5℃ (41 ℉);

Air-refrigerator (air-circulate) temperature below 4℃ (39 ℉);

Water freezes at the temperature of 0℃ (32 ℉);

Freezer temperature (legal frozen temperature) -18℃ (0 ℉) .

2. The converting formula between Celsius temperature and Fahrenheit temperature:

Celsius temperature × 9/5+ 32= Fahrenheit temperature

For example: 42℃ × 9/5+ 32= 107.6 ℉

(2) Time

① Bacteria will reproduce every 10-20 minutes at the right temperature;

② They reproduce by the way of binary fission;

③ The time bacteria take to grow: Every 10-20 minutes, one bacterium can divide into 2.

1min. =1

20min. =2

40min. =4

60min. =8

80min. =16

10hours=over 1billion

(3) Moisture

a. Bacteria's growth needs moisture: a thin film is enough.

b. Bacteria cannot multiply in dry foods such as flour, dried milk, spices and toast.

5.7.8 High Risk Foods

Defined as "Those foods which will support the growth of bacteria and may be eaten without further cooking." Also called potentially hazardous foods, bacteria grow easily in these foods.

High risk foods have the following characteristics in common.

① protein;

② moisture;

③ low salt and sugar;

④ low acid.

Examples are: cooked poultry, cooked meats; dairy products (not include hard cheese); soups, stocks and sauces, shellfish and seafood, cooked rice, raw eggs in food, e. g. mayonnaise (a thick yellowish sauce with eggs, oil, milk, etc. in it, which may be poured over cold foods) .

It is high priority that these foods are kept under refrigeration at the correct temperature. If these foods are being served or held hot, their temperature must be above 63℃. Failure to do these will result in the growth of any bacteria which may lead to food poisoning.

5.7.9 Safe or Low Risk Foods

These are foods on which bacteria cannot usually grow by virtue of the fact that the food is:

Too dry;

Too acid;

Too high in sugar;

Too high in salt;

Chemically preserved;

Too high in fat.

These should not be given priority in relation to refrigerated storage and display.

(1) The effect of acid on bacteria

①The acidity of food has an important effect on the growth of bacteria, therefore decide how long food will keep;

②This is called the ph;

③Strong acid foods are: lemon juice; vinegar; limes; rhubarb (a type of broad-leaved garden plant whose thick juicy stems are boiled with sugar and eaten as food) .

(2) The effect of sugar and salt on bacteria

① salt: e. g. brine;

② sugar: e. g. jam, treacle.

They shrivel the bacteria up.

5.7.10 Dealing with Poultry Safely

Fresh and frozen poultry can harbour both salmonella and campylobacter. This may be of the order of 40%. The situation is improving a little due to efforts mainly made by the large retailers who have improved standards at farms, slaughter and processing plants. However, you must assume that all poultry you deal with is contaminated.

Frozen poultry (unless processed goods) should always be thawed completely. Ideally, this should be done in a covered container in a fridge (think time needed). It should be checked with a skewer or similar.

Thawing should be done well away from any cooked foods.

Hands, equipment and surfaces used for raw poultry must be cleaned and disinfected after use (avoid cross contamination).

Poultry should be cooked thoroughly and checked with probe (well above 63℃).

Make sure cooked poultry is not allowed to come into contact with raw (or hands, surfaces, etc.).

If cooling is required, it should be done as quickly as possible in a blast chiller or more likely in a cool room. The aim is refrigeration within 1.5 hours.

Potentially, poultry is probably the most risky food you deal with and is very popular with customers. Be careful with it.

Notes

1. **If dealing with hot chicken, we must use 1/2 hour to cool it down and then put it into refrigerator;**
2. **If dealing with the food taken out of freezer, firstly we must put it into refrigerator.**

5.7.11 Avoiding Food Danger

(1) How to avoid food danger

The methods of avoiding food danger are as follows:

① Don't leave food at room temperature;

② keep food hot or cold;

③ Try not to prepare or cook foods too long in advance. If you must do like this, please cool hot food quickly (<1.5hours), cover it and then refrigerate it (below 5℃/41 ℉);

④ keep hot food hot (above 60℃/140 ℉), reheat thoroughly (above 60℃/140 ℉);

⑤ Transport food safely (refrigerated);

⑥ It is important to cook food thoroughly in order to destroy bacteria;

⑦ It is important to deal with frozen food correctly, and correct thawing practices and subsequent cooking times must be given, especially for poultry.

(2) The safety methods for dealing with eggs

The bacteria salmonella are very common in eggs, most eggs are contaminated. The following are the methods for dealing with eggs:

① We should store eggs in refrigerator;

② According to USPH standards, pasteurized eggs for most dishes must be used;

③ We should wash hands after preparation.

(3) Safe handling of raw vegetables

We should use 50 PPM (parts per million) solution to wash and sterilize vegetables.

(4) Safe handling of cooked food during preparation

Safe handling of cooked food is as follows:

① Cooked food must be covered;

② When thawing cooked food, we must get ready to eat it;

③ When mixing ingredients with cooked food, we should not use hand to contact it;

④ We should contact cooked food only with sanitized clean equipment.

Generally speaking, cooked food must be protected from contamination.

(5) Correct use of plastic gloves

①We should use plastic gloves only for the foods which are cooked and ready to eat;

②We should wash hands before and after using gloves;

③The aim of using plastic gloves is to minimize hands contact on cooked food.

5.7.12 Bacterial Spores

Some types of bacteria can produce spores e. g. clostridium.

These spores are formed when conditions are not suitable for survival and growth.

These spores protect the bacteria in a tough case which is extremely difficult to be destroyed by heat, drying or chemicals.

As soon as conditions improve, the spore detects this and germinates back to a normal bacterium which can then multiply again.

Spores cause particular problems in reheated foods.

Major problems are caused to food canners by spores. Another spore former is c. botulinum, which is deadly. It grows especially well in the absence of air inside a can or bottle. Canners take extreme care to ensure that their processes destroy these spores. The safety standard is called botulinum cook.

Spores protect the bacteria from:

① High temperature;

② Chemical disinfectant;

③ Dehydration

If we want to kill spores, we'd better use press cooker to cook for 20 minutes.

Note

Spore is a very small seedlike usu. single cell produced by some plants and simple animals and able to develop into a new plant or animal, often after living through bad conditions for a time .

5.7.13 Main Food Poisoning Bacteria

There are many different bacteria capable of causing illness. The following three are generally recognized as the main ones.

(1) Salmonella

① It is mainly caused by poultry and eggs;

② It possibly cause abdominal pains, fever, diarrhoea, vomiting and death;

③ It is the most common type of food poisoning bacteria (80-90%);

④ It comes from all animals, raw meat/poultry, eggs and humans.

(2) Clostridium

① It is mainly caused by reheated large meat dishes;

② It possibly cause abdominal pain, diarrhoea (usually mild), it is rarely fatal;

③ It is the second most common of food poisoning bacteria (5-15%);

④ It comes from raw meat, soil, insects, excretion and humans.

(3) Staphylococcus

① It is mainly caused by poorly handled cooked food—meats, trifle, sandwiches;

② It possibly cause vomiting and abdominal pains;

③ It is the third most common type of food poisoning bacteria (1-5%);

④ It comes from nose and throat, cuts and sores, boils, raw milk.

(4) Others which can cause illness are:

① Bacillus. It is caused by reheated rice.

② Botulinum. It is caused by badly canned food, deadly.

Notes

1. single celled organisms 单细胞微生物
2. make them very hard to detect their presence in food 让他们很难检测到他们在食物中的存在
3. moist condition 潮湿的环境
4. a single cell 一个单细胞
5. pathogenic bacteria 病菌，病原菌
6. grow crops 种植庄稼
7. binary fission 二元裂变
8. danger zone 危险区间
9. freezer temperature 冷冻温度
10. The converting formula between Celsius temperature and Fahrenheit temperature. 摄氏温度和华氏温度之间的转换公式。
11. thin film 薄膜
12. the two extremes of the danger zone 危险区的两极
13. dairy products 乳制品
14. They shrivel the bacteria up. 它们使细菌枯萎。
15. slaughter and processing plants 屠宰加工厂
16. blast chiller 鼓风冷却机
17. room temperature 室温
18. correct thawing practices and subsequent cooking times 正确解冻的做法和随后的烹调时间
19. pasteurized eggs 巴氏消毒鸡蛋
20. 50 PPM (parts per million) solution 百万分之五十的溶液
21. bacterial spores 细菌孢子
22. in the absence of air 在没有空气的环境下
23. botulinum cook 高压蒸煮

New words & expressions

microorganism [maikrəu'ɔːgəniz(ə)m] n. [微生] 微生物，微小动植物
parasite ['pærəsait] n. 寄生虫，食客
mould [məuld] n. [亦作 mold] 肥土，霉，模具 v. 发霉，铸造
fungus ['fʌŋgəs] n. 菌类，蘑菇
cheese [tʃiːz] n. 干酪，〈俚〉头等的人或事物
microbe ['maikrəub] n. 微生物，细菌
cell [sel] n. 单元，细胞，蜂房，(尤指监狱或寺院的) 单人房间，电池
pathogens ['pæθədʒəns] n. 病原体 (物)
spoilage ['spɔilidʒ] n. 损坏
detect [di'tekt] vt. 察觉，发觉，侦查，探测 v. 发现
presence ['prezns] n. 出席，到场，存在
characteristic [ˌkæriktə'ristik] adj. 表示特性的，典型的 n. 特性，特征
pin [pin] n. 钉，销，栓，大头针 vt. 钉住，别住，阻止
moist [mɔist] adj. 潮湿的 n. 潮湿
pathogenic [ˌpæθə'dʒenik] adj. 致病的，病原的，发病的
shellfish ['ʃelfiʃ] n. 贝，甲壳类动物
insect ['insekt] n. 昆虫，卑鄙的人 adj.. 虫的，虫子一样的，对付虫子的
pet [pet] n. 宠物，受宠爱的人 adj. 宠爱的，亲昵的 vt. 宠爱 vi. 拥抱
digest [di'dʒest; dai'dʒest] n. 分类，摘要 vi. 消化 vt. 消化，融会贯通
sewage ['sju (ː) idʒ] n. 下水道，污水 v. 用污水灌溉，装下水道于
drug [drʌg] n. 药，麻药，麻醉药，滞销货 vi. 〈俗〉吸毒 vt. 使服毒品
binary ['bainəri] adj. 二进位的，二元的
fission ['fiʃən] n. 裂开，分裂，分体，[原] 裂变 v. [原] (使) 裂变
split [split] v. 劈开，(使) 裂开，分裂，分离 n. 裂开，裂口，裂痕
invisible [in'vizəbl] adj. 看不见的，无形的
infection [in'fekʃən] n. [医] 传染，传染病，影响，感染
release [ri'liːs] n. 释放，发行的书，释放证书 vt. 释放，发表 n. 版本
toxin ['tɔksin] n. [生化] [生] 毒素
vary ['veəri] vt. 改变，变更，使多样化 vi. 变化，不同，违反
extent [iks'tent] n. 广度，宽度，长度，范围，程度，区域
To some extent 在某种程度上
moisture ['mɔistʃə] n. 潮湿，湿气
dormant ['dɔːmənt] adj. 睡眠状态的，静止的，隐匿的
Celsius ['selsjəs] adj. 摄氏的
extreme [iks'triːm] adj. 尽头的，极端的，极度的 n. 极端，极端的事物
warm up 加热
gravy ['greivi] n. 肉汁，不法利润，肉汤
vehicle ['viːikl] n. 交通工具，车辆，媒介物，传达手段
circulate ['səːkjuleit] v. (使) 流通，(使) 运行，(使) 循环，(使) 传播

freezer [ˈfriːzə] n. 制冰淇淋者, 冷藏工人

Fahrenheit [ˈfærənhait, ˈfaːr-] adj. 华氏温度计的 n. 华氏温度计

reproduce [ˌriːprəˈdjuːs] v. 繁殖, 再生, 复制, 使……在脑海中重现

billion [ˈbiljən] n. adj. 十亿（的）

film [film] n. 薄膜, 胶卷, 影片, 薄雾 vt. 在…上覆以薄膜

flour [ˈflauə] n. 面粉

spice [spais] n. 香料, 调味品, 趣味, 意味, 情趣

toast [təust] n. 烤面包（片）, 干杯 vt. 敬酒, 烤（面包等）, vi. 烤暖, 烤火

risk [risk] vt. 冒 . . . 的危险 n. 冒险, 风险

define [diˈfain] vt. 定义, 详细说明

potentially adv. 潜在地

hazardous [ˈhæzədəs] adj. 危险的, 冒险的, 碰运气的

protein [ˈprəutiːn] n. [生化] 蛋白质 adj. 蛋白质的

acid [ˈæsid] n. [化] 酸, < 俚> 迷幻药 adj. 酸的, 讽刺的, 刻薄的

poultry [ˈpəultri] n. 家禽

dairy [ˈdεəri] n. 牛奶场, 奶品场, 售牛奶, 奶油, 奶制品

stock [stɔk] n. 树干, 库存, 股票, 股份, 托盘, 原料 vi. 出新芽, 采购

seafood [ˈsiːfuːd] n. 海产食品, 海味

mayonnaise [ˌmeiəˈneiz] n. 蛋黄酱

priority [praiˈɔriti] n. 先, 前, 优先, 优先权

virtue [ˈvəːtjuː] n. 德行, 美德, 贞操, 优点, 功效, 效力, 英勇

In relation to 关于，涉及，有关

acidity [əˈsiditi] n. 酸度, 酸性, [医] 酸过多, 胃酸过多

lemon [ˈlemən] n. 柠檬 adj. 柠檬色的

rhubarb [ˈruːbɑːb] n. 大黄, 大黄的叶柄

lime [laim] n. 酸橙, 石灰, 黏鸟胶

brine [brain] n. 盐水

treacle [ˈtriːkl] n. 糖蜜, 甜蜜, 过分甜蜜的声调

shrivel [ˈʃrivl] v. （使）起皱纹,（使）枯萎,（使）束手无策

harbour [ˈhaːbə] n. （= harbor）海港 vt. 隐匿，窝藏，包含

salmonella [ˌsælməˈnelə] [生] 沙门氏菌属

due to 由于

retailer [riːˈteilə] n. 零售商人, 传播的人

slaughter [ˈslɔːtə] n. 屠宰, 残杀, 屠杀 v. 屠宰, 残杀, 屠杀

assume [əˈsjuːm] vt. 假定, 设想, 采取, 呈现

ideally [aiˈdiəli] adv. 理想地, 在观念上地, 完美地

fridge [fridʒ] n. 电冰箱

skewer [ˈskjuə] n. （烤肉用的）串肉扦, 扦, 棒 vt. 上叉

similar [ˈsimilə] adj. 相似的, 类似的

surface [ˈsəːfis] n. 表面, 外表, 水面 adj. 表面的, 肤浅的

disinfect [ˌdisinˈfekt] vt. 消毒
probe [prəub] n. 探针, 探测器 vt. （以探针等）探查, 查明
come into contact with 接触
make sure v. 确定，确信, 证实
blast [blɑːst] n. 一阵（风), 一股（气流), 鼓风, 送风 vt. 爆炸, , 毁灭
chiller [ˈtʃilə] n. 使寒冷之人或事物, 冷却器
avoid [əˈvɔid] vt. 避免, 消除
in advance 预先
thoroughly [ˈθʌrəli] adv. 十分地, 彻底地
subsequent [ˈsʌbsikwənt] adj. 后来的, 并发的
pasteurize [ˈpæstəraiz] vt. 用巴氏法灭菌
minimize [ˈmɪnɪmaɪz] vt. 将……减到最少 v. 最小化
glove [glʌv] n. 手套 vt. 戴手套
spore [spɔː, spɔə] n. 孢子 vi. 长孢子
clostridium [klɔsˈtridiəm] n. [生] 梭菌, 梭菌属
survival [səˈvaivəl] n. 生存, 幸存, 残存, 幸存者, 残存物
detect [diˈtekt] v. 察觉, 发觉, 侦查, 探测 v. 发现
germinate [ˈdʒəːmineit] v. 发芽, 发育, 使生长
canner [ˈkænə] n. 罐头制造商
bottler [ˈbɔtlə] 灌注机, 灌瓶机, 瓶装食品制造商
disinfectant [dɪsɪnˈfekt（ə）nt] n. 消毒剂
dehydration [ˌdiːhaiˈdreiʃən] n. 脱水
fatal [ˈfeitl] adj. 致命的, 重大的, 命运注定的, 不幸的, 致命的
deadly [ˈdedli] adj. 致命的, 势不两立的, 死一般的, 极度的, 必定的
excrete [eksˈkriːt] vt. 排泄, 分泌
staphylococcus [ˌstæfiləuˈkɔkəs] n. [微生物] 葡萄状球菌
trifle [ˈtraifl] n. 琐事, 少量, 蛋糕, 小事 v. 开玩笑, 玩弄, 浪费, 嘲弄
sore [sɔ, sɔə] adj. 疼痛的, 痛心的, 剧烈的 n. 痛的地方, 痛处
boil [bɔil] n. 沸点, 沸腾, 疖子 v. 煮沸, 激动
bacillus [bəˈsiləs] n. 杆状菌, 细菌
botulinum [bɔtʃəˈlainəm] n. [微] 肉毒（杆）菌

Exercises

1. Would you please list four main microorganisms?
2. Are all fungi harmful? Would you please give some examples?
3. What are bacteria?
4. What are the characteristics of bacteria?
5. What are the pathogenic bacteria?
6. Where do pathogenic bacteria come from?
7. What are the spoilage bacteria?
8. What are the differences between pathogenic and spoilage bacteria?

9. What are the useful bacteria?
10. How do bacteria grow?
11. What are toxins?
12. What are the conditions for bacterial growth?
13. How to divide the effect of temperature on food poisoning pathogens?
14. What conditions can likely make foods to be in the danger zone?
15. What are the hot hold temperature and cold hold temperature? What is danger temperature zone?
16. How to convert Celsius temperature into Fahrenheit temperature?
17. How do bacteria reproduce at the right temperature?
18. In which foods can bacteria not multiply?
19. What are the high risk foods?
20. What are the common characteristics of the high risk foods? Please give some examples.
21. How to hold and serve the high risk foods?
22. What are the safe or low risk foods?
23. What are the common characteristics of the safe or low risk foods
24. What is the effect of sugar and salt on bacteria?
25. How to deal with the frozen poultry?
26. How to deal with the cooked poultry?
27. How to avoid food danger?
28. What is the safety procedure for eggs?
29. What is the safe handling of cooked food during preparation?
30. How to use plastic gloves correctly?
31. What are bacteria spores?
32. How to destroy bacteria spores?
33. What are the features of salmonella?
34. What are the three main food poisoning bacteria ?

5.8 Contamination of Food

We can stop food contamination if we know the ways in which it occurs. Deliberate contamination is rare, accidental contamination is not rare. It is illegal to sell contaminated food.

5.8.1 Where Do Bacteria Come from

They mainly come from:

① people;

② air;

③ animals;

④ raw foods;

⑤ insects;

⑥ food waste;

⑦ dust and dirt;

⑧ Water.

5.8.2 How Do Bacteria Get into Food

(1) Direct contamination This may occur from direct contact with the sources of bacteria, e.g. raw food—cooked food; dirty hand contaminates food directly.

(2) Indirect cross contamination This may occur from one food to another via surfaces, equipment, cloths, clothing, utensils, etc. e.g. raw food—chopping board—cooked food.

This may also occur, and frequently does via hands as the vehicle. e.g. egg—hand—beef.

5.8.3 Identify the Three Types of Contamination

When we handle food, we must identify the ways in which food can be contaminated during production and service, and identify the methods to prevent biological, chemical and physical contamination.

(1) Biological contamination It is caused by microorganisms such as bacteria, viruses, etc. The harmful things that can get into foods are microorganisms.

(2) Chemical contamination It is caused by detergent, disinfectant, pesticide, insecticide, lubricants, air-freshener, etc.. This can be avoided by the following ways.

① Label decanted chemicals;

② Discard damaged containers;

③ Never reuse food container for chemical storage;

④ Store chemicals away from food areas.

(3) Physical contamination It is caused by physical substances, such as plastic, pen, hair, fly, etc. Physical contamination sometimes called foreign body contamination. Foreign bodies in food almost always result in complaints and possibly prosecution. All of the following have ever been found in food.

① pieces of metal;

② packaging materials (rubber band, thin film, etc.);

③ insects and animals (or parts of these);

④ cigarette ends;

⑤ hair of human and animals;

⑥ jewellery and buttons;

⑦ glass;

⑧ wood splinters;

⑨ mould;

⑩ rust.

plus many more.

Unless it can be shown that this contamination occurred before receipt of the foods, the seller is legally liable.

5.8.4 Prevention of Contamination

The methods of preventing contamination are as follows.

① Use warranted suppliers which has good quality;

② Cover foods;

③ Handle foods as little as possible;

④ Keep raw and cooked foods separate, particularly meats;

⑤ Keep animals out of food workplaces;

⑥ Good waste disposal;

⑦ Thorough cleaning & disinfection;

⑧ Good personal hygiene and habits;

⑨ Wash all equipment, surface, etc. between uses;

⑩ Use disposable cloths, wipes, etc. ;

⑪ Separate all clean and dirty processes as far as possible;

⑫ Color coding.

5.8.5 Avoid Cross Contamination by Cleaning

Cleaning equipments such as buckets, cloth, mops, etc. can spread bacteria, we must deal with them carefully.

5.8.6 Preventing Cross Contamination During Food and Drink Service

The prevention methods are as follows.

① Hold equipment by the handles when setting tables;

② Take ice with metal wares;

③ Don't touch the ice with hands;

④ Dirty plates—wash hands—clean plates.

5.8.7 The Ten Main Reasons for Food Poisoning

Food poisoning can be caused by a lot of reasons, the ten main reasons are as follows.

① Food is prepared too far in advance and stored wrongly at warm temperature;

② Food is cooled too slowly before refrigeration;

③ Food is not reheated properly;

④ Cooked food is contaminated by food poisoning bacteria;

⑤ Food is undercooked;

⑥ Poultry is thawed incorrectly;

⑦ Caused by cross contamination from raw to cooked food;

⑧ Hot food is kept below 63 degrees Celsius;

⑨ Caused by infected food handlers;
⑩ Caused by use of leftover.

5.8.8 The Food Poisoning Chain

There are three main ways of breaking the food poisoning chain.
① Protecting food from contamination;
② Preventing any bacteria within food from multiplying;
③ Destroying these bacteria present within the food.

Notes

1. Deliberate contamination is rare, accidental contamination is not rare. 故意的感染很少见，但意外的感染不少见。
2. raw foods 生的食物
3. indirect cross contamination 间接交叉感染
4. chopping board 砧板
5. This may also occur, and frequently does via hands as the vehicle. 这也可能发生，并经常以手为媒介。
6. label decanted chemicals 给可倾倒的化学品作标签
7. foreign body contamination 外来物体的感染
8. rubber band 橡皮圈
9. cigarette ends 烟头
10. use warranted suppliers which has good quality 使用质量好、有保证的供应商
11. waste disposal 废物处理
12. use disposable cloths, wipes, etc. 使用一次性的桌布、抹布等
13. color coding 彩色编码
14. hold equipment by the handles when setting tables 摆台时拿器皿的手柄
15. undercooked 未煮熟的
16. caused by use of leftover 由使用残羹剩菜所引起的

New words & expressions

contamination [kənˌtæmiˈneiʃən] n. 玷污，污染，污染物
deliberate [diˈlibəreit] adj. 深思熟虑的，故意的，预有准备的 v. 商讨
accidental [ˌæksiˈdentl] adj. 意外的，非主要的，附属的 n. 非本质属性
illegal [iˈliːgəl] adj. 违法的，不合规定的
identify [aiˈdentifai] vt. 识别，鉴别，把……和……看成一样 v. 确定
biological [baiəˈlɔdʒikəl] adj. 生物学的
surface [ˈsəːfis] n. 表面，外表，水面 adj. 表面的，肤浅的
via [ˈvaiə, viːə] prep. 经，通过，经由
utensil [ju(ː)ˈtensl] n. 器具
frequently [ˈfriːkwəntli] adv. 常常，频繁地 n. 经常地
vehicle [ˈviːikl] n. 交通工具，车辆，媒介物，传达手段
pesticide [ˈpestisaid] n. 杀虫剂

insecticide [in'sektisaid] n. 杀虫剂

lubricant ['lu:brikənt] n. 滑润剂

air-freshener 空气清新剂

label ['leibl] n. 标签，商标，标志 vt. 贴标签于，指……为，分类，标注

decant [di'kænt] vt. 轻轻倒出，移入其他容器

discard [dis'kɑ:d] vt. 丢弃，抛弃 v. 放弃

reuse ['ri:'ju:z] vt. 再使用 n. 重新使用

container [kən'teinə] n. 容器（箱，盆，罐，壶，桶，坛子），集装箱

prosecution [ˌprɔsi'kju:ʃən] n. 进行，经营，检举，起诉

splinter ['splintə] n. 裂片，尖片，小事，碎片 v. 裂成碎片，分裂

rust [rʌst] n. 铁锈 vt. （使）生锈

liable ['laiəbl] adj. 有责任的，有义务的，易……的，有……倾向的

warrant ['wɔrənt] n. 授权，批准，许可证 vt. 保证，辩解，担保，批准

supplier [sə'plaiə] n. 供应者，补充者，厂商，供给者

workplace 工作场所，车间

disposal [dis'pəuzəl] n. 处理，处置，布置，安排，配置，支配

disinfection [ˌdisin'fekʃən] n. 消毒

coding ['kəudiŋ] n. 译码

undercook ['ʌndəkuk] vt. 轻煎，微煎

leftover n. 剩余物，残留物，剩菜 adj. 剩余的

handler ['hændlə] n. 处理者，管理者，训练者，（尤指拳击）教练

Exercises

1. Where do bacteria come from?
2. What are the three types of contamination? Please give some examples.
3. How do bacteria get into food?
4. How to avoid chemical contamination?
5. What is physical contamination? Please give some examples.
6. How to prevent contamination?
7. What are the ten main reasons for food poisoning?
8. How to break the food poisoning chain?
9. How to prevent cross contamination during food and drink service?

5.9 Food Preservation and Personal Hygiene

5.9.1 Food Preservation

This is any process which extends the life of a food and ensures its safety. There are many methods used as follows.

① Heating: pasteurization, ultra heat treatment;

② Drying (dehydration);

③ Salt;

④ Sugar;

⑤ Other chemicals;

⑥ Cold: refrigeration (chilling), deep freezing;

⑦ Vacuum packing and related processes;

⑧ Smoking;

⑨ Irradiation.

5.9.2 Personal Hygiene

(1) People contaminate food Personal hygiene is vital. The public also expect to see clean, hygienic staff working in food areas, who don't display inappropriate habits when handling foods.

(2) Please observe the following points

① Outdoor clothing should be covered unless no open food is handled.

② Lockers should be provided and used.

③ Hair should be clean. On open food work, it should be covered.

④ Mouth, nose and ears harbor harmful bacteria, so

Don't cough or sneeze over food;

Don't pick at food;

Don't bite your nails;

Don't pick your nose or ears;

Don't spit or smoke (in food areas);

Wash your hands if you need to touch any of these facial areas.

⑤ Keep clean and take a shower or bath daily; cover cuts and sores.

In some foreign countries, people use blue water-proof plaster or bandage, dressing on cuts and sores in order to distinguish from food.

⑥ Hands are wonderful at spreading bacteria, so we must

a. wash them frequently and always:

Before work;

After using the "Loo";

After handling raw foods;

After handling rubbish;

After breaks or a smoke;

After using chemicals.

b. Keep nails clean and not bitten.

c. Use separate wash basins for hands. These should be provided. (In galley, a lot of stations are ready for washing hands.)

How do bacteria get onto your hands?

From toilet; nose; hands of a food handler, etc.

According to USPH regulations, wash your hands 20 seconds because time is limited; food employees must keep their hands and exposed portions of their arms clean.

⑦ Avoid wearing jewellery and watches on open food works.

⑧ Wash thoroughly and dry (using hot air-dryers or disposable tissue).

⑨ Clothing should be clean and smart and suitable for the job.

(3) Report to supervisor any skin or stomach problems This must then be dealt with by appropriate medical authority.

(4) It is the responsibility of managers & supervisors to ensure that all staff abide by the relevant parts of the hygiene regulations. Dirty food handlers will be prosecuted.

Notes

1. ultra heat treatment 超高温处理
2. vacuum packing 真空包装（封罐）
3. inappropriate habits 不恰当的习惯
4. outdoor clothing 户外服装
5. On open food work, it should be covered. 在处理敞开的食物时，应将户外服装遮盖起来。
6. Don't pick your nose or ears. 不要掏你的鼻子或耳朵。
7. harbor harmful bacteria 隐藏有害细菌
8. facial areas 面部区域
9. cover cuts and sores 将伤口和溃疡包起来
10. blue water-proof plaster or bandage, dressing 蓝色防水膏药或绷带、敷料
11. using hot air-dryers or disposable tissue 使用热空气干燥器或一次性纸巾
12. appropriate medical authority 有关医疗机构
13. abide by the relevant parts of the hygiene regulations 遵守卫生条例的有关规定
14. Dirty food handlers will be prosecuted. 不卫生食品的经营者将被绳之以法。

New words & expressions

preservation [ˌprezə(ː)'veiʃən] n. 保存

extend [iks'tend] v. 扩充，延伸，伸展，给予，提供，演化出的全文，对（地产等）估价

pasteurization [ˌpæstəraiˈzeiʃən] n. 加热杀菌法，巴斯德杀菌法

ultra ['ʌltrə] adj. 过激的，极端的 n. 过激论者，急进论者

dehydration [ˌdiːhaiˈdreiʃən] n. 脱水

chill [tʃil] n. 寒意，寒战，寒心 adj. 寒冷的，扫兴的 v. 使冷，变冷，冷藏

vacuum ['vækjuəm] n. 真空，真空吸尘器 adj. 真空的，产生真空的

pack [pæk] n. 包裹，包装 vt. 包装，捆扎，塞满，压紧 vi. 包装货物，挤

irradiation [iˌreidiˈeiʃən] n. 放射，照射

vital ['vaitl] adj. 生死攸关的，重大的，生命的，生机的，所必需的

inappropriate [ˌinə'prəupriit] adj. 不适当的，不相称的

outdoor ['autdɔː] adj. 室外的，户外的，野外的

pick at 用手拨

loo [luː] n. 一种纸牌游戏，〈英俚〉厕所，洗手间
air-dryer 干手机
abide by 遵守
prosecute ['prɔsikjuːt] vt. 实行，从事，起诉 vi. 告发，起诉，作检察官
relevant ['relivənt] adj. 有关的，相应的
plaster ['plɑːstə] n. 石膏，灰泥，膏药 vt 敷以膏药，减轻，粘贴，重创
bandage ['bændidʒ] n. 绷带
dressing ['dresiŋ] n. 穿衣，装饰，敷裹，敷料，调味品

Exercises

1. What is food preservation?
2. What are the methods to preserve the food?
3. Please name three dirty habits to avoid when working.
4. When you handle food, how to deal with your cuts and sores?
5. When you handle food, how to deal with skin and stomach problems?
6. What is the responsibility of managers and supervisors about hygiene?
7. Explain where bacteria on your hands come from.
8. Why do some people use blue plasters?

5.10 Premises

5.10.1 Premises Design and Construction

(1) Principles of hygienic design The hygienic design of food premises should abide by the following principles:

① Eliminate cross-contamination;
② Logical work flow;
③ Proper facilities for personal hygiene, e.g. locker room, washing basin;
④ Cleaning allowed for;
⑤ Proper temperature control facilities;
⑥ Suitable for pest control;
⑦ Suitable for waste disposal;
⑧ Conducive to the welfare and safety of the staff and customers.

Most food businesses must be registered with the local authority.

(2) Constructional details The construction and installation of the following parts of food premises should be suitable:

① Floors;
② Walls;
③ Ceiling;
④ Windows and doors;
⑤ Services of water, gas and electricity;

⑥ Drainage;

⑦ Lighting and ventilation.

(3) Food equipment The food equipment should be as follows:

① Easy to clean and maintain;

② Non-toxic, corrosion resistant, durable and chip free;

③ Non absorbent—avoid wood;

④ Metal (non-toxic) and plastic are best;

⑤ Large equipment should be movable;

⑥ Color code if appropriate.

5.10.2 Cleaning Premises and Equipments

(1) Why do we do cleaning Generally there are two reasons:

① To reduce harmful bacteria;

② To keep out of pests.

(2) The cleaning process Cleaning is the application of energy to a surface in order to remove grease and dirt.

The types of energy used are:

① Physical energy—manual labor or machine;

② Chemical energy—cleaning agents, detergents, etc. ;

③ Thermal energy—hot water.

Most cleaning uses all the three to some extent or another. Cleaning as you go is the best approach (As you go, if you find dirt, clean it immediately.).

(3) The rinsing process Rinsing is the process of washing in clean water so as to take away soap, dirt, etc..

(4) The sanitizing process Sanitizing is the process of reducing the number of micro-organisms on a surface to a safe level.

The methods of sanitizing:

① Heat sanitizing—Used by hot water;

② Chemical sanitizing—Used by chlorine solution.

Sanitizing requires clean, tepid water and correct strength. Direct sanitizing requires correct contact time (Need some time to kill microorganisms, then wash.).

Notes

When work with chemicals (sanitizing solution), do according to manufacturers' instructions. Chemical sanitizing is done in two ways.

1. By immersing a clean object in a specific concentration of sanitizing solution for a required period of time;

2. By rinsing or spraying an object with sanitizing solution.

(5) Management should draw up cleaning schedules.

① These schedules should indicate:

What is to be cleaned;

When it is to be cleaned;

How it is to be cleaned;

What with;

Health and safety considerations;

Who is to clean.

② The concept of ownership of cleaning responsibilities can be a useful tool.

It is a legal requirement that all parts of food premises are kept clean, the manager will be responsible for arranging the cleaning of your work area.

A good cleaning schedule should be specific to your work area; should be split into daily, weekly and monthly tasks; should be completed to help maintain a high standard of cleanliness.

(6) Technical terms

① Bactericide—a chemical which destroys bacteria;

② Detergent—a chemical which removes grease and dirt prior to disinfection;

③ Disinfectant—a chemical which reduces microorganisms to a safe level;

④ Sterilizer—an instrument which destroys all living microorganisms;

⑤ Sanitizer—a chemical which both cleans and disinfects.

Notes

1. logical work flow 合理的工作流程

2. locker room 衣帽间，更衣室

3. cleaning allowed for 考虑到清洗

4. Most food businesses must be registered with the local authority. 大多数食品企业必须在地方当局注册。

5. Non-toxic, corrosion resistant, durable and chip free. 无毒、耐腐蚀、经久耐用、无碎片剥落。

6. To keep out of pests. 远离害虫

7. thermal energy 热能

8. chlorine solution 氯溶液

9. Sanitizing requires clean, tepid water and correct strength. 消毒需要清洁的温水和合适的力度。

10. By immersing a clean object in a specific concentration of sanitizing solution for a required period of time. 通过将一个干净的物体在特定浓度的消毒液里浸泡所需的一段时间（的方式）。

11. draw up cleaning schedules 制定清洁计划

12. The concept of ownership of cleaning responsibilities can be a useful tool. 清洁责任制的理念可能是一个有用的工具。

New words & expressions

premise [ˈpremis] n. 场所，[逻][法]前提，房屋连地基

eliminate [iˈlimineit] vt. 排除，消除 v. 除去

facility [fəˈsiliti] n. 容易，简易，灵巧，熟练，便利，敏捷，设备，工具

welfare [ˈwelfɛə] n. 福利，安宁，福利事业，社会安全 adj. 福利的

disposal [dis'pəuzəl] n. 处理，处置，布置，安排，配置，支配

installation [ˌinstə'leiʃən] n. [计] 安装，装置，就职

drainage ['dreinidʒ] n. 排水，排水装置，排水区域，排出物，消耗

ventilation [venti'leiʃən] n. 通风，流通空气

toxic ['tɔksik] adj. 有毒的，中毒的

corrosion [kə'rəuʒən] n. 侵蚀，腐蚀状态

durable ['djuərəbl] adj. 持久的，耐用的

absorbent [əb'sɔːbənt] adj. 能吸收的 n. 吸收剂

appropriate [ə'prəupriit] adj. 适当的

removal [ri'muːvəl] n. 移动，免职，切除

grease [griːs] n. 油脂，贿赂 vt. 涂脂于，〈俗〉贿赂

manufacturer [ˌmænju'fæktʃərə] n. 制造业者，厂商

application [æpli'keiʃən] n. 请求，申请，申请表，应用，运用，施用

approach [ə'prəutʃ] n. 接近，方法，途径，通路 vt. 接近，动手处理

draw up v. 草拟，停住，逼近，追上，整队

chlorine ['klɔːriːn] n. [化] 氯

tepid ['tepid] adj. 微温的，温热的，不太热烈的，不热情的

immerse [i'məːs] vt. 沉浸，使陷入

specific [spi'sifik] n. 特效药，细节 adj. 详细而精确的，明确的，特殊的

be responsible for 为……负责，是造成……的原因

ownership ['əunəʃip] n. 所有权，物主身份

bactericide [bæk'tiərisaid] n. 杀菌剂

disinfectant [disin'fekt(ə)nt] n. 消毒剂

Exercises

1. What are the principles of hygienic design of food premises?
2. What are the constructional details of food premises that we must consider?
3. What kind of food equipment should we use in food premises?
4. What is cleaning? What are the three types of energy used for cleaning?
5. What is sanitizing? What are the methods of sanitizing?
6. What are the two ways of chemical sanitizing?
7. What is detergent? What is disinfectant?
8. State the reasons of importance to keep food area clean.
9. Please make difference between cleaning，rinsing and sanitizing.
10. Please list the main stages of cleaning.

5.11 Pest Control

Pests are animals，including insects，which live on our food. They carry and spread pathogenic bacteria as well as causing much food to be thrown away. All employees should be able to detect the means and signs of access and inform management accordingly. Management must take immediate steps to remove any problem.

5.11.1 The Main Pests

Rodents—e. g. mice;

Insects—e. g. flies, cockroaches, beetles, mites, weevils, moths, wasps and ants;

Birds—e. g. feral pigeons, sparrows, starlings and seagulls;

Domestic pets—e. g. dogs, cats.

5.11.2 Pests Should Be Effectively Controlled

Pests should be effectively controlled to minimize their presence in the following areas aboard a vessel.

① Food storage areas;

② Food preparation areas;

③ Food service areas;

④ Food ware-washing areas;

⑤ Food utensils storage areas.

5.11.3 Reasons for Attracting Pests to Food Premises

① food (received deliveries);

② moisture;

③ warmth;

④ shelter.

5.11.4 Cockroaches

(1) Cockroach is the most prevalent pest onboard, it gets on the ship by two ways.

① From infested deliveries;

② From passengers' luggage.

(2) Cockroaches are only active and drop eggs in the dark. They usually breed in:

① False ceiling;

② Boxed pipes;

③ Cracked decks;

④ Drainage.

(3) Methods of preventing cockroaches

① Keep clean;

② Don't give food;

③ Set a trap to kill it;

④ Spray pesticide to kill it.

5. 11. 5 Houseflies

(1) Houseflies are a serious heath hazard, they carry bacteria on their guts and feet, they transfer bacteria to food.

(2) Methods of control houseflies

① Clear away decaying vegetables matter;

② Tightly cover waste bins;

③ Empty bins frequently—especially in hot weather;

④ Use insectocution to kill them where possible.

Notes

1. All employees should be able to detect the means and signs of access and inform management accordingly. 所有员工应能及时发现害虫进入的方式和迹象并通知相应的管理部门。

2. Management must take immediate steps to remove any problem. 管理部门应该立即采取措施解决任何问题。

3. to minimize their presence in the following areas 尽量减少它们在以下区域出现

4. infested deliveries 被感染的已交付的货物

5. drop eggs 产卵

6. boxed pipes 盒装管道

7. They carry bacteria on their guts and feet. 它们在它们的内脏和脚上携带细菌。

8. decaying vegetables matter 腐烂的蔬菜

New words & expressions

pest [pest] n. 有动害物，害虫

insect [ˈinsekt] n. 昆虫，卑鄙的人 adj. 虫的，虫子一样的，对付虫子的

throw away v. 扔掉，丢弃

accordingly [əˈkɔːdiŋli] adv. 因此，从而，相应地

rodent [ˈrəudənt] adj. 咬的，嚼的，[动物] 啮齿目的 n. 啮齿动物

creature [ˈkriːtʃə] n. 人，动物，傀儡，创造物

cockroach [ˈkɔkrəutʃ] n. 蟑螂

wasp [wɔsp] n. 黄蜂

moth [mɔθ] n. 蛾，蛀虫

beetle [ˈbiːtl] n. 甲虫 vi. 悬垂，突出

mite [mait] n. 微小的东西，〈口〉小孩，力所能及的微小贡献

weevil [ˈwiːvil] n. [昆] 象鼻虫

feral [ˈfiərəl] adj. 野生的，未驯服的，凶猛的，野兽的

starling [ˈstɑːliŋ] n. 八哥

seagull [ˈsiːgʌl] n. 海鸥

minimize [ˈminimaiz] vt. 将……减到最少 v. 最小化

prevalent [ˈprevələnt] adj. 普遍的，流行的

shelter [ˈʃeltə] n. 掩蔽处，身避处，掩蔽，庇护所，掩体 v. 掩蔽，躲避

infest [in'fest] v. 大批滋生，寄生于

hazard ['hæzəd] n. 冒险，危险，冒险的事 vt. 冒……的危险，使遭危险

gut [gʌt] n. [复] 内脏，勇气，剧情，肚子，内脏，海峡 vt. 取出内脏

decay [di'kei] vi. 腐朽，腐烂，衰减，衰退 n. 腐朽，腐烂，衰减 v. 衰落

frequently ['fri:kwəntli] adv. 常常，频繁地 n. 经常地

insectocution [in,sektə'kju:ʃən] n. 通电杀虫

trap [træp] n. 圈套，陷阱，诡计 vi. 设圈套，设陷阱 vt. 诱捕，诱骗

Exercises

1. What is pest? Would you please list four main pests?
2. Which pest is the most prevalent onboard? How to prevent it?
3. How to control houseflies and mosquitoes?
4. Would you please list four main food areas?

5.12 Food Waste Disposal and Food Safety Law

5.12.1 Food Waste Disposal

Waste attracts pest, it must be done properly.

① Keep food and packaging waste separate;

② Keep foods for return separate from ordinary food, waste and any stored food, whether it is packaged or not;

③ Consider health and safety, be careful with sharp objects in waste;

④ Empty and clean any waste bins regularly;

⑤ Recycle if possible, but don't allow items to become a source of food contamination or personal safety risk;

⑥ Waste containers should have lids to deter pests;

⑦ Arrange collection as frequently as needed.

Note

It is against the law to allow the buildup of refuse.

5.12.2 Food Safety Law

The main law concerning food hygiene is the Food Safety Act 1990. While this act does contain some details, it is what is known as an "enabling" act, it enables government to make all sorts of regulations to deal with the details.

It also deals with such things as enforcement, penalties, defences in law (due diligence), powers of officers, etc.

The main offences under the act are as the follows.

(1) Rendering food injurious to health.

(2) Selling or possessing for sale food that doesn't meet the food safety requirement, in that it:

① has been rendered injurious to health;

② is unfit for human consumption;

③ is so contaminated that it would be unreasonable to expect it to be eaten.

(3) Selling food not of the nature, quality or substance demanded.

Notes

1. packaging waste 打包的废物
2. foods for return 返回的食物
3. sharp objects 尖锐的物体
4. to deter pests 阻止害虫
5. Arrange collection as frequently as needed. 经常不断地按需要安排收集（废物）。
6. an "enabling" act 一个授权法案
7. defences in law 法律抗辩
8. due diligence 尽职调查，应有的注意
9. Selling food not of the nature, quality or substance demanded. 卖的食品与要求的性质、质量或内容不符。

New words & expressions

disposal [dis'pəuzəl] n. 处理，处置，布置，安排，配置，支配

package ['pækidʒ] n. 包裹，包

buildup ['bild,ʌp] n. 组合，集结，累积，形成

regularly ['regjuləli] adv. 有规律地，有规则地，整齐地，匀称地

recycle ['riː'saikl] v. 使再循环，反复应用 n. 再循环，再生，重复利用

lid [lid] n. 盖子，〈美口〉限制，眼睑 vt. 给……盖盖子

deter [di'təː] v. 阻止

act [ækt] n 法案，法令 vi. 担当，表演，假装 vt. 扮演，装作

refuse [ri'fjuːz] vt. 拒绝，谢绝 n. 废物，垃圾

enable [i'neibl] vt. 使能够，授予权利或方法

enforcement [in'fɔːsmənt] n. 执行，强制

penalty ['penlti] n. 处罚，罚款

defence [di'fens] n. 防卫，防卫设备 n. [律]（被告的）答辩、辩护

offence [ə'fens] n. 犯罪，冒犯，违反，罪过，过错 n. [军] 攻击

render ['rendə] vt. 呈递，归还，着色 vi. 给予补偿 n. 交纳，粉刷，打底

in that 由于，因为，既然

unfit ['ʌn'fit] adj. (～for) 不适宜的，不适当的 v. 不适合

consumption [kən'sʌmpʃən] n. 消费，消费量，肺病

Exercises

1. How to deal with waste?
2. Why should waste containers have lids?
3. What is refuse?
4. What is the main law concerning food hygiene?

5.13 Environmental Protection

5.13.1 The Shipboard Organizational Structure

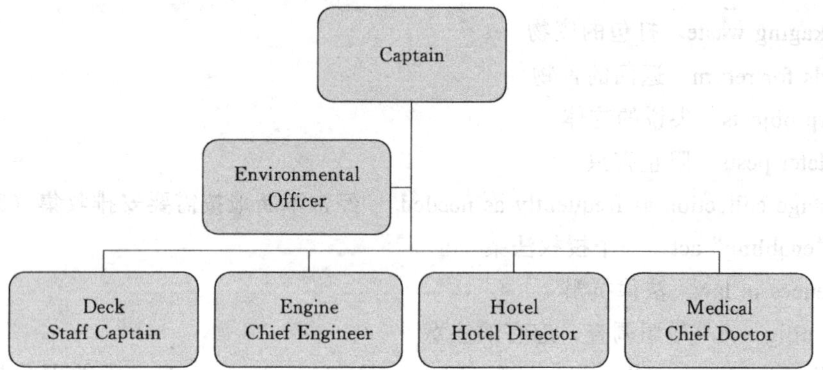

① Captain is responsible, along with the Environmental Officer and with the shore departments, for implementing the environmental protection system.

② Environmental Officer reports directly to the captain and is responsible for checking, supporting and monitoring the shipboard environmental management.

③ Department heads (hotel, deck, engine and medical) are responsible for properly managing the environmental aspects within their department.

5.13.2 Applicable Environmental Laws

(1) International Laws

① MARPOL: International Convention for the Prevention of Pollution from Ships.

② SOLAS: International Convention for the Protection of Life at Sea.

(2) National Laws There are a number of national laws that our vessels need to comply with when they are in the territorial waters of each respective country.

(3) Local Laws There are also local laws, which our ships need to comply with depending upon each individual port.

5.13.3 Environmental Aspects & Impacts

Every shipboard activity produces effects on the environment. The environmental aspect is the element of the activity that interacts with the environment. The impact is the effect, positive or negative, on the environment. Therefore, there is a cause-effect relationship between aspect and impact.

Environmental Aspects:

① Production of (Marpol and non-Marpol) Waste. Waste discharge at sea, production of waste.

② Production of waste water (grey, black, bilge water). Discharging of polluting substances at sea (oils and fats).

③ Discharge of ballast water. Sea water discharged for the purpose of maintaining the ships stability. This water can contaminate or impact on the ecosystem of each local sea water our ships visit.

④ Consumption of non-renewable raw materials. Most of the man-made fibres are made out of synthetic polymers. Water/electric power consumption.

⑤ Air emission. CO_2 (Carbon Dioxide), NOX (Nitrogen Oxides), SOX (Sulphur Oxides), fumes.

⑥ Electromagnetic emission. Emissions from radar antennas, telephones.

5.13.4 Waste Disposal

(1) There are different kinds of waste

① Marpol waste or garbage. this refers to waste that is covered by the Marpol convention. They are as follows: plastic, metal, paper, aluminum, glass, ashes, food, porcelain.

② Special waste. all waste not covered by the Marpol convention, which can be hazardous or non-hazardous. They are as follows: spray cans, hospital wastes and needles, neon, used cooking oil, fireworks, photo developer liquid, batteries, oily engine rags, dry cleaning machines residues, electronic parts.

Note: It is strictly prohibited to discharge or throw into the sea any waste from a vessel. Currently only food waste is permitted to be discharged from ships, which is done so by authorized personnel respecting all applicable laws and standards.

(2) To guarantee effective environmental protection you must identify and separate waste at the origin.

Identifying wastes and separating them is particularly important, not only because disposal system differ, but because some wastes can be recycled such as: Used cooking oil, Lead batteries, Glass, Aluminum, Electric/electronic material.

(3) Garbage waste disposal MARPOL allows some liquid and solid wastes to be discharged into the sea, taking into account: Distance from the coast, "En route" navigation, Speed, If the ship is within or outside special areas, The type of waste.

Regulations for Garbage Disposal at Sea(Annex V of MARPOL 73/78)

Garbage Type	Outside Special Areas	In Special Areas
Plastics-includes synthetic ropes and fishing nets and plastic garbage bags	Disposal is prohibited	Disposal is prohibited
Floating dunnage, lining and packing material	Disposal is permitted only if the distance from the nearest land is more than 25 nautical miles	Disposal is prohibited
Paper, rags, glass, metal, bottles, crockery and similar refuse	Disposal is permitted only if the distance from the nearest land is more than 12 nautical miles	Disposal is prohibited

continued

Regulations for Garbage Disposal at Sea(Annex V of MARPOL 73/78)		
Garbage Type	Outside Special Areas	In Special Areas
All other garbage including paper, rage, glass, etc. comminuted or ground*	Disposal is permitted only if the distance from the nearest land is more than 3 nautical miles	Disposal is prohibited
Food waste not comminuted or ground*	Disposal is permitted only if the distance from the nearest land is more than 12 nautical miles	Disposal is permitted only if the distance from the nearest land is more than 12 nautical miles
Food waste comminuted or ground*	Disposal is permitted only if the distance from the nearest land is more than 3 nautical miles	Disposal is permitted only if the distance from the nearest land is more than 3 nautical miles
Mixed refuse types	**	**

* Comminuted or ground garbage must be able to pass through a screen (mesh size no more than 25mm).

** When garbage is mixed with other harmful substances having different disposal or discharge requirements, the more stringent disposal requirements shall apply.

(4) Waste treatment system

① Pulper: food waste.

The food processing equipment (known as a pulper) is the system used onboard to process food. Collection stations can be found in: Food preparation areas, Galleys, Room service, Dishwashing areas.

② Comminuter: bones.

③ Glass crusher: glass.

④ Compactor: cans, cardboard, plastic.

Note: Plastic can never be discharged into the sea, we must separate carefully and correctly!

⑤ Incinerator: paper, cardboard, wood, food, some types of plastic and oily rags.

⑥ Can Crusher: spray cans, tins.

(5) Waste water

① Black water: Shipboard toilets. Hospital sinks. Hospital showers.

Before being discharged, black water is collected and treated with special equipment called a marine sanitation device.

② Oily bilge water: liquids produced by normal engine operation and cleaning.

Bilge water is collected, treated with bilge separators and monitored so that it complies with lawful parameters before being discharged.

③ Grey water: Sinks; Showers; Jacuzzis.

Greywater (also spelled graywater) or sullage is all wastewater generated in households or office buildings without fecal contamination. Sources of greywater include, e.g. sinks, showers, baths, clothes washing machines or dish washers. As greywater contains fewer pathogens than domestic wastewater, it is generally safer to handle and easier to treat and reuse onsite for toilet flushing, landscape or crop irrigation, or other non-potable uses.

Notes

1. MARPOL: International Convention for the Prevention of Pollution from Ships 国际防止船舶造成污染公约

2. SOLAS：International Convention for the Protection of Life at Sea 国际海上人身安全公约
3. environmental aspect 环境状况，环境方面
4. production of waste 废物的产生
5. bilge water 舱底水
6. ballast water 压载水
7. man-made fibres 人造纤维
8. Carbon Dioxide 二氧化碳
9. Nitrogen Oxides 氮氧化物
10. SOX（Sulphur Oxides） 硫氧化物
11. oily engine rags 擦引擎的油抹布
12. lead batteries 铅电池
13. "En route " navigation. 航行中
14. Floating dunnage，lining and packing material 浮垫、衬垫及包装材料
15. comminuted or ground 粉碎的或磨碎的
16. mesh size 网格尺寸
17. Can Crusher 易拉罐粉碎机
18. bilge separators 舱底水分离器
19. lawful parameters 合法参数
20. fecal contamination 粪便污染

New words & expressions

implement [ˈimplimənt] vt. 实施，执行，使生效，实现，落实（政策）n. 工具，器械
monitor [ˈmɔnitə] n. 显示屏，监测仪，监控人员 vt. 监控，监听 vi. 监视
applicable [ˈæplikəbl] adj. 适当的，可应用的
comply [kəmˈplai] vi. 遵守，顺从，遵从，答应
bilge [bildʒ] n. 舱底，舱底污水 vt. 使船底漏水 vi. 船底穿洞，搁浅
ballast [ˈbæləst] n. 压舱物，[建] 压载物 vt. 给……装压舱物，给……铺道渣
ecosystem [ˈsistəm] n. 体系，系统，制度，身体，方法
renewable [riˈnjuːəbl] adj. 可继续的，可更新的，可再生的，可翻新的
synthetic [sinˈθetik] n. 合成物 adj. 综合的，合成的，人造的
polymer [ˈpɔləmə] n. 多聚物，[高分子] 聚合物
nitrogen [ˈnaitrədʒən] n. [化] 氮，氮气
oxide [ˈɔksaid] n. [化] 氧化物
sulphur [ˈsʌlfə] n. 硫黄，硫黄色，黄绿色 v. 使硫化，用硫黄处理，在……中加硫黄
fume [fjuːm] n. 烟，愤怒，烦恼 vt. 熏，冒烟 vi. 冒烟，发怒
electromagnetic [iˌlektrə(ʊ)mægˈnetik] adj. 电磁的
emission [iˈmiʃən] n. 排放，辐射，排放物，散发物，（书刊）发行，发布（通知）
antenna [ænˈtenə] n. [电讯] 天线，[动] 触角，[昆] 触须
aluminum [əˈluminəm] n. 铝
neon [ˈniːɒn] n. 〈化〉氖，霓虹灯

rag [ræg] n. 破布，碎布 vt. 嘲笑，捉弄，糟蹋，指责，欺负人

annex [ə'neks] n. 附加物，附属建筑物 vt. 附加，获得，并吞

compactor [kəm'pæktə] n. 压土机，垃圾捣碎机，夯土机，[建] 压实器

incinerator [in'sinəreitə] n. [环境] [炉窑] 焚化炉，焚尸炉，焚烧装置

mesh [meʃ] n. 网孔，网状物，罗网，[机] 啮合

residue ['rezidjuː] n. 残渣，剩余，滤渣

dunnage ['dʌnidʒ] n. 填充，捆扎，包装

lining ['lainiŋ] n. 里料，里布，内衬

comminute ['kɔminjuːt] vt. 粉碎，分割

mesh [meʃ] n. 网孔，网状物，罗网，[机] 啮合

screen [skriːn] n. 屏幕，银幕，屏风 vt. 筛（煤、矿石等），拍摄

stringent ['strindʒənt] adj. 严格的，迫切的，（货币）紧缩的

comminuter [kɔ'minjuːtər] n. 粉碎器

pulper ['pʌlpə] n. 碎浆机

compactor [kəm'pæktə] n. 压土机，垃圾捣碎机，夯土机，[建] 压实器

incinerator [in'sinəreitə] n. [环境] [炉窑] 焚化炉，焚尸炉，焚烧装置

separator ['sepəreitə(r)] n. 分离器，分离装置，防胀器

parameter [pə'ræmitə] n. [数] 参数，〈物〉〈数〉参量，限制因素，决定因素

jacuzzis [dʒə'kuːziːz] n. 极可意浴缸，极可意水流按摩浴缸（Jacuzzi 的名词复数）

household ['haushəuld] n. 家庭，户，（集合词）全家人 adj. 家庭的，家内的

fecal ['fiːkl] adj. 排泄物的，渣滓的，糟粕的

onsite ['ɔnsait] adj. 在场的，就地的

potable ['pəutəbl] adj. 可以喝的，适合饮用的 n. 饮料

Exercises

1. What are the main duties of environmental officer onboard?
2. What are the main international laws concerning environmental protection?
3. What are the main environmental aspects?
4. What is Marpol waste or garbage? What kinds of waste does Marpol waste or garbage mainly refer to?
5. Why is identifying wastes and separating them very important?
6. Which devices does Waste treatment system include onboard?
7. How to deal with black water onboard?
8. What is bilge water? How to deal with it before being discharged onboard?
9. What is Greywater?

Part 6

Safety Practice on the Cruise Ships

6.1 General Safety Precautions—All Departments

(1) Keep hands off all electrical circuits unless your duties require it, then use the proper gloves. Stand on a dry rubber mat or board if possible, when working on electrical equipments, never bridge a fuse.

(2) Never touch machines without previous training and carefully reading the operating instructions and manuals. Make sure you understand the safety instructions and follow them all closely.

(3) Prior to plugging in electrical equipment, make sure about the voltage and plug it into the proper socket, if in doubt, always ask an electrician.

(4) Extension cable should be without cuts and mends or bends, and usage of proper junction boxes is recommended.

(5) If working with electrical machines, see that your hands are not wet and that you are not standing in wet areas.

(6) Do not leave electrical equipments exposed to leaks or in wet weather or rain.

(7) Make sure you switch off and cut off current supply after each use.

(8) Store equipments and cables properly in their storage areas after use.

(9) Do not wear loose or flapping clothing.

(10) Keep the decks clean. Keep stairways and all emergency escapes clean, clear and

unobstructed.

(11) Proper shoes must be worn during work. No sandals are allowed anywhere.

(12) Wear proper clothes, when exposed to the weather.

(13) Paint and volatile solvents, thinners, glue, etc. may be kept onboard a vessel only in approved paint lockers.

(14) Keep all paints and other items, such as paint thinners or other inflammables covered closely and sealed tightly.

(15) Painters and helpers should wear protective goggles, paint respirators and suitable protective clothing.

(16) In case painting is carried out in confined quarters, ensure good ventilation and get the men to fresh air frequently.

(17) Safety belts should be worn whenever necessary, and whenever you work on stages or in places where your feet do not touch the deck.

(18) Watch your step and always hold onto handrails while ascending or descending the stairways; always remember to have one hand to the railing.

(19) Watch out and take proper care and posture, when lifting heavy weights. Use proper lifting techniques, request assistance when necessary.

Always consult the material safety data manual.

(20) Do not run or shout around.

(21) Observe good hygiene code.

(22) Observe all signs for safety throughout the ship.

(23) Observe the smoking restrictions on board and the "NO SMOKING" signs, do not throw light cigarettes or matches over the ship's side. Smoke only in designated area.

(24) Secure all moving equipments & gears before ship proceeds to sea.

(25) Clean-up all spills immediately.

(26) Always consult the material safety data manual.

(27) Observe the closed Porthole/Deadlights and W. T. D order of the bridge during bad weather.

(28) Observe all heavy weather routines as required.

Notes

1. when working on electrical equipments, never bridge a fuse 在使用电气设备工作时,(电气设备)不要通电
2. reading the operating instructions and manuals 阅读操作说明书和指南手册
3. prior to plugging in electrical equipment 在将插头插进电器设备之前
4. usage of proper junction boxes 使用合适的接线盒
5. cut off current supply after each use 每次用完后切断电源
6. loose or flapping clothing 宽松或飘动的衣服
7. when exposed to the weather 当暴露在天气下时
8. volatile solvents, thinners, glue 易挥发的溶剂、稀释剂、胶水
9. protective goggles, paint respirators and suitable protective clothing 护目镜、打油漆的

口罩和适当的防护衣物

10. safety belt 安全带

11. hold onto handrails 紧紧抓住护栏

12. do not throw light cigarettes or matches over the ship's side 不要沿着船边乱扔点燃的烟头和火柴

13. Observe the closed Porthole/Deadlights and W. T. D order of the bridge during bad weather. 注意恶劣天气下驾驶台发出的关闭舷窗盖和水密门的指令。

14. Observe all heavy weather routines as required. 按要求留意恶劣天气下的日常操作规程。

New words & expressions

precaution [priˈkɔːʃən] n. 预防，警惕，防范

circuit [ˈsəːkit] n. 电路，一圈，周游，巡回

mat [mæt] n. 席子，垫子 v. 铺席子

fuse [fjuːz] n. 保险丝，熔丝 v. 熔合

previous [ˈpriːvjəs] adj. 在前的，早先的 adv. 在……以前返回上一级菜单

manual [ˈmænjuəl] n. 手册，指南 adj. 手的，手动的，手工的，体力的

prior [ˈpraiə] adj. 优先的，在前的 n. 预先 adv. 在

plug [plʌg] vt. 堵，塞，插上，插栓 n. 塞子，插头，插销

instruction [inˈstrʌkʃən] n. 指示，用法说明（书），教育，指导，指令

voltage [ˈvəultidʒ] n. [电工] 电压，伏特数

socket [ˈsɔkit] n. 窝，穴，孔，插座，牙槽 v. 给……配插座

electrician [ilekˈtriʃ(ə)n] n. 电工，电学家

extension [iksˈtenʃən] n. 延长，扩充，范围 n. 扩展名 adj. 客观现实的

mend [mend] n. 改进，改良，补丁，好转 vt. 修改，修理，修补 vi. 好转

bend [bend] v. 弯曲，专心于，屈服 n. 弯曲

junction [ˈdʒʌŋkʃən] n. 连接，接合，交叉点，汇合处

leak [liːk] n. 漏洞，漏出，〈俚〉撒尿 vi. 漏，泄漏 vt. 使渗漏

current [ˈkʌrənt] adj. 当前的，流通的，最近的 n. 涌流，趋势，电流

cable [ˈkeibl] n. 电缆，海底电报，缆，索 v. 打（海底）电报

flap [flæp] n. 拍打，拍打声，副翼 v. 拍打，鼓翼而飞，飘动，扔，掷

sandal [ˈsændl] n. 凉鞋，檀香，便鞋 v. 穿上便鞋

volatile [ˈvɔlətail] adj. 飞行的，挥发性的，可变的，不稳定的，轻快的

solvent [ˈsɔlvənt] adj. 溶解的，有偿付能力的 n. 溶媒，溶剂，解决方法

thinner [ˈθinə] n. 稀释剂

glue [gluː] n. 胶，胶水 vt. 胶合，粘贴，粘合

flammable [ˈflæməbl] adj. 易燃的，可燃性的

goggle [ˈgɔgl] n. （复数）风镜，护目镜 adj. 睁眼的 vi. 眼珠转动，瞪眼看

respirator [ˈrespəreitə] n. 呼吸器

confine [ˈkɔnfain] vt. 限制，禁闭 n. 界限，边界

quarter [ˈkwɔːtə] n. 四分之一，方向，地区，方面，季，季度，一刻钟

stage [steidʒ] n. 舞台，戏剧，活动场所，阶段或时期 vt. 上演，筹备

handrail ['hændreil] n. 栏杆，扶手
ascend [ə'send] v. 攀登，上升
descend [di'send] vi. 下来，下降，遗传（指财产，气质，权利）v. 下去
railing ['reiliŋ] n. 栏杆，扶手
posture ['pɔstʃə] n. （身体的）姿势，体态 v. 令取某种姿势，作出姿态
shout around 到处乱喊
code [kəud] n. 代码，代号，密码，编码 v. 编码
restriction [ris'trikʃən] n. 限制，约束
secure [si'kjuə] adj. 安全的，可靠的，放心的，无虑的 v. 保护
gear [giə] n. 齿轮，传动装置 v. 调整，（使）适合，换挡
spill [spil] n. 溢出，溅出 vt. 使溢出，使散落，洒 vi. 溢出，涌流，充满
data ['deitə] n. datum 的复数，[计] 资料，数据
deadlight ['dedlait] n. 舷窗盖
routine [ru:'ti:n] n. 例行公事，常规，日常事务，程序

Exercises

1. How to do precautions when you work with machines on the cruise ships?
2. What do you do before you plug in electrical equipment?
3. Why should we keep stairways and all emergency escapes clear and unobstructed?
4. Where should you store paint and volatile solvents，thinners，glue，etc. onboard?
5. When should you wear safety belts?
6. What should we do during bad weather?

6.2 Safety Precautions for Cabins Stewards and Cleaners（Housekeeping）Department

（1）Never leave master keys in doors while working in cabins.

（2）Never leave chemicals，cleaning materials or equipments lying around unattended.

（3）Always lock door after leaving cabin for any period of time.

（4）Keep empty cabins locked at all times.

（5）Always report any damage or missing items immediately.

（6）When upper bunk is in use after preparing for the night，ensure that the ladder is in place.

（7）Always advise the passengers as to where the bed ladder is stored when it is not in position on the bunk.

（8）Prior to sailing instruct the new passengers in the operation of light switches，A/C diffusers and bunk ladders.

（9）Keep housekeeping lockers clean and neat，do not store inflammable materials.

（10）Use extreme caution when vacuuming public rooms，cabins，corridors and stairwells，making sure electric cords are in place so that no one can trip over them.

（11）Check electric plugs and wires on equipment adaptors，fixtures，etc. and report immediately if repair should be necessary.

(12) Promptly clean up spillages.

(13) Do not leave glasses lying around corridors; return to deck parties for collection.

(14) Use caution when using stairways in public areas and in service areas.

(15) Do not block passageways, stairways, WTD and FSD or block access to any fire fighting or fire prevention apparatus.

(16) Do not smoke at your station and make sure that ashtrays and cigarette butts are disposed in a proper and safe way.

(17) Secure all of your equipment during rough seas.

(18) Do not smoke in bed or in restricted areas. Smoke only in designated areas.

(19) Avoid inhalation of toxic fumes.

(20) Do not let debris accumulate onboard the ship. It is a fire hazard.

(21) When handling cleaning materials, wear gloves, eye protection, and face mask. If you are allergic, report it to your supervisor.

(22) Report all hazards and defects noted immediately.

(23) Turn off and disconnect electrical equipment before cleaning, repairing or adjusting.

(24) All chemical cleaning bottles must be labelled.

(25) Trolleys must be secured, when not in use.

(26) Do not store any items inside electrical lockers and electrical panels.

(27) Do not leave your hand or fingers between the door while closing.

Notes

1. master keys 主钥匙，总钥匙
2. lying around unattended 到处乱放，无人照管
3. upper bunk 上铺
4. in position 在适当的位置
5. A/C diffusers 交流电传播器
6. inflammable materials 易燃物质
7. trip over 被……绊倒
8. Check electric plugs and wires on equipment adaptors, fixtures, etc. 检查电插头、设备的适配器及固定装置上面的电线等。
9. return to deck parties for collection 归还给楼面的相关人员收起来
10. fire prevention apparatus 防火器、灭火器
11. make sure that ashtrays and cigarette butts are disposed in a proper and safe way 确保烟灰缸和烟头以一种适当而又安全的方式得到处理。
12. rough seas 波涛汹涌的大海
13. Avoid inhalation of toxic fumes. 避免吸入有毒烟雾。
14. fire hazard 火灾（隐患）
15. electrical lockers and electrical panels 电气柜、电气面板

New words & expressions

lie around 到处放

master [ˈmɑːstə] adj. 主人的，熟练的，主要的 vt. 征服，控制，精通

item [ˈaitem，ˈaitəm] n.（可分类或列举的）项目，条款，一则，一条

bunk [bʌŋk] n. （轮船，火车等）铺位
as to 关于，至于
diffuser [dIˈfjuːzə(r)] n. 散布者，扩散体，传播器
switch [switʃ] n. 开关，电闸，转换 vt. 转换，转变
inflammable [inˈflæməbl] adj. 易燃的，易怒的 n. 易燃物
caution [ˈkɔːʃən] n. 小心，谨慎，警告 vt. 警告
vacuum [ˈvækjuəm] n. 真空，空间，真空吸尘器 vt. 用真空吸尘器打扫
stairwell [ˈstɛəwel] n. 楼梯井，楼梯间
trip over 绊倒
adaptor [əˈdæptə(r)] n. 接头，结合器，附加器，〈美〉编剧者，改编者
fixture [ˈfikstʃə] n. 固定设备，附着物，[机] 装置器，工作夹具
spillage [ˈspilidʒ] n. 溢出，溢出量
butt [bʌt] n. 粗大的一端，靶垛，笑柄 v. 以头抵撞，碰撞
dispose [disˈpəuz] v. 处理，处置，部署 vt. 布置，安排，除去，使愿意
inhalation [ˌinhəˈleiʃən] n. 吸入
toxic [ˈtɔksik] adj. 有毒的，中毒的
fume [fjuːm] n. （浓烈或难闻的）烟，气体 v. 用烟熏，冒烟，发怒
debris [ˈdebriː,ˈdeib-] n. 碎片，残骸
allergic [əˈləːdʒik] adj. [医] 过敏的，患过敏症的
defect [diˈfekt] n. 过失，缺点
disconnect [ˌdiskəˈnekt] v. 拆开，分离，断开
label [ˈleibl] n. 标签，签条，商标 vt. 贴标签于，分类，标注
adjust [əˈdʒʌst] vt. 调整，调节，校准，使适合
trolley [ˈtrɔli] n. 电车，手推车，手摇车 vt. 用手推车运 vi. 乘电车
panel [ˈpænl] n. 面板，嵌板，仪表板，全体陪审员 vt. 嵌镶板

Exercises

1. How to deal with chemicals，cleaning materials or equipment?
2. How to deal with empty cabins?
3. Before the ship sets sail，what should cabin steward instruct the passengers to do?
4. How to deal with housekeeping lockers?
5. How to handle ashtrays and cigarette butts at your station?
6. When handling cleaning materials，if you are allergic，what should you do?
7. What are WTD and FSD?
8. While closing door，what should you pay attention to?

6. 3 Safety Precautions for Dealing with Substances Hazardous to Health

6. 3. 1 How to Deal with Substances Hazardous to Health

Under COSHH or Control of Substances Hazardous to Health Regulations 1988，all persons at work need to know the safety precautions to take so as not to endanger themselves or others through exposure substances hazardous to health. Below are four general classifications of risk, we should know the appropriate symbols, their meanings and their safety precautions.

(1) The meaning of toxic/very toxic substances May cause serious health risk or even death if inhaled, ingested or if it penetrates the skin.

Safety precautions for toxic/very toxic substances:

① Wear suitable protective clothing, gloves and eye/face protection.

② After contact with skin, wash immediately with plenty of water.

③ In case of contact with eyes, rinse immediately with plenty of water and seek medical advice.

④ In case of accident or if you feel unwell, seek medical advice immediately.

(2) The meaning of corrosive substances May cause destruction of living and burns if it is contacted.

Safety precautions for corrosive substances:

① Wear suitable gloves and eye/face protection.

② Take off immediately all contaminated clothing.

③ In case of contact with the skin, wash tissue immediately.

④ In case of contact with eyes, rinse immediately (for15 minutes) with plenty of water and seek medical advice.

(3) The meaning of harmful substances May cause limited health risk if inhaled, ingested or if it penetrates the skin.

Safety precautions for harmful substances:

① Do not breathe vapor/spray/dust.

② Avoid contact with the skin.

③ Wash thoroughly before you eat, drink or smoke.

④ In case of contact with the eyes, rinse immediately with plenty of water and seek medical advice.

(4) The meaning of irritant substances May cause inflammation and irritation on immediate or repeated or prolonged contact with the skin or if inhaled.

Safety precautions for irritant substances:

① In case of contact with eyes, rinse immediately with plenty of water and seek medical advice.

② In case of contact with the skin, wash immediately with plenty of water.

③ Do not breathe the vapor/spray/dust.

6.3.2 How Do Hazardous Substances Enter Your Body

① Ingest—take into stomach, eat or drink accidently.

② Inhale—breathe something in.

③ Absorb—take or suck in (liquids).

④ Inject—put liquid into someone with a special needle.

6.3.3 Safety Practices for Dealing with Hazardous Substances

① Make as instructed.

② Read the label.

③ Wear protective clothing (or equipment).

④ Keep separate from them.

⑤ Store correctly.

⑥ Keep good personal hygiene.

⑦ Don't eat or drink when you deal with them.

Notes

1. safety precautions 安全保障措施，安全预防
2. exposure substances hazardous to health 对健康有害的暴露物质
3. if it penetrates the skin 如果它渗入皮肤
4. seek medical advice 寻求医疗建议
5. corrosive substances 腐蚀性物质
6. wash tissue immediately 立即清洗组织
7. irritant substances 刺激性物质
8. suck in (liquids) 吸入（液体）
9. Safety practices 安全规范，安全方法

New words & expressions

hazardous [ˈhæzədəs] adj. 危险的，冒险的，碰运气的

substance [ˈsʌbstəns] n. 物质，实质，主旨

endanger [inˈdeindʒə] vt. 危及

exposure [iksˈpəuʒə] n. 暴露，揭露，曝光，揭发，揭露，方向，陈列

classification [ˌklæsifiˈkeiʃən] n. 分类，分级

appropriate [əˈprəupriit] adj. 适当的

toxic [ˈtɔksik] adj. 有毒的，中毒的

ingest [inˈdʒest] vt. 摄取，咽下，吸收

penetrate [ˈpenitreit] vt. 穿透，渗透，看穿，洞察 vi. 刺入，看穿，弥漫

inhale [inˈheil] vt. 吸入 vi. 吸气

protective [prəˈtektiv] adj. 给予保护的，保护的

seek [siːk] v. 寻找，探索，寻求

corrosive [kəˈrəusiv] adj. 腐蚀的，腐蚀性的 n. 腐蚀物，腐蚀剂

destruction [disˈtrʌkʃən] n. 破坏，毁灭

burn [bəːn] v. 烧，烧焦，点（灯），使感觉烧热 n. 烧伤，灼伤

tissue [ˈtisjuː] n. 薄的纱织品，薄纸，棉纸，[生] 组织，连篇

vapor [ˈveipə] n. 水汽，无实质之物 vi. 蒸发，自夸 vt. 使蒸发 n. 自夸者

spray [sprei] n. 喷雾，飞沫 vt. 喷射，喷溅

thoroughly [ˈθʌrəli] adv. 完全地，彻底地

irritant [ˈiritənt] n. 刺激物 adj. 刺激的

inflammation [ˌinfləˈmeiʃən] n. 怒火，发火，燃烧，[医] 炎症，发炎
prolong [prəˈlɔŋ] vt. 延长，拖延
absorb [əbˈsɔːb] vt. 吸收，吸引
inject [inˈdʒekt] vt. 注射，注入
label [ˈleibl] n. 标签，签条，商标，标志 vt. 贴标签于，分类，标注

Exercises

1. What does COSHH mean?
2. What are "toxic substances"? How to do safety precautions?
3. What are "corrosive substances"? How to do safety precautions?
4. What are "harmful substances"? How to do safety precautions?
5. What are "irritant substances"? How to do safety precautions?
6. How do hazardous substances enter your body?
7. What are the safety practices for dealing with hazardous substances?

6.4 Personal Booklet

PLACE OF EMERGENCY, FIRE AND BOATS STATION

NO. ……………………………………………………
RANK……………………………………………………
NAME……………………………………………………
SURNAME………………………………………………

STUDY THIS BOOKLET CAREFULLY

(1) This booklet must be carefully kept by each crew member and be returned in the event that the crew member signs off the ship.

(2) Each crew member must know exactly what to do in the case of an emergency—fire or abandon ship—all particulars can be found in this book.

(3) Read carefully all the notices and instructions which are posted around the ship.

INSTRUCTIONS AND REMARKS

IMPORTANT

(1) It is compulsory that all crew members attend to the life boat drills. During the drills the crew members must be serious and courteous.

(2) All crew members must be on time—No one can be absent without any serious reason unless certified by the head of each department.

(3) Crew members must be back aboard the vessel in time —at least one hour before sailing.

(4) In ports where passes must be returned to the local authorities, crew members must deliver them without delay, and also, in ports where the crew under medical examination must proceed on time to avoid any delay.

(5) Crew members are obliged to follow customs regulations in the ship's ports of call to avoid any complications.

(6) Keep the ship clean because it is your home.

(7) Do your duty by being courteous and cooperative with your colleagues of all ranks.

(8) Be tidy and wear the proper uniforms issued by the ship, and be punctual on duty.

(9) Do not waste water, electricity, or provisions, this is in your own interest.

(10) Follow carefully meal times arranged for you by the ship, if you are late, meals will not be provided.

(11) Smoking is forbidden in the cabins on retiring in order to avoid any chance of fire.

(12) Be quite and behave with your colleagues and do not disturb them when they are sleeping.

(13) It is very important to be polite to passengers and other crew members.

(14) Crew members are not allowed to have any explosives on board or any other articles that could endanger the safety of the ship.

(15) All crew members are not allowed:

① To be on deck at any port during the ship's arrival and departure unless they are on duty.

② To put their heads out of any porthole or window.

③ To remain at the gangways during embarkation and disembarkation.

④ To go ashore in port without having permission from the head of their departments.

⑤ To remain near the ship's swimming pool.

⑥ To sleep in other crew members' cabins.

⑦ To use the ship's passenger lift-except in the case of emergency.

(16) Crew members are not allowed to stay in the passengers' areas except during hours of duty and during the hours specified by the ship's regulations.

(17) Portholes must only be opened or closed following orders from the staff captain and their deadlights must not be removed without orders to do so.

(18) Make sure that all cigarettes are extinguished and never throw butts overboard from open decks or portholes.

(19) Crew members are not allowed to throw overboard any kind of rubbish from the open decks or through portholes. They may use the rubbish tins only.

Notes

1. be returned in the event that the crew member signs off the ship 如果船员离船时就要交还（船方）
2. abandon ship 弃船
3. all particulars can be found in this book 所有的细节都可在这本书中找到
4. attend to the life boat drills 参加救生艇演习
5. unless certified by the head of each department 除非得到每个部门领导的批准
6. the ship's ports of call 船舶的停靠港
7. to avoid any complications 避免任何纠纷
8. cooperative with your colleagues of all ranks 与你的各个级别的同事合作
9. be punctual on duty 准时上班

10. this is in your own interest 这是你自己的利益
11. on retiring 就寝
12. Be quite and behave with your colleagues 保持安静，在同事面前举止端正
13. embarkation and disembarkation 上船和离船（起岸）

New words & expressions

booklet [ˈbuklit] n. 小册子
rank [ræŋk] n. 等级，横列，阶级 adj. 繁茂的，下流的 vt. 排列，归类
surname [ˈsəːneim] n. 姓 v. 用姓称呼
in the event that 如果
particular [pəˈtikjulə] n. 细节，详细 adj. 特殊的，精确的，挑剔
post [pəust] n. 柱，邮件，岗位，职位，邮政 vt. 张贴，揭示，邮递，布置
remark [riˈmɑːk] n. 备注，评论，注意，注释 vt. 评论，注意 vi. 谈论
compulsory [kəmˈpʌlsəri] adj. 必需做的，必修的，被强制的，义务的
courteous [ˈkəːtjəs] adj. 有礼貌的，谦恭的
certify [ˈsəːtifai] v. 证明，保证
authority [ɔːˈθɔriti] n. 权威，威信，权威人士，权力，职权，著作权威
oblige [əˈblaidʒ] vt. 迫使，责成
complication [ˌkɔmpliˈkeiʃ(ə)n] n. 复杂化，（使复杂的）因素，纠纷
pass [pɑːs] n. 经过，关口，护照，通行证 及格 vt. 通过，审查通
be cooperative with 与……合作
punctual [ˈpʌŋktjuəl] adj. 严守时刻的，准时的
provision [prəˈviʒən] n. 供应，（一批）供应品，预备，防备，规定
retiring [riˈtaiəriŋ] adj. 退休的 n. 就寝
departure [diˈpɑːtʃə] n. 启程，出发，离开
arrival [əˈraivəl] n. 到来，到达，到达者
disembark [ˈdisimˈbɑːk] v. （使）起岸，（使）登陆
permission [pə(ː)ˈmiʃən] n. 许可，允许
specify [ˈspesifai] vt. 指定，详细说明，列入清单
deadlight [ˈdedlait] n. 舷窗盖
butt [bʌt] n. 粗大的一端，靶垛，笑柄 v. 以头抵撞，碰撞
overboard [ˈəuvəbɔːd] adv. 自船上落下，在船外
tin [tin] n. [化] 锡，马口铁，罐 vt. 涂锡于 adj. 锡制的

Exercises

1. What's a personal booklet?
2. Who must the personal booklet be kept by?
3. What's life boat drill?
4. After going ashore, what time should we be back aboard the vessel?
5. When doing your duty, how to get along with your colleagues of all ranks?
6. What are all crew members not allowed to do onboard? Please list seven points.
7. How to deal with cigarettes and cigarette butts onboard?

8. How to deal with rubbish onboard?

MAN OVERBOARD

SIGNAL: When you realize that a person is overboard, inform the bridge immediately on the phones ____ or ____ .

The ship's whistle will be sounded two (2) short and two (2) long blasts.

DUTIES: Look for the nearest ring buoy and throw it to the water towards the man overboard.

ABANDON SHIP

Continuous long blast from the ship's whistle and supplemented with the same ringing of the ship's alarm bells.

The order to "abandon ship" will be given only by the ship's master through the public address system.

All crew to life boats stations

BOAT NO. ____ LIFE RAFT NO. ____

ABANDON SHIP DUTIES

EMERGENCY AND FIRE SIGNAL

Seven or more short blasts followed by one (1) long blast from the ship's whistle supplemented by the same signal on the general alarm bells.

The operational command by the master will be announced through the public address system.

All crew to emergency/fire stations.

EMERGENCY FIRE STATION DUTIES

EQUIPMENT FOR THE SHIP'S LIFE BOATS

Your ship is fitted with life boats, in accordance with the International Convention of Safety of Life at Sea, 1960. The normal equipment of every lifeboat is as follows.

(1) A single banked complement of buoyant oars, two spare buoyant oars, and a buoyant steering oar; one and half sets of thole pins or crutches attached to the lifeboat by lanyard or chain; a boat hook (two hooks in motor boats).

(2) Two plugs for each hole (plugs are not required when proper automatic valves are fitted).

(3) A baler and two buckets of approved material.

(4) A rudder attached to the lifeboat, and a tiller.

(5) Two hatchets, one at each end of the lifeboat.

(6) A lamp with sufficient oil for 12 hours, two boxes of suitable matches in a watertight container.

(7) An efficient compass to be illuminated or fitted with suitable means of illumination.

(8) Lifeline becketed around the outside of the lifeboat.

(9) A sea anchor of approved size.

(10) Two painters of sufficient length. One shall be secured to the forward end of lifeboat with a stop and toggle so that it can be released, and the other shall be firmly secured to the stern of the lifeboat and ready for use.

(11) A vessel containing one gallon of vegetable, fish or animal oil. The vessel shall be so arranged that it can be attached to the sea anchor.

(12) A food ration for each person the lifeboat is certified to carry. These rations shall be kept in airtight receptacles which are to be stowed in a watertight container.

(13) Watertight receptacles containing six pints (or three liters) of fresh water for each person the lifeboat is certified to carry, a rustproof graduated drinking vessel.

(14) Four parachute signals of approved type capable of giving a bright red light at a high altitude, six hand flares giving a bright red light.

(15) Two smoke signals (for daytime use) capable of giving off a volume of orange-colored smoke.

(16) Grab lines secured from gunwale to gunwale under the keel.

(17) First aid outfit in a watertight case.

(18) Electric torch suitable for signaling in Morse Code together with one spare set of batteries and one spare bulb.

(19) A daylight signaling mirror.

(20) A jack knife fitted with a tin opener.

(21) Two buoyant heaving lines.

(22) One manual pump of an approved type.

(23) A suitable locker for the stowage of small items of equipment.

(24) One whistle.

(25) One set of fishing tackle.

(26) One approved cover of a high visible color capable of protecting the occupants against injury or exposure.

(27) One copy of the illustrated table of life-saving signals.

All lifeboats are fitted with suitable means to enable persons in the water to climb into the lifeboat. Every motor lifeboat carries a portable fire extinguisher.

Notes

1. throw it to the water towards the man overboard 朝着落水那个人，把（救生圈）扔到水里
2. supplemented with the same ringing of the ship's alarm bells 辅之以相同的船上警报铃的铃声
3. through the public address system 通过公共播音系统
4. in accordance with the International Convention of Safety of Life at Sea，1960 按照“1960年国际海上安全公约”
5. a single banked complement of buoyant oars，two spare buoyant oars 一支定额的有浮力的专用桨，两支备用的有浮力的桨
6. thole pins or crutches 桨架或支架
7. automatic valves 自动阀门
8. watertight container 水密容器，防水容器
9. suitable means of illumination 合适的照明装置
10. Lifeline becketed around the outside of the lifeboat. 套在救生艇外围的救生索（生命线）。
11. Two painters of sufficient length. 两根足够长的系船索（船头缆绳）。
12. stop and toggle 栓柱和套索钉
13. airtight receptacles 密闭容器
14. a rustproof graduated drinking vessel 一个防锈的有刻度的饮水容器
15. Grab lines secured from gunwale to gunwale under the keel. 经过龙骨底下固定在两边船舷上缘的抓绳
16. first aid outfit 急救装备
17. A jack knife fitted with a tin opener. 装有开罐器的折刀
18. manual pump 手动抽水机
19. One copy of the illustrated table of life-saving signals. 一册救生信号说明表
20. a portable fire extinguisher 一个便携式的灭火器

New words & expressions

sound [saund] n. 声音，语音 vi. 发出声音，回响，测深 vt. 使发声，宣告
buoy [bɔi] n. （湖，河等中的）浮标，浮筒，救生圈 vt. 使浮起，支撑
whistle [(h)wisl] n. 口哨，汽笛，口哨声，汽笛声 v. 吹口哨，鸣汽笛
blast [blɑːst] n. 一阵（风），爆炸，冲击波 vt. 爆炸，毁灭，使枯萎，损害
address [ə'dres] n. 地址，致辞，演讲，说话的技巧 vt. 向……致辞，演说
supplement ['sʌplimənt] n. 补遗，补充，附录，增刊 v. 补充
operational [ˌɔpə'reiʃənl] adj. 操作的，运作的

in accordance with 一致，和谐，符合
convention [kən'venʃən] n. 大会，协定，习俗，惯例
bank [bæŋk] n. 银行，堤，岸，沙洲，浅滩，一堆（土），（云）层
buoyant ['bɔiənt] adj. 有浮力的，轻快的
oar [ɔː,ɔə] n. 桨，橹
steer [stiə] v. 驾驶，掌舵
thole [θəul] n. [船] 桨架，钉桨架的钉 vt. 〈英方〉忍受 vi. 〈古〉有耐心
pin [pin] n. 钉，销，栓，大头针，别针，腿 vt. 钉住，扣牢，止住，牵制
crutch [krʌtʃ] n. （跛子用的）拐杖，支撑，帮助 vt. 支撑
lanyard ['lænjəd] n. 系索
valve [vælv] n. 阀，[英] 电子管，真空管
baler ['beilə] 打包工 打包机，压捆机
rudder ['rʌdə] n. 舵，方向舵
tiller ['tilə] n. 耕者，农夫，（船的）舵柄
hatchet ['hætʃit] n. 短柄斧
sufficient [sə'fiʃənt] adj. 充分的，足够的
watertight ['wɔːtətait] adj. 不漏水的，水密的
compass ['kʌmpəs] n. 罗盘，指南针，圆规 v. 包围
illuminate [i'ljuːmineit] vt. 照明，照亮，阐明，说明 vi. 照亮
lifeline ['laiflain] n. 救生索，生命线，重要的交通线（或通信联络线）
becket ['bekit] n. 小环索，把手环
painter ['peintə] n. 画家，油漆匠，系船索，船头缆绳
stop [stɔp] n. 停止，车站，逗留 vi. 停止，被塞住 vt. 塞住，堵塞，阻止
toggle ['tɔgl] n. [海] 绳针，套索钉 vt. 拴牢
gallon ['gælən] n. 加仑
ration ['ræʃən] n. 定量，配给量，定量配给 v. 配给，实行定量配给
airtight ['eətait] adj. 密封的，无懈可击的
receptacle [ri'septəkl] n. 容器，[植] 花托，[电工] 插座
stow [stəu] v. 装载
pint [paint] n. 品脱
rustproof ['rʌstpruːf] adj. 不锈的 vt. 使不生锈
parachute ['pærəʃuːt] n. 降落伞，降落伞状的东西
altitude ['æltitjuːd] n. （尤指海拔）高度，高处，（等级，地位等）高等
flare [flεə] n. 闪光，闪耀，照明弹，焰火 vi. 闪光，闪耀 vt. 使闪耀，使张开
give off v. 发出（蒸汽、光等），长出（枝、杈等）
volume ['vɔljuːm; (*US*)-jəm] n. 卷，册，体积，量，大量，音量
gunwale ['gʌnl] n. 船舷上缘
keel [kiːl] n. 龙骨（船的脊骨），平底船 vt. 装以龙骨，使倾覆 vi. 倾覆
outfit ['autfit] n. 用具，配备，全套装配，vt. 配备，装备 vi. 得到装备
torch [tɔːtʃ] n. 火把，启发之物 vi. 像火炬一样燃烧 vt. 用火炬点燃

Morse [mɔːs] n. 莫尔斯式电码（用点和划表示字母，可用灯光或无线电发送）
jack knife 大折刀
heave [hiːv] v. 举起 n. 举起
manual ['mænjuəl] n. 手册，指南 adj. 手的，体力的，手册（性质）的
tackle ['tækl] n. 工具，辘轱，用具，装备，扭倒 vt. 固定，应付 vi. 捉住
occupant ['ɔkjuːpənt] n. 占有者，居住者，占用者
portable ['pɔːtəbl] adj. 轻便的，手提（式）的，便携式的
extinguisher [ik'stiŋgwiʃə(r)] n. 熄灭者，灭火器

Exercises

1. What's the signal for man overboard?
2. What's the signal for abandon ship?
3. Only who can give the order of "abandon ship"?
4. What's the signal for emergency and fire?
5. What's lifeline?
6. What's watertight container?
7. What's first aid outfit?
8. How many liters does one gallon equal to?

INFLATABLE LIFE RAFTS

Every inflatable life raft is so constructed that, when fully inflated and floating with the cover uppermost, it is stable in a sea way.

The life rafts are so constructed that if they are dropped into the water from a height of 60 feet, their equipments will be undamaged.

The total weight of a life raft and its equipment does not exceed 400 pounds.

The life rafts are made of approved material and constructed to be capable of being 30 days afloat in all sea conditions and are fully operational through a temperature range of 150 degrees F to minus 22 degrees F.

All the inflatable life rafts onboard have a capacity of 25 persons each.

Equipments of inflatable life rafts.

1 buoyant rescue quoit attached to at least 100 feet of buoyant line.

2 sponges.

2 paddles.

1 repair outfit capable of repairing punctures in the buoyant compartments.

Approximately the same rations and other equipments as a lifeboat.

1 instruction booklet on how to survive in a life raft.

INSTRUCTIONS IN CASE OF FIRE

(1) The greatest danger on every ship is fire-which is usually caused by a lighted cigarette, a match, a short circuit, or negligence of any person onboard.

(2) Everyone onboard is obliged to be careful not to cause any fire, and to be careful not to put in danger those lives onboard, and their own, and all crew are obliged to know how to use the fire extinguishers provided by the ship.

(3) Only a very well prepared crew can definitely face the danger of fire and observe a fire at its onset before it has a chance to spread.

(4) Each great fire naturally starts from a small one and no matter how small, it must be observed in time and extinguished immediately.

(5) Anyone observing smoke or flame or smelling anything burning must urgently inform the bridge, either by telephone or verbally, or (on observing a fire) by breaking the glass in the nearest manual fire alarm. Be calm in order not to cause panic among passengers.

(6) When we are near a fire and the whole area is full of smoke, we must realize that the area closest to the floor is more breathable than the area higher up. For this reason we must crawl on our knees when using fire hoses and extinguishers.

(7) When we use a fire hose in order to extinguish fire, we must remember that by holding the hose close to the face while hosing, we are getting clearer air to breathe near the water.

(8) When a room is full of smoke, whether we are wearing breathing apparatus or not, we must find exactly our position in the room so that we may leave quickly when necessary. Touching the walls or furniture helps to guide the way out in the limited visibility.

(9) Everyone wearing the breathing apparatus and his assistant holding a contact safety rope must know the signals to be given with the rope which are as follows:

① One pull on the rope means to give more length.

② Two pulls on the rope means "hold tight" onto the rope.

③ Three pulls on the rope means "lead me out" .

The signals mentioned above must be known by heart by all crew members as they are very important.

(10) Everyone using a fire hose must know that as the water is under high pressure and being forced out of a small nozzle, the end of the nozzle must be kept pressed down. For this reason the hose should be held under one arm with one hand holding the nozzle pressed down, thus avoiding the water jetting upwards, instead of down onto the fire.

(11) Crew must make sure that every single passenger is wearing his life jacket properly and also carries a blanket in the event of emergency or fire. Children under the age of 10 years must have children's life jackets, which are provided by the stewards at the beginning of every voyage.

(12) Crew must make sure that all passengers have evacuated all passengers accommodation and have proceeded to their muster stations before they leave for their emergency stations. Only when instructed to do so, may crew proceed to their lifeboats after informing the officer in charge of their particular areas that all passengers have evacuated their cabins.

(13) The personnel in charge of the emergency stations must check and make sure that no passengers leave these stations without the captain's order.

(14) In case of any misunderstanding or for any other questions, apply to safety officer or staff captain for any serious matter.

GENERAL INFORMATION ON TYPES OF FIRES AND FIRE FIGHTING EQUIPMENTS TO BE USED

To use the fire hoses in the fire stations you must connect the hose to the hydrant and turn the valve anti-clockwise. If it is necessary you can make a longer length of hose by connecting two together.

WATER EXTINGUISHERS

Can be used by turning the extinguisher upside down or by pressing the button on the head of the extinguisher. These extinguishers can be used in the case of a 1st class fire (wood, papers, rubbish, etc.) but never on a fire caused by electrical equipment or liquid fuel.

FOAM EXTINGUISHERS

Can be used also by turning them upside down (After first being shaken and turned anti-clockwise fully the top valve). Turn the nozzle towards the base of the fire and do not move the position until the cylinder is empty. These extinguishers can be used on a 2nd class fire (liquid fuel, paints, etc.)

CO_2 EXTINGUISHERS

These extinguishers are with a cone-shaped attachment. They can be operated by pressing the handle or turning the valve. Point the cone directly to the fire, holding the extinguisher by the wooden handle and spray from left to right onto the fire. These extinguishers can be used for all types of fires and especially for 3rd class fire (electrical equipment, motors, etc.).

DRY CHEMICAL EXTINGUISHER

These extinguishers come in three types which operate as follows:

Remove the plug and switch on.

Remove the plug and pump.

Remove the plug and turn the extinguisher upside down, knock the base and then direct the nozzle to the fire.

The main types are NO. 1 and 2. They can be used in the case of 2nd or 3rd class fires (fuel, paint, electrical apparatus, etc.).

WATERTIGHT DOORS (W. T. D.)

The ship is divided into watertight compartments by transverse bulkheads. For the purpose of isolating one or more of these compartments, that may have become damaged by collision, grounding, etc. the vessel has been designed with watertight doors in various positions from the keel to watertight deck.

These doors are made from steel and may be closed from both sides of the door or from the bridge.

When the WTDs are about to be closed, a hooter sound is warning. This is to avoid accidents. Crew should take care on hearing the signal and keep clear of the doors.

The WTDs may be used as Fire Screen Doors (F. S. D.) if necessary.

Notes

1. inflatable life raft 充气救生筏
2. It is stable in a sea way. 在海上它很稳定
3. approved material 经批准的材料
4. buoyant rescue quoit 有浮力的救生圈
5. repairing punctures 修补刺孔
6. short circuit 短路
7. at its onset 在它一开始
8. smelling anything burning 闻到某东西烧焦
9. For this reason we must crawl on our knees when using fire hoses and extinguishers. 因为这个原因，当我们使用消防软管和灭火器时，我们必须跪着爬。
10. Touching the walls or furniture helps to guide the way out in the limited visibility. 触摸墙壁或家具有助于在有限的能见度内引导出路。
11. a contact safety rope 一根联系安全绳
12. avoiding the water jetting upwards 避免水往上喷
13. muster stations 集合站
14. apply to safety officer or staff captain for any serious matter 任何重大事情应向安全官员或副船长请示
15. turn the valve anti-clockwise 逆时针旋转阀门
16. turning the extinguisher upside down 把灭火器倒置
17. turned anticlockwise fully the top valve 逆时针彻底地旋转顶阀
18. cone-shaped attachment 锥形装置
19. transverse bulkheads 横向舱壁
20. watertight doors 水密门
21. watertight deck 水密甲板
22. hooter sound 汽笛声
23. keep clear of the doors 保持门的通畅
24. Fire Screen Doors（F. S. D.） 防火门

New words & expressions

inflatable [in'fleitəbl] adj. 通货膨胀，膨胀的

uppermost ['ʌpəməust] adj. 至上的，最主要的 adv. 在最上，首先

stable ['steibl] adj. 稳定的

construct [kən'strʌkt] vt. 建造，构造，创立

exceed [ik'siːd] vt. 超越，胜过 vi. 超过其他

afloat [ə'fləut] adj. adv. 飘浮的，在海上的，传播的

range [reindʒ] n. 山脉，行列，范围，射程 vt. 排列，归类于，使并列
minus ['mainəs] adj. 负的，减的 prep. 减去 n. 负数
quoit [kwɔit, kweit] n. 金属环，铁环，绳圈 vt. 掷（圈环）
paddle ['pædl] n. 短桨，划桨，明轮翼 vi. 划桨，戏水，涉水 vt. 用桨划
puncture ['pʌŋktʃə] n. 刺孔，刺痕 vt. 刺，揭穿
compartment [kəm'pɑːtmənt] n. 间隔间，车厢，水密箱
approximately [əprɔksi'mətli] adv. 近似地，大约
survive [sə'vaiv] v. 幸免于，幸存，生还
circuit ['səːkit] n. 电路，一圈，周游，巡回
negligence ['neglidʒəns] n. 疏忽
be obliged to 不得不
onset ['ɔnset] n. 攻击，进攻，有力的开始，肇端 n. [医] 发作
calm [kɑːm] adj. 平静的，镇静的，沉着的 v. （使）平静，（使）镇定，平息
panic ['pænik] n. 惊慌，恐慌，没有理由的
breathable ['briːðəbl] adj. 适宜呼吸的，（衣料）透气的
hose [həuz] n. 软管，水龙带，长筒袜 v. 用软管浇水
apparatus [ˌæpə'reitəs] n. 器械，设备，仪器
furniture ['fəːnitʃə] n. 家具，设备，储藏物
visibility [ˌvizi'biliti] n. 可见度，可见性，显著，明显度，能见度
nozzle ['nɔzl] n. 管口，喷嘴
jet [dʒet] n. 喷射，黑玉 v. 喷射 adj. 黑玉色的，墨黑的喷气机
blanket ['blæŋkit] n. 毯子 vt. 覆盖
evacuate [i'vækjueit] v. 疏散，撤出，排泄
particular [pə'tikjulə] n. 细节，详细 adj. 特殊的，详细的，挑剔
apply [ə'plai] vt. 申请，应用 vi. 申请，适用
clockwise ['klɔkwaiz] adj. 顺时针方向的 adv. 顺时针方向地
hydrant ['haidrənt] n. 消防栓，消防龙头
valve [vælv] n. 阀，[英] 电子管，真空管
turn…upside down 倒置
cylinder ['silində] n. 圆筒，圆柱体，汽缸，柱面
cone [kəun] n. [数、物] 锥形物，圆锥体，（松树的）球果 vt. 使成锥形
attachment [ə'tætʃmənt] n. 附件，附加装置，配属
operate ['ɔpəreit] v. 操作，运转，起作用，动手术 n. [军] 作军事行动
transverse ['trænzvəːs] adj. 横向的，横断的
collision [kə'liʒən] n. 碰撞，冲突
grounding ['graundiŋ] n. [电] 接地，基础，（染色的）底色，搁浅
hooter ['huːtə(r)] n. 汽笛
keep clear of v. 不接触

Exercises

1. What's the biggest weight of a life raft?
2. What are the equipments of each life raft?
3. What's the biggest danger on the ship?
4. Why must we crawl on our knees when using fire hoses and extinguishers?
5. When a room is full of smoke, how to guide the way out in the limited visibility?
6. Why should we hold the hose close to the face?
7. What's the first class fire?
8. What's the second class fire?
9. What's the third class fire?

6.5 Safety Training Induction Programme

Objectives

This Safety Induction Programme is intended to encourage safety awareness for all new personnel serving onboard Kyma Ship Management Passenger ships.

The Programme will commence as soon as possible after you have joined the ship, and will be conducted as quickly as possible.

The overall objective of the programme is to ensure new personnel onboard Kyma Ship Management Passenger ships are familiar with emergency procedures and have knowledge and ability to correctly use the available safety equipment.

Particular emphasis will be given to safety equipment and procedures specific to shipboard duties, specifically in the areas of:

Personal survival techniques.
Fire prevention and fire fighting.
Elementary First Aid.
Emergency Procedures.

After successfully passing a short test you will be issued with a certificate stating that you have completed and passed a programme of basic training to enable you to take immediate action and to react in a correct manner during any emergency.

PROGRAMME OUTLINE

Ship Safety Familiarization

1.1 Ship Familiarization
1.2 Emergency plan/organization
1.3 Safety Equipment
1.4 Survival Craft/Equipment
1.5 I. S. M. Familiarization

Basic Personal Survival

2.1 General Principles

2. 2 Emergency Stations

2. 3 Communications

2. 4 Evacuation

2. 5 Survival Craft and Life Saving Appliances

Basic Fire Fighting

3. 1 General Principles

3. 2 Fire Situations

3. 3 Fire Fighting Equipment

3. 4 Breathing Apparatus

3. 5 Important Considerations

Basic First Aid

4. 1 General Principles

4. 2 Elementary First Aid

4. 3 Transportation of Casualties

4. 4 Company Drug and Alcohol Policy

Ship Safety Familiarization

1. 1 Ship Familiarization

Be familiar with the ship through repeated guided tours onboard and verbal instructions.

1. 2 Emergency Plan/Organization

Know what to do if a person falls overboard.

Recognize instructions on the muster list, be able to identify individual duties in conjunction with individual's muster card.

Know the location of the approved muster lists posted onboard.

Recognize the meaning of emergency signals and coded messages/broadcasts.

Know how to use the emergency instruction card and ensure it is attached to your lifejacket at all times.

1. 3 Safety Equipment

Know the type of safety equipment onboard, its location and how to use it.

1. 4 Survival Craft/Equipment

Have knowledge of the location and basic operation of survival craft and the equipment they carry.

1. 5 I. S. M. Familiarization

Be familiar with the International Safety Management System (I. S. M.) and how it affects you.

Basic Personal Survival

2. 1 General Principles

Demonstrate the importance of:

(1) Regular training and drills.

(2) Being prepared for any emergency.

Take appropriate action when:

(1) Called to survival craft stations.

(2) Required to abandon ship.

(3) In the water.

(4) Aboard a survival craft.

2.2 Emergency Stations

Demonstrate an understanding of how the effective use of equipment depends upon the ability of you to use and know:

(1) The location and use of all types of firefighting equipment.

(2) Escape routes.

(3) Emergencies involving the use of watertight doors and damage control.

(4) Understand survival techniques onboard ship and in the survival craft.

2.3 Communications

Apply communications and understand the importance of:

(1) Internal communication systems onboard.

(2) Raising the alarm.

(3) Alerting passengers and fellow crew members.

(4) Reporting and notification of an incident onboard.

(5) Being able to communicate in English, guidance instruction for passengers.

2.4 Evacuation

(1) Recognize the alarm signals.

(2) Prepare yourself for abandoning ship.

(3) Demonstrate a knowledge of the number and location of passenger muster stations.

(4) Understanding the importance of keeping order and avoiding panic in emergency situations.

(5) Recognize the routes from muster stations to embarkation of survival craft.

(6) Be familiar with the location of evacuation supplies, e. g. lifejacket, warm clothing, blankets, essential medicines.

(7) Understand the need to exercises control of the movements of passengers and crew in corridors, staircases and passageways.

(8) Recognize and apply methods of evacuation for disabled persons and persons requiring special assistance.

(9) Recognize the restrictions of the use of elevators.

(10) Understand the need for alternative routes if a part of the ship is inaccessible as a result of an emergency situation.

(11) Apply search routines for personnel in accommodation spaces filled with smoke.

(12) Recognize when a passenger is wearing suitable clothing, and when they have donned their lifejackets correctly.

(13) Know that the order to abandon ship comes from the Master.

The following requirements arc essential for survival after the ship has been abandoned:

(1) Means of staying afloat.

(2) Means of protection from the elements, i. e. Temperature extremes.

(3) Drinking water and food.

(4) Communication with other survivors, ships and rescue services.

(5) First aid supplies.

Be aware of the following dangers that may occur in a survival craft:

(1) Heat stoke, sun stroke, hypothermia and exposure to cold.

(2) Effects of seasickness.

(3) Failure to maintain body fluids causing dehydration.

(4) Drinking sea water.

(5) Sea surface fire.

2. 5 Survival Craft and Life Saving Appliances

(1) Recognize and describe a lifeboat and its equipment.

(2) Understand the precautions which have to be taken to ensure personal safety while launching lifeboats.

(3) Describe the two types of life raft (davit launched and throw over) and the launching equipment for each.

(4) Recognize and be able to use survival craft facilities to get clear away from the ship when waterborne.

(5) Identify the distribution of lifebuoys throughout the ship, and the operation of additional equipment attached to lifebuoys.

(6) Demonstrate an awareness of the location of adult and infant lifejackets.

(7) Demonstrate unaided how to put on a non inflatable lifejacket correctly and without assistance, and understand the use of equipment on the lifejacket, e. g. whistle and light.

(8) Demonstrate the correct procedure for entering the water wearing a lifejacket.

Basic Fire Fighting

3. 1 General Principles

Demonstrate an understanding of the three elements that are required for a fire to occur:

(1) Presence of material which acts as a fuel.

(2) A source of ignition.

(3) The Presence of oxygen.

Action to be taken on discovering a fire:

(1) Find-the fire.

(2) Inform-raise the alarm.

(3) Restrict-remove the cause if possible, the fuel or restrict ventilation, starve.

(4) Extinguish if possible.

3. 2 Fire Situations

(1) Recognize the general emergency signal consisting of seven or more short blasts followed

by one long blast on the ship's whistles or alarm bells.

(2) Recognize the alarm activated from the bridge to muster specific emergency parties such as fire teams.

(3) Understand the muster list, the information contained within it, and be able to identify duties of individual crew members.

(4) Know the communications used during a fire emergency:

① Verbal instructions.

② Telephones.

③ Public Address Systems.

④ Hand held Radios.

(5) Recognize the different types of fire doors onboard and demonstrate the closing operation.

3. 3 Fire Fighting Equipment

Hoses

(1) Understand how hoses are joined together and connected to fire hydrants.

(2) Know the application of a nozzle and how it can be adjusted to produce a concentrated jet, a spray or mist, and in what situation each application should be used.

(3) Demonstrate the use of a hose with jet or spray nozzle.

(4) Understand the correct stowage of hoses and nozzles.

Portable Extinguishers

(1) Recognize the different types carried onboard and understand the colour coding system:

① Water-Red.

② Foam-Cream.

③ CO2-Black.

④ Dry Power-Blue.

(2) Identify which type of fire each extinguisher is suitable for and hence the reasons for its location.

(3) Understand and demonstrate the operation of each type of extinguisher.

Fire blankets

Identify where they are normally located, and demonstrate how they are used.

Sprinkler system

Have a basic understanding of the operational principle of a sprinkler system.

3. 4 Breathing Apparatus

(1) Have a basic operational knowledge of a breathing apparatus (BA) set, and demonstrate its use.

(2) Recognize the safety procedures to follow when using a BA set.

(3) Understand search techniques in a smoke filled environment using BA.

3. 5 Important Considerations

(1) Smoke inhalation.

(2) Heat.

(3) Humidity.

(4) Fatigue of firefighters.

(5) Recognize when breathing protection is required.

Basic First Aid

4.1 General Principles

Recognize life threatening medical emergencies.

4.2 Elementary First Aid

(1) Understand the basic principles of airway, breathing, circulation (ABC).

(2) Understand the correct procedure for dealing with a choking casualty.

(3) Understand the correct procedure for positioning casualties.

(4) Demonstrate the recovery position of a patient.

(5) Know how to keep air passages clear.

(6) Recognize the hazards of bleeding.

(7) How to stop excessive bleeding.

(8) Understand how to apply exhaled air and other methods of artificial resuscitation.

(9) Apply the appropriate measures for burns and scalds, including cooling the area as quickly as possible.

(10) To be aware of the dangers of electric shock and potential hazards to first aiders.

(11) When reporting a medical incident give clear and concise details of location of incident and symptoms.

(12) When confronted with multiple casualties know how to categorize and prioritize.

4.3 Transportation of Casualties

(1) Know how to apply appropriate transportation alone and with assistance, being aware of the confined spaces and height restrictions onboard.

(2) Demonstrate stretcher transport.

4.4 Company Drug and Alcohol Policy

A short presentation on the company's policy.

Certification

The following check lists are to be completed by the relevant instructor for each particular unit of the course.

After a brief verbal examination the sections will be ticked off. When a section is completed it will be signed off as complete by the instructor and dated. The rear copy is to be kept in the book as a personal record.

The second and top copies are to be presented to the training officer onboard. One will be kept onboard and one will be returned to the Marine Operations Department.

Once all four units are complete and the tickets are presented to the Master, a certificate will be issued.

Please be aware that it is the responsibility of the individual to ensure that the 4 units of the course are completed and returned as soon as possible. Any items included in the programme that are not fully understood are to be referred to the instructor for further tuition.

CHECK LIST

Date: ____________ Certificate NO. 1018

Ships Safety Familiarization

Section	Number	Items	Checked
1	1. 1	Ship Familiarization	
	1. 2	Emergency plan/organization	
	1. 3	Safety Equipment	
	1. 4	Survival Craft/Equipment	
	1. 5	I. S. M. Familiarization	

Candidate Name: ____________ (Please Print) Instructor's Name: ____________

Signature: ____________ Signature: ____________

Position: ____________ Ship: ____________

CHECK LIST

Date: ____________ Certificate NO. 1018

Ships Safety Familiarization

Section	Number	Items	Checked
2	2. 1	General Principles	
	2. 2	Emergency Stations	
	2. 3	Communications	
	2. 4	Evacuation	
	2. 5	Survival Craft and Life Saving Appliances	

Candidate Name: ____________ (Please Print) Instructor's Name: ____________

Signature: ____________ Signature: ____________

Position: ____________ Ship: ____________

CHECK LIST

Date: ____________ Certificate NO. 1018

Ships Safety Familiarization

Section	Number	Items	Checked
3	3. 1	General Principles	
	3. 2	Fire Situations	
	3. 3	Fire Fighting Equipment	
	3. 4	Breathing Apparatus	
	3. 5	Important Considerations	

Candidate Name: ____________ (Please Print) Instructor's Name: ____________

Signature: ____________ Signature: ____________

Position: ____________ Ship: ____________

CHECK LIST

Date: ____________ Certificate NO. 1018

Ships Safety Familiarization

Section	Number	Items	Checked
4	4. 1	General Principles	
	4. 2	General Principles	
	4. 3	Elementary First Aid	
	4. 4	Company Drug and Alcohol Policy	

Candidate Name: ____________ (Please Print) Instructor's Name: ____________

Signature: ____________ Signature: ____________

Position: ____________ Ship: ____________

Notes

1. safety awareness 安全意识
2. correctly use the available safety equipment 正确使用现有安全设备
3. particular emphasis 特别强调
4. Personal survival techniques. 个人生存技巧。
5. Elementary First Aid. 初级急救。
6. Emergency Procedures. 应急程序。
7. Survival Craft 救生载具
8. Breathing Apparatus 呼吸装置
9. Transportation of Casualties 伤亡人员的运送
10. Be familiar with the ship through repeated guided tours onboard and verbal instructions. 通过反复的船上导览和口头说明来熟悉船舶。
11. muster list 应变部署表
12. to identify individual duties in conjunction with individual's muster card 确定个人职责与个人集合部署卡一致
13. coded messages 编码信息
14. the emergency instruction card 紧急指示卡
15. regular training 定期培训
16. survival craft stations and drills 救生载具站和演习
17. escape routes 逃生线路
18. damage control 损害控制
19. raising the alarm 发警报
20. alerting passengers and fellow crew members 向乘客和船员同事发警报
21. keeping order and avoiding panic in emergency situations 在紧急情况下保持秩序，避免恐慌
22. essential medicines 基本药物
23. temperature extremes 极端温度
24. the elements 大自然的力量（风、雷、雨等），风雨
25. Failure to maintain body fluids causing dehydration 未能保持体液造成脱水

26. launching lifeboats 放救生艇

27. Describe the two types of life raft (davit launched and throw over) and the launching equipment for each 描述两种类型的救生筏（一种用吊艇柱具放，一种直接抛）和每一种下水设备。

28. to use survival craft facilities to get clear away from the ship when waterborne 在水上时，用救生艇筏设施逃离船舶。

29. presence of material which acts as a fuel 作为燃料的材料的存在

30. Hand held Radios. 手持无线电报话机

31. Fatigue of firefighters. 消防员疲劳

32. Understand the basic principles of airway, breathing, circulation (ABC). 了解气道、呼吸、血液循环的基本原理。

33. Understand how to apply exhaled air and other methods of artificial resuscitation. 了解如何应用人工呼吸和其他人工复苏方法。

34. electric shock 电击，电震

35. being aware of the confined spaces and height restrictions onboard 了解在船上的空间限制和高度限制

36. the Marine Operations Department 海事处

New words & expressions

induction [in'dʌkʃən] n. 首次经验，入门，归纳（法），就职，就职典礼

objective [əb'dʒektiv] n. 目标，任务 adj. 客观的，实体的

commence [kə'mens] vt. & vi. 开始，着手，获得学位

familiarization [fəˌmiliərai'zeiʃn] n. 亲密，熟悉，精通

survival [sə'vaivəl] n. 幸存，生存，幸存者，遗物，遗风

evacuation [iˌvækju'eiʃn] n. 撤空，撤离，撤退，疏散

appliance [ə'plaiəns] n. 器具，器械，装置

casualty ['kæʒuəlti] n. 伤亡（人数），事故，横祸，受害者，死伤者，损坏

conjunction [kən'dʒʌŋkʃən] n. 连词，连接，联合，结合物

broadcast ['brɔːdkɑːst] vt. 广播，播放 vi. 播放节目 n. 广播 adj. 广播的，广泛散布的

affect [ə'fekt] vt. 影响，假装 n. 感情，情感，心情

route [ruːt] n. 常规路线，航线，渠道，途径 vt. 按某路线发送

alert [ə'ləːt] adj. 警觉的，警惕的 n. 警报，警戒状态 vt. 向……报警

panic ['pænik] n. 恐慌，惊慌 vt. 使恐慌 vi. 十分惊慌 adj. 恐慌的，惊慌失措的

essentia [i'senʃəl] adj. 基本的，必要的 n. 必需品，基本要素，必不可少的东西

staircase ['stɛəkeis] n. 楼梯，楼梯间

passageway ['pæsidʒwei] n.（尤指两面有墙的）通道，走廊

don [dɔn] n. 大学教师，（牛津、剑桥大学的）导师，特别研究员 vt. 穿上，披上

extreme [iks'triːm] adj. 极端的，过激的 n. 极端，[常用复数] 在两末端的事物

survivor [sə'vaivə (r)] n. 幸存者，残存者，生还者，遗物，残存物

fluid ['fluːid] n. 液体，流体 adj. 流体的，流动的，流体的，液体的

dehydration [ˌdiːhai'dreiʃn] n. 脱水，干燥，极度口渴，失水

unaided [ʌn'eidid] adj. 无外援的，独立的

fuel [fjuəl] n. 燃料 vt. 给……加燃料，给……加油，激起 vi. 补充燃料

ignition [ig'niʃn] n. 着火，燃烧，点火，点燃

ventilation [ˌventi'leiʃn] n. 空气流通，通风设备，通风方法，公开讨论

starve [stɑːv] vi. 挨饿，受饿，[古语] 冻死 vt. 使挨饿，饿死

stowage ['stəuidʒ] n. 堆装物，配载货物

fatigue [fə'tiːg] n. 疲劳，疲乏 vt. 使疲劳，使疲乏 vi. 疲劳

firefighter ['faiəfaitə (r)] n. 〈美〉消防队员

choking ['tʃəukiŋ] adj. 窒息的，憋闷的 v. 填塞（choke 的现在分词），（使）窒息

exhale [eks'heil] vt. 发散出，放出 vi. 呼气，放出，发散

artificial [ˌɑːti'fiʃəl] adj. 人造的，人工的，虚假的 n. 人造肥料，〈美〉假花

resuscitation [riˌsʌsi'teiʃn] n. 恢复知觉，苏醒

scald [skɔːld] vt. （沸水等）烫伤（皮肤）n. （沸水或蒸汽造成的）烫伤

concise [kən'sais] adj. 简明的，简洁的，简约，精炼

categorize ['kætəgəraiz] vt. 把……归类，把……分门别类

prioritize [prai'ɔrətaiz] vt. 按重要性排列，划分优先顺序，优先处理

stretcher ['stretʃə(r)] n. 担架，延伸器，顺边砖，框架结构的横档

tick off [tik ɔf] v. 用记号勾出，列举，简略地描述，〈英口〉责备

sign off [sain ɔf] 停止广播，签字结束书信

tuition [tju'iʃən] n. 学费，教学，讲授

Exercises

1. What is the overall objective of the Safety Induction Programme?
2. What is the main content of the Safety Induction Programme?
3. What is the main contents of Emergency Plan/Organization?
4. What does I. S. M. Familiarization mean?
5. What are the essential requirements for survival after the ship has been abandoned?
6. What are the dangers that may occur in a survival craft?
7. What are the three elements that are required for a fire to occur?
8. What action should be taken on discovering a fire?
9. What is the color of foam extinguisher?
10. Generally speaking, how many types of portable extinguishers are carried onboard? What are they?
11. What should we do when reporting a medical incident?
12. What should we know when confronted with multiple casualties?
13. Whom will the second and top copies be presented to onboard?
14. How can we get the certificate of the Safety Induction Programme?

Appendix 1

General Rules & Regulations for Officers, Staff & Crew Onboard

The following rules and regulations as outlined and prescribed by management require compliance by all officers, staff and crew members. The disregard of, or failure to comply with these regulations by the vessel's management will result in disciplinary action that could result in a fine or dismissal. Refusal to obey a lawful order will result in immediate dismissal. The master, staff captain, chief engineer, hotel manager and all department heads are directed to maintain and enforce compliance of these regulations at all times.

1. Definition Of All Officers, Staff And Crew Members

Senior officers

Hotel officers

Officers

Staff

Crew

The above ever mentioned before.

2. Procedures

If any member of the ship's complement breaks the rules and regulations, the master will take the necessary action and record the facts in the Log Book. At all times ship's personnel have the opportunity to lay before the master any complaint; the procedure to follow: Department head reports to the staff captain, who will bring the case to the attention of master. All matters concerning discipline and order will be investigated and if necessary action will be taken in these matters by the staff captain. All members of the ship's complement are under the master's command. They will follow orders. They will follow orders given by the master, department heads and officers on duty.

3. Conduct

All members of the ship's complement must be polite and helpful to passengers at all times and at no time argumentative or discourteous even if provoked. All vessels' personnel will conduct themselves at all times in a manner, which will not discredit or cause harmful consequences to the ship and/or to the company. They will refrain from any acts, which may adversely affect the ship, and especially will avoid any act, which might entail risk or injury to themselves and/or other crew members, and or passengers. Failure to conform to this regulation will result in immediate dismissal without exception.

All vessel's personnel will require reporting for duty at their stations at lease 15 minutes before their assigned duties begin.

All personnel will report for each duty or work period in clean uniforms or work clothes and name badge.

No personnel, officers, staff and crew members are permitted to enter passenger cabins or invite passengers to their cabins, except on specified ship's business, or in the line of duty. When in public rooms or gangways passengers must always be given top priority.

Large concentrations of crew members in any space in the ship should be avoided at all times. All members of the ship's complement will behave properly toward other crew members and respect those who retire. Use of foul language is not permitted. No member of the ship's complement is allowed to use passenger toilets. These are for passengers only.

4. Dress/Appearance

All members of the ship's complement must at all times be properly dressed in accordance with the uniform regulation: clean, clean-shaven and well groomed. Hair must be neatly trimmed, and for male crew members the length of hair will not exceed the shirt collar. Those crew members assigned to service duties to passengers are not allowed to grow beards (only a moustache) .

5. Work Dress In Public Areas

Any member of the ship's complement who is conducting work in public areas in work dress times must wear a clean white boiler suit or other assigned uniform.

6. Smoking

Smoking is strictly forbidden:

(1) When on duty;

(2) When in bed;

(3) When near ventilator intakes;

(4) When in the holds/storerooms/galley/pantries;

(5) When in the elevator;

(6) When passing through passenger accommodations.

7. Alcohol

Excess consumption of alcoholic beverages is prohibited at any time. Personnel found drunk or intoxicated are subject to disciplinary action. (Dismissal)

8. Working Conditions

All members of the ship's complement must report for duty on time. No member of the ship's complement is allowed to be absent from his/her work duties unless on doctor's written orders. Questions regarding working conditions, hours, overtime, etc shall be directed to the department head.

9. Shore Leave

No member of the ship's complement is allowed to go ashore without prior authorization from the department heads, and when necessary, staff captain. chief engineer or master. When leaving or boarding the vessel, all members of the ship's complement will carry ID card and show it to the officer on duty at gangway or quarter master. Senior officers and department heads will sign in and out in the prescribed logbook that is at the gangway. All members of the ship's complement must board the vessel 30 minutes prior to departure. Failure in doing so will result in a written warning.

The master can, at any time forbid any member of the ship's complement to go shore leave. In this case the master will make the reason for his action known and write it down in the ship's log. It is required that at least one third of each department be on vessel at all times. The respective department heads will designate these crew members. The staff captain must approve any deviation from this. It is understood that department heads will be on board the majority of the time and in their absence the second in command after being advised.

10. Boat And Fire Drills

All members of the ship's complement shall attend the drills. There are exceptions to this rule, which is to be strictly enforced. It is imperative that all members of the ship's complement be familiar with their duties in case of emergency. Each and every member of the ship's complement must be familiar with the boat station and the shortest route thereto. Life jackets must be stored in cabins at all times when not in use.

11. Cabins

All members of the ship's complement must ensure that cabins, bathrooms and accesses are kept clean and tidy. For any changes in cabin arrangements permission from the staff captain must be obtained. Never shall any member of the ship's complement carry out these changes him/himself.

It is forbidden: To hang clothing, towels, etc. near any electrical appliance, whether connected or not.

To install auxiliary wires in cabins for extra lighting, etc.

To connect radio sets or any appliance other than those with regulation plugs and insulation. To open portholes/windows in air-conditioned spaces or in rough seas.

12. Gambling

No member of the ship's complement is allowed to indulge in public or private gambling of any nature. No member of the ship's complement is allowed to enter the ship's casino area at any time other than on specified duty.

13. Smuggling

Smuggling is strictly forbidden. Any form of smuggling will be followed by disciplinary action and is subject to prosecution in a criminal court.

14. Firearms/Weapons

It is forbidden for any member of the ship's complement to possess firearms of any nature or any other dangerous weapons. Failure to comply with this will result in fines and/or dismissal with a report to the appropriate authorities.

15. Drugs And/Or Narcotics

It is forbidden for any member of the ship's complement to bring on board or use or possess any drugs or narcotics. Personnel suspected of carrying or smuggling illegal drugs on themselves or in their cabins will be subject to examination. Failure to comply with this will result in heavy fines and/or dismissal with a report to the appropriate authorities.

16. Ship's Property

No items belonging to the vessel may be removed or taken ashore , unless authorized by the department heads and approved by the master. Any member of the ship's complement defacing, abusing or pilfering the ship's property is open to severe fine and immediate dismissal.

17. Garbage

Dumping of the garbage on the ship is not allowed. Any garbage must be put properly in the receptacles (Note: Never put paper waste in any ashtrays) . At no time should garbage be thrown overboard.

18. Fighting, Using Indecent Language

Any personnel bothered by another, should report such action to his/her department head or the officer on duty. When a problem is serious, it should be reported to the staff captain immediately. The staff captain with department heads concerned will investigate the matter and will take necessary steps to prevent the same problem for recurring. In case of serious fights the participating crew members will be dismissed.

19. Meals, Times And Supervision

All personnel must attend meals at assigned times and must use dining room according to their ratings. Never will food be taken to crew quarters unless authorized by the master. Members of the ship's complement who are entitled to use buffets should do so not prior to 30 minutes after the commencement of the buffet and always at the end of the line when passengers are still being served. The assistant F&B manager on duty and frequently the F&B manager must inspect crew food/meals. The assistant F&B manager is obligated to act immediately on complaints that food portions are insufficient. Officers, staff and crew are not permitted to enter the galley at any time. The galley area is for authorized personnel only, unless work crew is performing maintenance and repairs. Any unauthorized person found in the galley will be reported to the staff captain and will be warned.

Dining room and buffet services for guests/visitors

Guests and/or visitors, department heads and staff officers will be able to use the above services only after authorization from the staff captain and the hotel manager. The F&B manager must see to it that only authorized visitors and guests are served meals. Special care must be exercised in implementing the above so as to eliminate abuse of this privilege by unauthorized persons.

20. Elevators

The use of passenger elevators are prohibited for all members of the ship's complement, unless specified business, or authorized by the master.

21. Customs And Immigration

All personnel will report to immigration in any port that they are signing on or off in. In the US port where immigration takes place you must be in the designated lounge at the time advised by the crew purser, with proof of citizenship for the United States citizens and your I-95 (if signing off the vessel for non-United States citizens) . No member of the ship's complement is allowed to leave the vessel until Customs and Immigration have cleared the vessel.

All personnel face fines and/or imprisonment for failure to obey customs laws, and deportation or fines and imprisonment for failure to obey immigration laws.

(1) Personal Items To Be Cleared By Customs Any crew member wishing to take items ashore (i. e. package, stereo, etc) in US ports must submit a declaration in writing to the purser's office no later than noon on Friday. If for any reason you decided not to take the manifested items ashore you must advise the chief purser immediately to insure proper cancellation with United States Customs. Failure to do so could result in any further items being cleared by denial of Customs declaration.

Items that are to be landed in Nassau must be given in writing to the Purser's Office one day prior to arrival. Forms are supplied through Department Head of Purser' Office.

(2) Items To Be Landed Any ship's property that is to be sent shoreside for any reason must be submitted with the proper paper work to the purser's office no later than 5:00p. m. on Friday. Failure to do so will only result in items not being landed. In a case where items that are cleared are not taken from the vessel you must contact the chief purser immediately so proper formalities can be conducted with the United States Customs. Failure to abide by this could result in fines being imposed to the ship. When items that have been landed for repair are returned back to the vessel, proper paper work must be completed to enable United States Customs to be informed.

22. Missing The Ship-not Reporting On Sailing Day

Any personnel missing the vessel are subject to immediate warning or dismissal. All personnel must be onboard one-half-hour prior to sailing, or will be subject to a warning. Crew members missing the vessel should notify address and phone number on back of crew pass.

23. Pay-day

Salaries will be paid in the crew purser's office at designated times.

24. Request To See Ship's Doctor

Any member of the ship's complement who wishes to see the doctor must have the appropriate form from the department head. Anyone failing to do so will be turned away. This of course does not apply to emergency situations.

25. Crew Berthing Book And Cabins

The crew purser will keep the existing crew-berthing list. For any changes in cabin assignment, the staff captain and hotel manager must give permission and notification. At the end of each month it is the responsibility of the crew purser to update the Berthing Book and submit copies to the master, staff captain and main office.

The following is forbidden in cabins:

(1) Opening portholes

(2) Nails, screws, or pictures on the wall unless approved by the staff captain.

(3) Antennas or similar devices hung from portholes.

(4) Furniture added or removed.

(5) Cooking or eating.

(6) Gambling or smuggling.

(7) Illegal drugs or offensive weapons.

(8) Installing flammable materials over light fixtures.

(9) Bringing passengers into cabins.

26. Sunbathing And Pool

Sunbathing by officers and staff is only permitted on Sun Deck around funnel. No member of the ship's complement is allowed in the ship's swimming pool.

27. P. A. System

No one except authorized persons shall use the ship's P. A. System.

28. Officer's Regulations

Officers will wear their prescribed uniforms while on or off duty and not appear in public areas in civilian clothes. Officers will wear their evening uniforms after 19: 00 hours when visiting public areas.

(1) Public Rooms And Passenger Areas All officers may stay in these rooms and areas for recreational and entertaining purposes. While in the public lounges, officers are not allowed to use bar stools or crowd around bar service areas at any time and shall not walk around public areas carrying glasses or bottles. Passengers always have priority and should never be left standing, always remember to vacate seats to accommodate passengers.

All officers are permitted in the Disco until 02: 00 a. m. Officers who are on watch standing duties should not be in pubic rooms during hours intended for their rest

Officers are allowed to dance with passengers and should limit dancing with other officers and staff.

(2) Loitering

Avoid loitering in the following areas:

① purser's square

② Shore Excursion Office

③ Housekeeping Desk

④ Casino

⑤ Gift Shop

⑥ Photo Gallery

29. Staff Regulations

The following rules and regulations are in addition to those previously stated;

(1) Dress All staff members must be immaculately dressed in prescribed uniforms and well groomed. Dress must be in keeping with standards on a cruise ship, Please remember that you are a representative of your company. At no time may staff members appear in see-through apparel. T-shirts, shorts, sweats or other civilian clothes while on board unless otherwise prescribed is part of the uniform. Evening attire should consist of smart dresses for female staff members and jacket and tie for the male staff members.

(2) Meals Staff members will take their meals in the Staff Dining Room at posted times.

(3) Public Rooms And Passengers' Areas All staff members may stay in these rooms and areas for recreational and entertaining purposes. While in the pubic lounges staff members are not allowed to use bar stools or crowd around the bar service areas at any time and shall not walk around public areas carrying glasses and bottles.

All staff members are permitted in the Disco until 02:00a. m. staff members are to be immaculately dressed and well groomed. Staff members are allowed to dance with passengers and should limit dancing with other officers and staff.

30. Crew Regulations

The following rules and regulations are in addition to those previously stated.

(1) Dress Uniforms must be as clean and neat as possible.

(2) Public Areas And Decks Crew ratings are not permitted to wander around in passenger accommodations, public rooms or passenger open deck spaces. When on duty in these areas make it as brief as possible. Do not make unnecessary noise. Passing through public areas shall be avoided as much as possible. Never shall a crew-rating member pass through public areas inside the accommodation carrying articles for his work such as paint cans, brushes, etc.

(3) Cabins/Lavatories Each crew member is responsible for keeping his cabin and lavatory clean and tidy. All crew members must behave properly towards other crew members and respect each other.

31. Laundry

Uniforms will be laundered on board free of charge. Private laundry for crew members and officers will be done on board at reduced rates as stated on the Crew Laundry Slip.

Crew members and staff are responsible to take their uniforms and private wash to the laundry themselves. Officers with a steward servicing their cabins will fill a laundry slip and place their uniforms or private wash in a laundry bag, which is supplied in their cabins. the steward will then take to and from the laundry.

Dry cleaning of uniforms will be done by shoreside operator and charged to the company for which the officers or crew members are working onboard. There is no dry cleaning of private clothing.

32. Beepers

Department heads and other designated crew have been issued beepers. The beepers must remain with the department heads and crew at all times. Periodic checks must be made to insure that batteries are charged and in perfect working order. If other personnel are on duty and have the beeper, the department head must give it directly to them. The beeper has been allotted to the department head and it is their responsibility.

In conclusion, it is the responsibility of the department head to make sure that all the above rules and regulations are known and abided by his/her personnel. All those failing to abide by the rules and regulations have to face consequences.

Notes

1. outlined and prescribed by management 管理部门列举和规定的
2. require compliance by all officers, staff and crew members 要求所有领导、员工和船员服从
3. disciplinary action 违纪惩罚
4. to maintain and enforce compliance of these regulations at all times 随时维护和遵守这些规定
5. Log Book 航海日记，值班日记
6. to lay before the master any complaint 在船长面前投诉
7. at no time argumentative or discourteous even if provoked 即使受到挑衅，也绝不争辩无礼
8. assigned duties 分配的任务
9. name badge 姓名徽章
10. in the line of duty 执勤，值班
11. foul language 粗话，骂人的话
12. clean-shaven and well groomed 刮光胡子，干净整洁
13. boiler suit 连衫裤工作服
14. excess consumption of alcoholic beverages 饮用过多酒精饮料
15. ventilator intakes 通风口
16. report for duty on time 按时报到上班
17. without prior authorization 没有事先得到批准
18. quarter master 舵手
19. auxiliary wires 附加电线
20. to indulge in public or private gambling of any nature 沉溺于任何性质的公开或私密

的赌博

21. is subject to prosecution in a criminal court 收到刑事法庭的起诉
22. defacing, abusing or pilfering the ship's property 污损、滥用或偷窃船上的财产
23. to prevent the same problem for recurring 防止同样问题的再次发生
24. serious fights 严重斗殴
25. so as to eliminate abuse of this privilege by unauthorized persons 从而消除未经授权的人员滥用这一特权
26. No member of the ship's complement is allowed to leave the vessel until Customs and Immigration have cleared the vessel. 在移民局和海关结关之前，船上任何人都不得离开船舶。
27. submit a declaration in writing 提交书面申报
28. Failure to do so could result in any further items being cleared by denial of Customs declaration. 不这样做可能导致更多物品的申报被海关拒绝。
29. the existing crew-berthing list 现有的船员铺位分配表
30. to update the Berthing Book 更新铺位分配记录
31. Illegal drugs or offensive weapons. 不合法的药物和进攻性武器
32. civilian clothes 普通服装
33. see-through apparel 透明衣服
34. posted times 宣布的时间
35. periodic checks 定期检查

New words & expressions

prescribe [pris'kraib] v. 指示，规定，处（方），开（药）

compliance [kəm'plaiəns] n. 依从，顺从

disregard [ˌdisri'gɑːd] v. 不理漠视 n. 漠视，忽视

enforce [in'fɔːs] vt. 强迫，执行，坚持，加强

comply with v. 照做

definition [ˌdefi'niʃən] n. 定义，解说，精确度，（轮廓影像等的）清晰度

logbook ['lɔgbuk] n. 航海日志，飞行日志，飞机航程表

provoke [prə'vəuk] vt. 激怒，挑拨，煽动，惹起，驱使

argumentative [ˌɑːgju'mentətiv] adj. 好辩的，争论的

discredit [dis'kredit] n. 无信用，疑惑，不名誉，耻辱 vt. 不信，怀疑，使丢脸，使丧失信誉

adverse ['ædvəːs] adj. 不利的，敌对的，相反的

adversely adv. 逆地，反对地

entail [in'teil] vt. 使必需，使蒙受，使承担，遗传给 n. ［建］限定继承权

conform [kən'fɔːm] vt. 使一致，使遵守 . vi. 符合，相似，适应环境 adj. 一致的，顺从的

assign [ə'sain] vt. 分配，指派 v. 赋值

line of duty n. 公务（尤指军事任务），履行职责，尽职

retire [ri'taiə] vi. 退休，引退，退却，撤退，就寝

foul [faul] adj. 污秽的，邪恶的，肮脏的，淤塞的，恶劣的 vt. 弄脏，妨害，污蔑，犯

规，淤塞

in accordance with 根据，符合

groom [grum, gruːm] n. 马夫，新郎，男仆 vt. 喂马，推荐，整饰 vi. 修饰

moustache [məsˈtɑːʃ, mus-] n. 小胡子，（哺乳动物的）触须

boiler suit n. 连衫裤工作服

trim [trim] adj. 整齐的，整洁的 vt. 整理，修整，装饰

pantry [ˈpæntri] n. 餐具室，食品室

overtime [ˈəuvətaim] n. 超时，加班，延长时间 adj. 超时的，加班的

authorization [ˌɔːθəraiˈzeiʃən] n. 授权，认可

quarter [ˈkwɔːtə] n. 四分之一，方向，地区，方面，航（区间）

respective [risˈpektiv] adj. 分别的，各自的

deviation [ˌdiːviˈeiʃən] n. 背离，离开

exception [ikˈsepʃən] n. 除外，例外，反对，异议

imperative [imˈperətiv] n. 命令，诫命，需要，规则，祈使语气 adj. 命令的，强制的，紧急的

be familiar with 与……熟悉

thereto [ðεəˈtuː] adv. 另外，往那里，到那

auxiliary [ɔːgˈziljəri] adj. 辅助的，补助的

indulge in v. 沉湎于

narcotic [nɑːˈkɔtik] n. 麻醉药，致幻毒品，镇静剂 adj. 麻醉的，催眠的

smuggle [ˈsmʌgl] n. 走私，偷带 v. 走私

deface [diˈfeis] vt. 损伤外观，丑化，使失面子

abuse [əˈbjuːz] n. 滥用，虐待，辱骂，陋习，弊端 v. 滥用，虐待，辱骂

pilfer [ˈpilfə] v. 盗，偷，窃

dump [dʌmp] vt. 倾倒（垃圾），倾卸 n. 堆存处

receptacle [riˈseptəkl] n. 容器，[植] 花托，[电工] 插座

indecent [inˈdiːsnt] adj. 下流的，猥亵的，〈口〉不像样的，不妥当的

recur [riˈkəː] vi. 复发，重现，再来

rating [ˈreitiŋ] n. 等级级别（尤指军阶），额定，责骂，申斥

be obligated to do sth 有义务做某事

see to v. 负责，注意

immigration [ˌimiˈgreiʃən] n. 外来的移民，移居入境

citizenship [ˈsitizənʃip] n. 公民的身份，公民的职责和权力

deportation [ˌdipɔːˈteiʃən] n. 移送，充军，放逐

imprisonment [imˈprizənmənt] n. 关押

stereo [ˈstiəriəu] n. 立体声系统，立体声，[印] 铅版，立体照片

declaration [ˌdekləˈreiʃən] n. 宣布，宣言，声明

manifest [ˈmænifest] n. 载货单，旅客名单 adj. 显然的，明白的 vi. 出现 vt. 表明，证明

cancellation [kænsəˈleiʃən] n. 取消

denial [diˈnaiəl] n. 否认，否定，谢绝，拒绝

Nassau [ˈnæsɔː] 拿骚（巴哈马首都）

formality [fɔːˈmæliti] n. 拘谨，礼节，仪式，正式手续，拘泥形式

be subject to 服从，遭受

berthing 停泊地，船边或隔间的钢板

antenna [ænˈtenə] n. 天线

smuggling n. 走私

turn away v. 不准……入内，走开，转过脸，解雇，避免，防止

offensive [əˈfensiv] adj. 讨厌的，无礼的，攻击性的 n. 进攻，攻势

fixture [ˈfikstʃə] n. 固定设备，预定日期，比赛时间，工作夹具

sunbathe [ˈsʌnbeið] v. 日光浴，太阳灯浴

vacate [vəˈkeit] v. 腾出，空出，离（职），退（位）

watch [wɔtʃ] n. 注视，注意，手表，看守，守护，监视，值班人 vt. 看，注视，照顾，监视

loiter [ˈlɔitə] v. 闲荡，虚度，徘徊

immaculate [iˈmækjulit] adj. 完美的

see through v. 看穿，识破

apparel [əˈpærəl] n. 衣服，装饰

attire [əˈtaiə] n. 服装

as brief as possible 尽可能简单

launder [ˈlɔːndə, ˈlɑːndə] n. 流水槽 v. 洗涤，清洗，洗黑钱

beeper n. 能发出哔哔声音的仪器

consequence [ˈkɔnsikwəns] n. 结果，[逻] 推理，推论，因果关系

abide by v. 坚持，遵守

Appendix 2

Disciplinary Rules, Regulations & Procedures

Offences	1st step	2nd step	3rd step
Assault on fellow crew member	Discharge		
Cooperating with or overlooking smugglers	Discharge		
Dishonesty	Discharge		
Drinking while on duty	Discharge		
Fighting	Discharge		
Going to passenger's cabin(except in the line of duty)	Discharge		
Misconduct towards passengers	Discharge		
Possession of illegal weapons	Discharge		
Reporting for work under the influence of alcohol & drugs	Discharge		
Smuggling	Discharge		
Smuggling stowaways	Discharge		
Solicitations of tips	Discharge		
Taking passengers to crew areas	Discharge		
Theft of company's or other crew members' property	Discharge		
Threatening fellow crew members	Discharge		
Use of other crew member's ID card	Discharge		
Solicitation of good comments	Discharge		
Sexual harassment	Discharge		
Use of public or passenger areas (crew)	Discharge		
Failure to abide by any ship's rules and regulations	Written warning	Discharge	
Losing crew pass	Written warning	Written warning	Discharge
Missing the ship on departure from port	Written warning	Written warning	Discharge
Having food in cabin	Written warning	Written warning	Discharge

continued

Offences	1st step	2nd step	3rd step
Failure to comply with immigration and customs rules	Written warning	Written warning	Discharge
No reporting to immigration officials when requested	Written warning	Written warning	Discharge
Late for immigration crew check	Written warning	Written warning	Discharge
Failure to report to crew purser when returning from leave or vacation	Written warning	Written warning	Discharge
Insubordination	Written warning	Written warning	Discharge
Misuse or damage of company's property	Written warning	Written warning	Discharge
Refusal to follow supervisor's order	Written warning	Written warning	Discharge
Smoking in unauthorized areas or while on duty	Written warning	Written warning	Discharge
Passing through passenger areas where not allowed	Written warning	Written warning	Discharge
Using passenger elevators	Written warning	Written warning	Discharge
Not taking salary on pay-day	Written warning	Written warning	Discharge
Being absent from fire and boat drill	Written warning	Written warning	Discharge
Cabin found dirty during inspection	Written warning	Written warning	Discharge
Abusive language	Written warning	Written warning	Discharge
Not wearing name tag	Written warning	Written warning	Discharge
Not having safety booklet during drills	Written warning	Written warning	Discharge
Boarding vessel late	Verbal warning	Written warning	Discharge
Failure to report injury or accident to self or others	Verbal warning	Written warning	Discharge
Inability to cooperate with other crew members	Verbal warning	Written warning	Discharge
Late for duty	Written warning	Written warning	Discharge
Leaving duty without proper permission	Written warning	Written warning	Discharge

Take a cruise ship as an example.

Notes

1. Assault on fellow crew member. 攻击船员同事。
2. Cooperating with or overlooking smugglers. 与走私者合作或放任走私者。
3. Misconduct towards passengers. 对乘客行为不当。
4. Smuggling stowaways. 偷运偷乘船者。
5. Solicitations of tips. 索要小费。
6. Sexual harassment. 性骚扰。
7. Not taking salary on pay-day. 发薪日不领薪水。
8. Abusive language. 辱骂性语言。

New words & expressions

assault [əˈsɔːlt] n. 攻击，袭击 v. 袭击

smuggler [ˋsmʌglə(r)] n. 走私者，走私船，走私犯

in the line of duty 执行公务（尤指军事任务），履行职责，尽职

dishonesty [disˈɔnisti] n. 不诚实，不老实，欺骗，欺诈

overlook [ˌəuvəˈluk] vt. 放任 耸出，远眺，没注意到 n. 眺望，俯瞰中的景色

misconduct [misˈkɔndʌkt] vt. 处理不当，干坏事 n. 不正当的行为，明知故犯

stowaway [ˈstəuəˈwei] n. 偷渡者，匿身处

drug [drʌg] n. 药，麻药，麻醉药，滞销货 vi. 〈俗〉吸毒 vt. 使服毒品，毒化

solicitation [səˌlisiˈteiʃən] n. 恳求，恳请，诱惑，引发

theft [θeft] n. 偷，行窃，偷窃的事例，偷窃行为

harassment [ˈhærəsmənt] n. 折磨，骚扰

immigration [ˌimiˈgreiʃən] n. 外来的移民，移居入境

insubordination [ˈinsəˌbɔːdiˈneiʃən] n. 不顺从，反抗

misuse [ˈmisˈjuːz] v. 误用，错用，滥用，虐待 n. 误用，错用，滥用

unauthorized [ˈʌnˈɔːθəraizd] adj. 未被授权的，未经认可的

abusive [əˈbjuːsiv] adj. 辱骂的，滥用的

refusal [riˈfjuːzəl] n. 拒绝，推却，优先取舍权，优先取舍的机会

name tag 胸牌

pass through v. 经过，通过

property [ˈprɔpəti] n. 财产，所有物，所有权，性质，特性，(小) 道具

failure [ˈfeiljə] n. 失败，失败者，缺乏，失灵，故障，破产，疏忽

permission [pə(ː)ˈmiʃən] n. 许可，允许

Appendix 3

Code of Appearance for Crew Members Onboard

It is important that passengers have every confidence in the staff who are going to give service to them. The passenger's expectations will be of staff who are neat, clean, and tidy and show that they have taken as much care of themselves as they are likely to take care of the customers. They will expect similar standards to those who offer professional service in high quality hotels ashore.

The objective of a set of standards is consistency. When consistency is applied to people it is called 'fairness'. People who feel they are being treated fairly have greater respect for supervision and company requirements. The following code will lead to a consistent standard of appearance to our customers. To make it fair, exceptions cannot be allowed.

Entertainers must also adhere to the appearance standards as laid out below when in public spaces. It is recognized that standards of makeup and costume will be different when performing on stage.

The standards are split into Grooming, Jewellery and Uniforms (take a cruise ship as an example).

1. Grooming

Every crew member should present themselves, when on duty, with a smart and clean appearance. Mirrors are posted at all entrances to passenger areas onboard and these should be used each time when you enter such an area to check if your appearance is up to standard.

(1) Hair A neat natural style with a conservative cut. If bleached or dyed, to be maintained as natural looking as possible with no unnatural colors e. g. blue, green, silver. If hairsprays and gels are used they should be kept to a minimum.

Ladies-Hair should be off the face and if longer than shoulder length, to be tied at back of head or plaited when on duty, using company supplied bow. If a hair band is used for shorter hair, it should be black in color.

Men-Length never to exceed shirt collar. Hair can be short but no totally shaved 'skinhead' look.

(2) Facial hair Men are to be clean-shaven when on duty. An unshaven appearance offends. Daily shaving is required and for those who have a heavy growth they may have to shave twice daily. Moustaches are acceptable, but they must be fully grown and kept neatly trimmed. Beards including goatee beards are not acceptable. (Exceptions to this are for those individuals hired before the establishment of this policy)

(3) Body Hair Female staff who wear shorts as part of their uniforms must make sure their legs are free from hair.

(4) Tattoos Exposed tattoos offend in a service situation. Any tattoos should be covered when on duty.

(5) Makeup Lipstick. Only company approved lipstick (on sale in the crew shop at cost price) may be worn on duty. This should be applied sparingly and not outside the natural lip line. No separate lip outline is used.

Company approved lipsticks: Margaret Astor, Soft Sensation 410; Margaret Astor, Soft Sensation 497; Margaret Astor, Soft Sensation 800.

Eyeliners and shadow. These are acceptable when applied in neutral colors that are close to the skin tone and create a natural blended look. Eye shadow should not extend beyond the natural eye area. Eyeliner should not extend beyond the corner of the eye. Mascara may be applied lightly in shades of brown or black and eyebrow pencil should only applied lightly to highlight the brows in shades as close to the natural hair color as possible.

Foundation. Neutral colors should be chosen in a shade complimentary to the skin tone. No use of any form of makeup is acceptable for men.

(6) Nails Fingernails should be kept trimmed. They should be no longer than the end of the fingertip. Accumulated dirt under the fingernail is unacceptable. For females, company approved varnishes may be used from the slop chest. Chipped varnish should be removed or replaced. False nails are unacceptable.

Company approved nail varnishes; Margaret Astor, '60sec' Wonderlast 08; Margaret Astor, Ultra Diamond 220; Margaret Astor, Ultra Diamond 800.

(7) Fragrances Due to close contact with customers and fellow crew members, the use of underarm antiperspirant or deodorant is required. For the same reasons, the use of strong heavy scents or fragrances is unacceptable. If you choose to wear after-shave, perfume or eau de toilette, please be considerate to others and use a light, mild scent.

(8) Personal Cleanliness In warm climate it is essential to shower once a day and in warm service environments it is recommended to shower at least twice a day. Not only does showering freshen up the body but it removes bacteria and sweat from the skin which can cause offensive smells, especially if strong flavored foods have been consumed. Areas that need most attention are under the arms, between the legs and the feet. Hot water showers, towels and soap are freely provided by the ship.

2. Jewellery

Service staff are not allowed to wear excessive jewellery. They collect dirt and bacteria and can become hazardous in a service environment. Additionally excessive jewellery can give the customer the impression that the crew are "well off" and this could negatively affect the customer's decision to pay a tip.

(1) Watches Service staff can wear a watch. Straps, faces and backs should be kept clean.

Food handlers i. e. galley staff should not wear watches when working with food.

(2) Earrings Ladies-a single stud or ring worn on the earlobe is acceptable when on duty. Multiple studs, dangle or hoop rings are unacceptable.

Men - no earrings allowed.

(3) Piercings No visible pierced jewellery is acceptable to customers and is not to be worn on duty

(4) Rings Staff should not wear an excessive number of rings or oversized rings when on duty. One ring per hand on middle or ring finger. A ring should be no wider than 1/2 cm. The exception being a wedding set.

Food handlers i. e. galley staff should remove any rings when working with food.

(5) Chains & pendants If worn on duty, any neck jewellery visible to the customers, should be limited to a simple chain necklace.

(6) Bangle & Bracelets Wrist and arm jewellery is not to be worn on duty. This includes ankle bracelets and belly chains.

3. Uniforms

Uniforms and the free laundering of those uniforms are to provide a standardized and professional image of our crew. They should be kept clean, repaired and worn correctly.

(1) Shirts/Blouses On open necked shirts or blouses, only the top (neck) button will be left undone.

Shirts or blouses that are worn with a tie should be buttoned completely.

Long sleeved shirts or blouses should have their sleeves rolled down and be buttoned at the cuff during service. Sleeves may only be rolled up when handling stores or working in pantries.

(2) Jackets When a jacket is part of the uniform, this should be buttoned at all times.

(3) Skirts A skirt should be flat fronted without pleats or pockets. It may have a single slit at the back, but no more 4 inches (10cm) . The bottom of a skirt should be worn

no higher than 4 inches (10cm) above the kneecap. A simple black belt must be worn with a skirt. Officer's dress skirts should be worn no longer than ankle length.

(4) Trousers Black trousers provided to crew members should be flat fronted with pleats, have no side stripe or turn-ups. They should not be a jeans type, baggy or flared. The trouser leg bottom should cover the back of the shoe. Trousers are to be worn with a plain black belt.

(5) Tights & Stockings Black tights or stockings should be worn with black and green skirts. Flesh colored tights or stockings should be worn at all other times including the time of wearing a white skirt. Self-grip stockings, if used, should be strong enough not to slide down the leg. If suspenders are worn, clips should not outline in a skirt or dress.

Exception: staff whose duties require them to wear shorts when plain white socks without logo or colored tops should be worn.

(6) Socks Men—Black socks must be worn when on duty at all times.

Exception: Staff whose duties require them to wear shorts when plain white socks without logo or colored tops should be worn.

(7) Shoes It is recommended that leather shoes be worn as they allow feet to breathe. They should be comfortable, as service staff will spend many hours on their feet. It is also recommended that rubber-soled shoes be worn in food areas for a safety precaution.

It is also advisable to have two pairs of the same style shoes so that they can be rested.

Male—Smart black, slip on or laced shoe, with plain toe is acceptable. If heeled this should not be more than 3 cm high. No thick or heavy soles, no buckles, no patent (shiny) leather.

Exception—Staff whose duties require them to wear shorts. Plain white, low-heeled trainers with no obvious logos should be worn.

Female service staff—Smart plain black flat shoe or with a heel to a maximum of 3 cms. high. No thick soles or platform heels. No open toes or open back and without ankle strap.

Exception—Staff whose duties require them to wear shorts. Plain white, low-heeled trainers with no obvious logos should be worn.

Female housekeeping staff—Plain white flat slip on shoes or with a heel to a maximum of 3 cms. high. No open toes or open back and without ankle strap.

For those positions requiring safety shoes, these will be provided on board.

(8) Additional points for officers Daytime uniforms are white. Plain white shoes of canvas or leather should be worn. These may be flat but any heel should not be more than 3 cms. high.

Men should wear plain white socks with no colored tops or logo.

A white belt with simple buckle needs to be worn with trousers or skirt.

In the evening high collared white jackets are worn. White T-shirts without logo will make wearing these more comfortable.

For formal evenings when mess uniforms are worn, a black cummerbund should be worn between shirt and trousers/skirt. Males should have a set of plain black dress studs and cuff links.

Notes

1. offer professional service in high quality 提供高质量专业服务
2. The objective of a set of standards is consistency. 一套标准的目标是一致性。
3. consistent standard 一致标准
4. Entertainers must also adhere to the appearance standards as laid out below when in public spaces. 在公共区间时，款待者（服务人员）也必须遵循以下列举的外貌标准。
5. make sure their legs are free from hair 确保他们的腿没有毛发
6. Exposed tattoos offend in a service situation. 在服务工作状况下，暴露文身是违规的。
7. at cost price 以成本价
8. the natural lip line 天然唇线
9. No separate lip outline is used. 不要使用单独的唇轮廓线。
10. Eyeliners and eye shadow. 眼线和眼影。
11. skin tone 肤色
12. create a natural blended look 创造一个自然协调的外观
13. eyebrow pencil 眉笔
14. slop chest （船上供应日用品的）小卖部
15. eau de toilette 淡香水
16. Chipped varnish should be removed or replaced. 有缺口的指甲油应该去掉或重新上。
17. false nails 假指甲
18. the use of underarm antiperspirant or deodorant is required. 腋下止汗剂或除臭剂的使用是必需的。
19. offensive smells 令人讨厌的气味
20. well off 富裕的
21. a single stud or ring worn on the earlobe is acceptable when on duty 上班时耳垂上可带一个耳钉或耳环
22. Multiple studs，dangle or hoop rings are unacceptable. 戴多个耳钉、耳环和戒指是不可接受的。
23. oversized rings 太大的戒指
24. This includes ankle bracelets and belly chains. 这包括脚踝手镯和腹部链。
25. Bangle & Bracelets 手镯和手链
26. free laundering 免费洗烫（衣物等）
27. Long sleeved shirts or blouses should have their sleeves rolled down and be buttoned at the cuff during service. 服务时，长袖衬衫或上衣应该把袖子放下来，将袖口扣好。
28. A simple black belt must be worn with a skirt. 穿裙子时必须配一条简单的黑色腰带。
29. have no side stripe or turn-ups 不要有边纹或翻边（卷边）
30. They should not be a jeans type，baggy or flared. 裤子不能是牛仔裤，也不能过于宽大或向外翻出。
31. Trousers are to be worn with a plain black belt. 穿裤子时应配一条简洁的黑皮带。
32. flesh colored tights 肉色紧身裤
33. self-grip stockings 有弹性（能自己固定）的长袜

34. rubber-soled shoes　橡胶底鞋

35. Plain white，low-heeled trainers with no obvious logos should be worn. 应该穿纯白色的低跟运动鞋，并且不要有太明显的标志。

New words & expressions

appearance [ə'piərəns] n. 出现，露面，外貌，外观

confidence ['kɔnfidəns] n. 信心

objective [əb'dʒektiv] n. 目标，目的

consistency [kən'sistənsi] n. 联结，结合，坚固性，一致性，连贯

fairness ['fɛənis] n. 公平，正直，美好，明亮，清晰，适当，顺利性

laid out below　以下列举的

makeup ['meikʌp] n. 天性，化妆品，补充，组成，结构，补考，体格

costume ['kɔstjuːm，-'tjuːm] n. 装束，服装

adhere [əd'hiə] vi. 黏附，胶着，坚持 v. 坚持

be up to　一直到，等于

bleach [bliːtʃ] v. 漂白，变白

gel [dʒel] n. 凝胶体 v. 成冻胶

hairspray　n. 头发定型剂

plait [plæt] n. 辫子 vt. 把……打成辫

skinhead ['skinhed] n. 理平头的男人

offend [ə'fend] v. 犯罪，冒犯，违反，得罪，使……不愉快

beard [biəd] n. 胡须

goatee [gəu'tiː] n. 山羊胡子，(只留于下颚的) 胡子

tattoo [tə'tuː，tæ'tuː] v. 刺花样 n. 纹身

sparingly　adv. 节俭地，保守地

lipstick ['lipstik] n. 〈美〉口红，唇膏

outline ['əutlain] n. 大纲，轮廓，略图，外形，要点，概要 vt. 描画轮廓，略述

eyeliner ['ailainə(r)] n. 眼线膏

tone [təun] n. 音调，音质，语调，色调 vt. 调和，增强

mascara [mæs'kɑːrə] n. 染眉毛油 vi. 涂染眉毛油

fingernail ['fiŋgəneil] n. 手指甲

varnish ['vɑːniʃ] n. 清漆，凡立水，光泽面，掩饰 v. 修饰

slop chest　发给海员的储备商品

ultra ['ʌltrə] adj. 过激的，极端的 n. 过激论者，急进论者

underarm ['ʌndərɑːm] adj. 手臂下的，腋下的

antiperspirant ['ænti'pəːspirənt] n. [医] 止汗药，防汗药

deodorant [diː'əudərənt] n. 除臭剂 adj. 除臭的

fragrance ['freigrəns] n. 芬芳，香气，香味

perfume ['pəːfjuːm] n. 香味，芳香，香水 vt. 使发香，洒香水于

strap [stræp] n. 带，皮带 vt. 用带缚住，用带捆扎

stud [stʌd] n. 大头钉，饰纽，柱头螺栓，马群 v. 用饰纽装饰，散布

earlobe [ˈiələub] n. 耳垂 n. [解] 耳垂

dangle [ˈdæŋgl] v. 摇摆

hoop [huːp] n. 箍，铁环，戒指，篮 v. 加箍于，环绕

pierce [piəs] vt. 刺穿，刺破，穿透，突破，深深感动

bangle [ˈbæŋgl] n. 手镯，脚镯

bracelet [ˈbreislit] n. 手镯

blouse [blauz] n. 宽松的上衣，似衬衫的上衣

undone [ˈʌnˈdʌn] adj. 未完成的，破灭的 v. undo 的过去分词

cuff [ˈkʌf] n. 袖口，裤子翻边，护腕，手铐 vt. 给……上袖口（或翻边）

pleat [pliːt] n. 褶，褶状物 vt. 使……打褶

slit [slit] vt. 切开 n. 裂缝，狭长切口

kneecap [ˈniːkæp] n. 膝盖骨，护膝

turn-ups 衣服的卷起部分

baggy [ˈbægi] adj. 袋状的，松垂的

flare [flɛə] n. 闪光，闪耀 vt. 使闪耀，使张开

grip [grip] vt. 紧握，紧夹 n. 掌握，控制，把手 v. 抓住

self-grip stockings 紧身袜

suspender [səˈspendə(r)] n. 吊裤带，悬挂物，吊杆，袜吊

clip [klip] n. 夹子，回形针，子弹夹 vt. 夹住，剪短，修剪

rubber-soled shoes 橡胶底鞋

heel [hiːl] n. 脚后跟，踵，跟部

laced [leist] adj. 有花边的，绑带子的，加酒的

buckle [ˈbʌkl] n. 带扣 v. 扣住，变弯曲

patent [ˈpeitənt，ˈpætənt] adj. 显著的，明白的，新奇的

trainer [ˈtreinə] n. 训练者，驯服者，驯马师，软运动鞋

ankle [ˈæŋkl] n. [解] 踝

canvas [ˈkænvəs] v. 彻底讨论探究 n. 帆布

cummerbund [ˈkʌməbʌnd] n. （印度男人的）腹带，徽带，装饰带

cuff links 袖口连扣

Appendix 4

ISM Code Booklet

This Booklet is an introductory guide to the International Safety Management Code and its principal requirements. The contents of this booklet are intentionally kept very simple so that everybody reading it will understand the philosophy of the ISM Code. If you require more details on a specific part of the code, please refer to the full official text reprinted at the end of this booklet.

This is a personal copy for you to keep. Please write your name in the space provided.

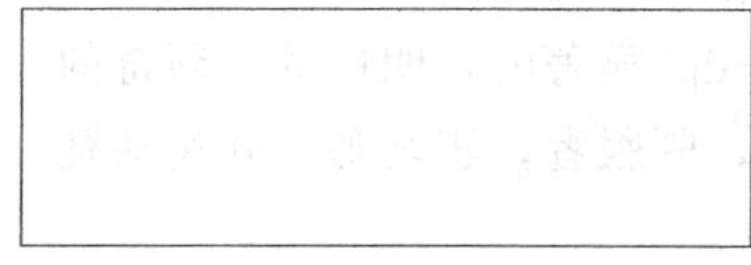

1. What Is The ISM Code

The ISM Code is the standard for establishing a system for the SAFE management and operation of vessels and for POLLUTION PREVENTION. This system will have to be approved by the flag administration, or an organization recognized by it, then a certificate is issued. Think of it as a license to be a ship operator.

2. Your Company Will Have To Be Certificated

For the first time in history-the company ashore (the office-not just the ship) has to be approved and have a certificate. (Like the license an airline needs to be an aircraft operator). Would you fly on an airplane run by a company which is not certificated?

3. There Are At Least 4 Reasons To Adopt The ISM Code

(1) It makes your ship a safer place to work It provides for safe working practices and develops a safe working environment on board for your ship.

(2) It protects the sea and the marine environment.

(3) It clearly defines your job and therefore it makes it easier for you.

(4) It's the law. Compliance to the ISM Code is required by Chapter IX of SOLAS 74 Convention. It is therefore mandatory. Deadline for tankers, bulk carriers and passenger ships is not later than July 1998. For all other ships July 2002.

Notes

1. understand the philosophy of the ISM Code 理解 ISM 规则的哲理
2. ISM Code (International Safety Management Code) 国际安全管理规则
3. be approved by the flag administration 经船旗国管理部门批准
4. marine environment 海洋环境
5. compliance to the ISM Code 遵守 ISM 规则
6. SOLAS (Convention on the Safety of Life at Sea) 国际海上人命安全公约
7. IMO (International Maritime Organization) 国际海事组织
8. IMCO (Intergovernmental Maritime Consultative Organization) (联合国) 政府间海事协商组织

4. What Is The Role Of The Seafarer

The seafarers are very important in working with the system. They are the ones who make it work/happen. They are the end user of the system. Their participation and involvement is required during the development and implementation stage.

5. ISM Code Requirements

The ISM Code is divided in 13 sections

(1) Section 1 "General". An introduction to the general purpose of the code and its objectives.

(2) Section 2 "Safety and environmental protection policy". The Company must put in writing its policy on the safety and the protection of the marine environment and make sure that everyone knows it and follows it.

(3) Section 3 "Company's responsibilities and authorities". The company must have sufficient & suitable people (in the office and on vessels) with clearly defined roles & responsibilities (who is responsible for what).

(4) Section 4 "Designated person ashore". The Company must appoint a person in the office responsible for monitoring and following all "SAFETY" matters of the vessels.

(5) Section 5 "Master's responsibility & authority". The Master is responsible for making the system work on board. He must help his crew in following the system and give them instructions when necessary.

The Master is the boss on the ship and he can override the office on "SAFETY" and "POLLUTION PROTECTION" matters.

(6) Section 6 "Resources & personnel". The Company must employ the "right" people on board and in the office and make sure that all of them:

① know what their duties are;

② receive instructions on how to carry out their duties;

③ get trained when and if necessary.

(7) Section 7 "Development of plans for shipboard operations". "*Play What You Do-Do What You Plan*", You need to plan your work on the ship and follow your plan when working.

(8) Section 8 "Emergency Preparedness". You should be prepared for the unexpected (emergency). It can happen any time. The company should develop plans for responding to emergency situations on board its vessels and practice them.

(9) Section 9 "Report and analysis of non-conformities, accidents and hazardous occurrences". No person and system is perfect. The good thing about this system is that it gives you a way to correct it and improve it. When you find something wrong (including accidents and hazardous situations), report it. It will be analyzed and the whole system can be improved.

(10) Section 10 "Maintenance of the ship and equipment". The vessel and its equipment must be maintained in a good condition. You should always comply with the rules and regulations. Always maintain and frequently test those pieces of equipment important for your safety.

Keep records of the work carried out.

(11) Section 11 "Documentation". Your working system (Safety Management System-SMS) must be put in writing (documented), and controlled. Such documents must be available both in the office and on the ships. You must also control all your paperwork related to the system. (i. e. record and forms)

(12) Section 12 "Company verification review and evaluation". The Company must have its own internal methods for making sure that the system works and is improving.

(13) Section 13 "Certification, verification and control". The flag administration or an organization recognized by it, will have to send external auditors to check the company's system in the office and on board each ship. After it has satisfied itself that the system is working the flag administration will issue a certificate of compliance for the office and a safety management certificate for each ship.

ISM "SAFETY MANAGEMENT CERTIFICATE" (VESSEL)	ISM "DOCUMENT OF COMPLIANCE" (OFFICE)

Notes

1. They are the end user of the system. 他们是这个制度的最终执行者。

2. the development and implementation stage 发展与实施阶段

3. The Company must put in writing its policy on the safety and the protection of the marine environment. 公司必须对安全及海洋环境保护的政策形成书面文件。

4. He can override the office on "SAFETY" and "POLLUTION PROTECTION" matters. 在"安全"和"环境保护"的问题方面，他可以凌驾于办公室之上。
5. Keep records of the work carried out. 将执行的工作记录在案。
6. external auditors 外部审计员

INTERNATIONAL MANAGEMENT CODE FOR THE SAFE OPERATION OF SHIPS AND FOR POLLUTION PREVENTION

[International Safety Management (ISM) Code]

SAFETY AND POLLUTION-PREVENTION MANAGEMENT REQUIREMENTS

Contents

Preamble

(1) The purpose of this code is to provide an international standard for the safe management and operation of ships and for pollution prevention.

(2) The assembly adopted resolution A. 443 (Ⅺ), by which it invited all governments to take the necessary steps to safeguard the ship master in the proper discharge of his responsibilities with regard to maritime safety and the protection of the marine environment.

(3) The assembly also adopted resolution A. 680 (17), by which it further recognized the need for appropriate organization of management to enable it to respond to the need of whose on board ships to achieve and maintain high standards of safety and environmental protection.

(4) Recognizing that no two shipping companies or shipowners are the same, and that

ships operate under a wide range of different conditions, the code is based on general principles and objectives.

(5) The Code is expressed in broad terms so that it can have a widespread application. Clearly, different levels of management, whether shore-based or at sea, will require varying levels of knowledge and awareness of the items outlined.

(6) The cornerstones of good safety management is commitment from the top. In matters of safety and pollution prevention it is the commitment, competence, attitudes and motivation of individuals at all levels that determines the end result.

1. General

1.1 Definitions

1.1.1 *International Safety Management* (*ISM*) *Code* means the International Management Code for the Safe Operation of Ships and for Pollution Prevention as adopted by the assembly, as many be amended by the organization.

1.1.2 *Company* means the owner of the ship or any other organization or person such as the manager, or the bareboat charterer, who has assumed the responsibility of operation of the ship from the shipowner and who on assuming such responsibility has agreed to take over all the duties and responsibility imposed by the code.

1.1.3 *Administration* means the government of the state whose flag the ship entitled to fly.

1.2 objectives

1.2.1 The objectives of the code are to ensure safety at sea, prevention of human injury or loss of life, and avoidance of damage to the environment, in particular to marine environment, and to property.

1.2.2 Safety-management objectives of the company:

Inter alia:

(1) provide for safe practices in ship operation and a safe working environment;

(2) establish safeguards against all identified risks;

(3) continuously improve safety-management skills of personnel ashore and aboard ships, including preparing for emergencies related both to safety and environmental protection.

1.2.3 The safety-management system should ensure:

(1) compliance with mandatory rules and regulations;

(2) that applicable codes, guidelines and standards recommended by the organization, administration, classification societies and maritime industry organization are taken into account.

1.3 Application

The requirements of this code may be applied to all ships.

1.4 Functional requirements for a Safety-Management System (SMS)

Every Company should develop, implement and maintain a safety-management system (SMS) which includes the following functional requirements:

(1) a safety and environmental-protection policy;

(2) instructions and procedures to ensure safe operation of ships and protection of the environment in compliance with relevant international and flag state legislation;

(3) defined levels of authority and lines of communication between, and amongst, shore and shipboard personnel;

(4) procedures for reporting accidents and non-conformities with the provisions of this code;

(5) procedures to prepare for and respond to emergency situations;

(6) procedures for internal audits and management reviews.

2. Safety and Environmental Protection Policy

2.1 The Company should establish a safety and environmental-protection policy which describes how the objectives given in paragraph 1.2 will be achieved.

2.2 The company should ensure that the policy is implemented and maintained at all levels of the organization, both ship-based as well as shore-based.

3. Company Responsibilities and Authority

3.1 If the entity who is responsible for the operation of the ship is other than the owner, the owner must report the full name and details of such entity to the administration.

3.2 The company should define and document the responsibility, authority and interrelation of all personnel who manage, perform and verify work relating to and affecting safety and pollution prevention.

3.3 The company is responsible for ensuring that adequate resources and shore-based support are provided to enable the designated person or persons to carry out their functions.

4. Designated Person(s)

To ensure the safe operation of each ship and to provide a link between the company and those on board, every company, as appropriate, should designate a person or persons ashore having direct access to the highest level of management. The responsibility and authority of the designated person or persons should include monitoring the safety and pollution-prevention aspects of the operation of each ship and ensuring that adequate resources and shore-based support are applied, as required.

5. Master's Responsibility and Authority

5.1 The Company should clearly define and document the master's responsibility with regard to:

(1) implementing the safety and environmental-protection policy of the company;

(2) motivating the crew in the observation of that policy;

(3) issuing appropriate orders and instructions in a clear and simple manner;

(4) verifying that specified requirements are observed;

(5) reviewing the SMS and reporting its deficiencies to the shore-based management.

5.2 The Company should ensure that the SMS operating on board the ship contains a clear statement emphasizing the master's authority. The company should establish in the SMS that the master has the overriding authority and the responsibility to make decisions with respect to safety and pollution prevention and to request the company's assistance as may be necessary.

6. Resources and Personnel

6.1 The company should ensure that the master is:

(1) properly qualified for command;

(2) fully conversant with the company's SMS;

(3) given the necessary support so that the master's duties can be safely performed.

6.2 The company should ensure that each ship is manned with qualified certificated and medically fit seafarers in accordance with national and international requirements.

6.3 The company should establish procedures to ensure that new personnel and personnel transferred to new assignments related to safety and protection of the environment are given proper familiarization with their duties. Instructions which are essential to be provided prior to sailing should be identified, documented and given.

6.4 The Company should ensure that all personnel involved in the company's SMS have an adequate understanding of relevant rules, regulations, codes and guidelines.

6.5 The Company should establish and maintain procedures for identifying any training which may be required in support of the safety management system and ensure that such training is provided for all personnel concerned.

6.6 The Company should establish procedures by which the ship's personnel receive relevant information on the safety management system in a working language or languages understood by them.

6.7 The Company should ensure that the ship's personnel are able to communicate effectively in the execution of their duties related to the safety management system.

7. Development of Plans for Shipboard Operations

The company should establish procedures for the preparation of plans and instructions for key shipboard operations concerning the safety of the ship and the prevention of pollution. The various tasks involved should be defined and assigned to qualified personnel.

8. Emergency Preparedness

8.1 The company should establish procedures to identify, describe and respond to potential emergency shipboard situations.

8.2 The company should establish programmes for drills and exercises to prepare for emergency actions.

8.3 The SMS should provide for measures ensuring that the company's organization can respond at any time to hazards, accidents and emergency situations involving its ships.

9. Reports and Analysis of Non-conformities, Accidents and Hazardous Occurrences

9.1 The SMS should include procedures ensuring that non-conformities, accidents and hazardous situations are reported to the company, investigated and hazardous situations are reported to the Company, investigated and analyzed with the objective of improving safety and pollution prevention.

9.2 The company should establish procedures for the implementation of corrective action.

10. Maintenance of the Ship and Equipment

10.1 The company should establish procedures to ensure that the ship is maintained in conformity with the provisions of the relevant rules and regulations and with any additional requirements which may be established by the company.

10.2 In meeting these requirements the company should ensure that:

(1) inspections are held at appropriate intervals;

(2) any non-conformity is reported, with its possible cause, if known;

(3) appropriate corrective action is taken;

(4) records of these activities are maintained.

10.3 The company should establish procedures in its SMS to identify equipment and technical systems the sudden operational failure of which may result in hazardous situations. The SMS should provide for specific measures aimed at promoting the reliability of such equipment or systems. These measures should include the regular testing stand-by arrangements and equipment or technical systems that are not in continuous use.

10.4 the inspections mentioned in 10.2 as well as the measures referred to in 10.3 should be integrated into the ship's operational maintenance routine.

11. Documention

11.1 The company should establish and maintain procedures to control all documents and data which are relevant to the SMS.

11.2 The Company should establish and maintain procedures to control all documents and data which are relevant to the SMS.

(1) valid documents are available at all relevant locations;

(2) changes to documents are received and approved by authorized personnel; and

(3) obsolete documents are promptly removed.

11.3 The documents used to describe and implement the SMS may be referred to as the Safety Management Manual. Documentation should be keep in a form that the company considers most effective. Each ship should carry on board all documentation relevant to that ship.

12. Company Verification, Review and Evaluation

12.1 The company should carry out internal safety audits to verify whether safety and pollution-prevention activities comply with the SMS.

12.2 The company should periodically evaluate the efficiency of and, when needed, review the SMS in accordance with procedures established by the company.

12.3 The audits and possible corrective actions should be carried out in accordance with documented procedures.

12.4 Personnel carrying out audits should be independent of the areas being audits unless this is impracticable due to the size and the nature of the company.

12.5 The results of the audits and reviews should be brought to the attention of all personnel having responsibility in the area involved.

12.6 The management personnel responsible for the area involved should take timely corrective action on deficiencies found.

13. Certification, Verification and Control

13.1 The ship should be operated by a company which is issued a document of compliance relevant to that ship.

13.2 A document of compliance should be issued for every company complying with the requirements of the SMS Code by the administration, by an organization recognized by the administration or by government of the country acting on behalf of the administration in which the company has chosen to conduct its business.

This document should be accepted as evidence that the company is capable of complying with the requirements of the code.

13.3 A copy of such a document should be placed on board in order that master, if so asked, may produce it for verification of the administration or organizations recognized by it.

13.4 A certificate, called a Safety Management Certificate, should be issued to a ship by the administration or organization recognized by the administration. The administration should, when issuing the certificate, verify that the company and its shipboard management operate in accordance with the approved SMS.

13.5 The administration or an organization recognized by the administration should periodically verify the proper functioning of the ship's SMS as approved.

Notes

1. to safeguard the ship master in the proper discharge of his responsibilities 保障船长（能够）适当地履行职责
2. operate under a wide range of different conditions 在各种不同的条件下运行
3. from the top 从一开始
4. the bareboat charterer 光船承租人
5. avoidance of damage to the environment 避免对环境造成损害
6. inter alia 除了别的以外，特别
7. relevant international and flag state legislation 有关国际和船旗国的立法
8. If the entity who is responsible for the operation of the ship is other than the owner, the owner must report the full name and details of such entity to the administration. 如果负责船舶作业的企业不是船主，船主必须向管理当局报告该企业的全称和详细情况。
9. motivating the crew in the observation of that policy 激励船员遵守那一政策
10. the overriding authority 高于一切的权利
11. fully conversant with the company's SMS 充分了解公司的安全管理制度
12. The company should establish procedures for the implementation of corrective action. 公司应制定纠正措施的实施程序。
13. Inspections are held at appropriate intervals. 检查在适当的间隔时间举行。
14. Obsolete documents are promptly removed. 作废的文件应被及时删除。
15. be independent of the areas 与这些区域无关
16. The administration or an organization recognized by the administration should periodically

verify the proper functioning of the ship's SMS as approved. 行政当局或政府认可的组织应定期按要求核实该船的正常运作情况。

New words & expressions

introductory [ˌintrəˈdʌktəri] adj. 介绍性的
intentionally [inˈtenʃənəli] adv. 有意地，故意地
philosophy [fiˈlɔsəfi] n. 哲学，哲学体系，达观，冷静
convention [kənˈvenʃən] n. 大会，协定，习俗，惯例
mandatory [ˈmændətəri] adj. 命令的，强制的，托管的
bulk carrier 散装货轮
involvement [inˈvɔlvmənt] n. 连累，包含
implementation [ˌimplimenˈteiʃən] n. 执行
put in v. 放进，提出，提交，插入，进入，使就职，种植，进港
sufficient [səˈfiʃənt] adj. 充分的，足够的
monitor [ˈmɔnitə] n. 班长，监听器，监视器，监控器 vt. 监控 v. 监控
override [ˌəuvəˈraid] vt. 制服，践踏，越过，n. 代理佣金
conformity [kənˈfɔːmiti] n. 一致，符合
occurrence [əˈkʌrəns] n. 发生，出现，事件，发生的事情
documentation [ˌdɔkjumenˈteiʃən] n. 文件
paperwork [ˈpeipəwəːk] n. 文书工作
verification [ˌverifiˈkeiʃən] n. 确认，查证，作证
evaluation [iˌvæljuˈeiʃən] n. 估价，评价，赋值
certification [ˌsəːtifiˈkeiʃən] n. 证明
auditor [ˈɔːditə] n. 计员，核数师
preamble [priːˈæmbl] n. 导言
objective [əbˈdʒektiv] n. 目标，目的 adj. 客观的，[语法] 宾格的
assembly [əˈsembli] n. 集合，装配，集会，集结，汇编
discharge [disˈtʃɑːdʒ] vt. 卸下，放出，清偿（债务），解雇 vi. 卸货，流注
express in broad terms 概括性地表述
in matters of 就……而论
commitment [kəˈmitmənt] n. 委托事项，许诺，承担义务
competence [ˈkɔmpətəns] n. 能力
bareboat [ˈbeəˈbəut] adj. 空船的
assume [əˈsjuːm] vt. 假定，设想，采取，呈现
charterer [ˈtʃɑːtərə] n. 租船者，租船主
shipowner n. 船主
take over v. 把……从一地带到另一地，接收，接管
impose [imˈpəuz] vt. 征税，强加，以……欺骗 vi. 利用，欺骗，施影响
audit [ˈɔːdit] n. 审计，稽核，查账 vt. 稽核，旁听 vi. 查账
other than adv. 不同于，除了
entity [ˈentiti] n. 实体

verify [ˈverifai] vt. 检验，校验，查证，核实

deficiency [diˈfiʃənsi] n. 缺乏，不足

adequate [ˈædikwit] adj. 适当的，足够的 adj. 适当的，足够的

conversant [kənˈvəːsənt] adj. 亲近的，有交情的，熟悉的

be manned with 给…配备人员

in support of 支持

execution [ˌeksiˈkjuːʃən] n. 实行，完成，执行，死刑，制作，杀伤力

shipboard [ˈʃipbɔːd] n. 舷侧，船

interval [ˈintəvəl] n. 间隔，距离，幕间休息 n. 时间间隔

obsolete [ˈɔbsəliːt] adj. 荒废的，陈旧的 n. 废词，陈腐的人

be referred to 参考

impracticable [imˈpræktikəbl] adj. 不可行的

Appendix 5

Basic Interview Questions about Cruise Ships

Ⅰ. Personal Information

1. How do you do? How are you? /How are you doing?

2. Could you introduce yourself? /Can you say something about yourself in English?

3. Could you tell me your name? /May I have your name? /Who name you?

Do you have English Name? /Who gave you the English name?

4. How old are you? When/where were you born? What is your age? Could you tell me your date of birth?

5. How tall are you? What is your weight/height?

6. Are you married or single? Have you got married?

7. What's your nationality?

8. What's your health condition? /How is your health?

Did you have any infected diseases before? Are you seasick?

9. What about your eyes sight? Are you wearing contact lenses?

Are you short-sighted or color blind?

10. Are your hands sweaty? / Are your palms sweaty?

11. What's date today? /What day is it today?

What is the weather like today? /How is the weather today?

Ⅱ. Introduce Hometown

12. Where do you live? /Where are you from? /where do you come from? /What's

your address? /Where is your hometown?

13. How long does it take you from your hometown to here by bus/train? /How far away from here to your hometown?

14. Is there any interesting place/place of interest in your hometown? Could you introduce some interesting place in your hometown? Can you tell me the most famous local food/snacks/flavor in your hometown?

Ⅲ. Like and Dislike (hobby)

15. What's your favorite color, would you tell me the reason?
Which season do you like the best , why?

16. what's your hobby/interest?

17. Who is your favorite star? /Why do you like him/ her?

18. What kind of film do you prefer? /Could you introduce it to me?

19. Are you interested in any TV programs?

20. Do you like music? What kind of music do you like best, why do you like it?

21. Do you like traveling? Have you ever been to any places before?

22. Do you like sports? Tell me more.

Ⅳ. Family Information

23. How many persons/people/ family members in your family?

24. Do you have any brothers or sisters/sibling (兄弟姐妹)? How old is he/ she?
What is your brother or sister doing?

25. Would you tell me your parents' age?
What is your father/mother doing? /What's the occupation of your parents?
What are your parents' jobs? /What kinds of job do they have?

26. Who will take care of/look after your parents when you are abroad/on board?

27. Have you told you parents that you want to work for us? What's their idea?
Do they agree/disagree with you?

28. If your parents do not allow/object/disagree you to work on ship. What will you do?

Ⅴ. Education Background

29. Which school did you graduate from? When/where did you graduate from?
What's your major?

30. Do you have bachelor's degree or diploma? /What degree do you get?

31. What subject did you learn at school? /Which course did you study?
What did you learn/study in the school?

32. What's your favorite classes/subjects at school, why?

33. Do you like English? Why? /Why do you think English is important?
How many years/ How long have you learned English?
How to improve your English?

34. Can you speak other foreign languages except English?
Can you speak Cantonese?

35. Can you operate/use computer? What programs can you use?

Ⅵ. Job Application

36. Which position/occupation are you going to take? / Which position/occupation are you applying for, why?

What job are you interested in, why?

37. Do you have any knowledge about Star Cruises?

Do you know something about our company?

38. Why do you want to work with Star cruise? For what reason you want to join us?

How many years do you plan to work for us?

39. Why do you want to work abroad/on board?

40. Do you have any registration of disciplinary violation? Did you ever breach/break country law?

41. If you work on board, will you be homesick? /will you miss your family?

42. Do you think it is dangerous/safe to work on ship?

43. Can you work on board? /Can you work overtime?

Can you work for long time standing?

44. Are you confident to take this job? Do you have confidence to work on board?

Do you think you are qualified/suitable for this job?

45. What's your expected salary? / What's your salary expectation?

Are you satisfied with the salary we offer, Why?

46. Why should we offer/provide/give you this position?

Why should we hire/employ you?

47. If we offer you a position in the casino, will you accept it?

48. How much is five plus seven? /How much is ten minus five?

How much is six times three? /How much is twelve divided by four?

Ⅶ. Working Experience

49. Do you have any (related) working experience? /What's your working experience background? /Can you describe your working experience?

50. What's your duty? /What did you do for this job? Would you please state your duty and responsibility?

Do you like your last/previous job? /Why did you quit/resign from/give up/leave your last/ previous job?

51. How much (money) did you get/earn per month? /What's your salary?

52. How did you deal with/handle the customers' complaint?

Have you got any complaints from the guests?

If the guest complaints to you , what do you do?

53. What do you think is the important thing in this job?

What did you learn from this job?

54. Do you have any questions for this job or our company?

Do you have any questions? /Do you want to know more about us?

55. Do you prefer to work independently or on a team?

Do you prefer to work alone or work with others?

56. Are you a leader or a follower?

57. What's your advantage/strength/strong points?

What's your weakness/disadvantage/weak points?

58. Do you think smiling is very important when you are working? Why?

59. Is this the first time you take the interview? Why are you so nervous?

60. If you cannot be recruited/employed/hired by Carnival/Royal Caribbean International this time , what will you do?

61. Are there many foreigners living in your hotel? Where are they from?

Appendix 6

The Pictures of Different Cruise Ships

VOYAGER
of the
SEAS℠
海洋航行者号
吨位：138.000吨 甲板楼层：15层
载客：3,840人 船员：176人
长度：310米 宽度：48米
吃水：9米 航行速度：22节
客房数：1,557间
游泳池与温水按摩池
皇家大道景观房
卫京皇冠酒廊
酒吧
蓝月光爵士吧
天光教堂
七心棋牌室
运动吧
直排轮滑道
模拟高尔夫
海上历奇@青少年活动中心
尊尼火箭美式餐厅
冒险海滩
迷你高尔夫
冰淇淋吧
日光浴馆
漫步咖啡厅
斯古诺吧
休闲走廊
健身中心
日间水疗
珊瑚大剧院
慢跑径
观景点
Island烧烤餐厅
帆船自助餐厅
波多菲诺意大利餐厅
主餐厅
篮球场
攀岩墙
图书馆
19洞俱乐部
商务中心
皇家网吧
中庭
精品免税店
香槟酒吧
Studio B
真冰滑冰场
皇家大道
真冰滑冰场
皇家娱乐场
会议中心
夜总会
会议室
中庭
雪茄俱乐部
VOYAGER OF THE SEAS

亚太区最大最豪华的超级邮轮
「处女星号」
StarVirgo

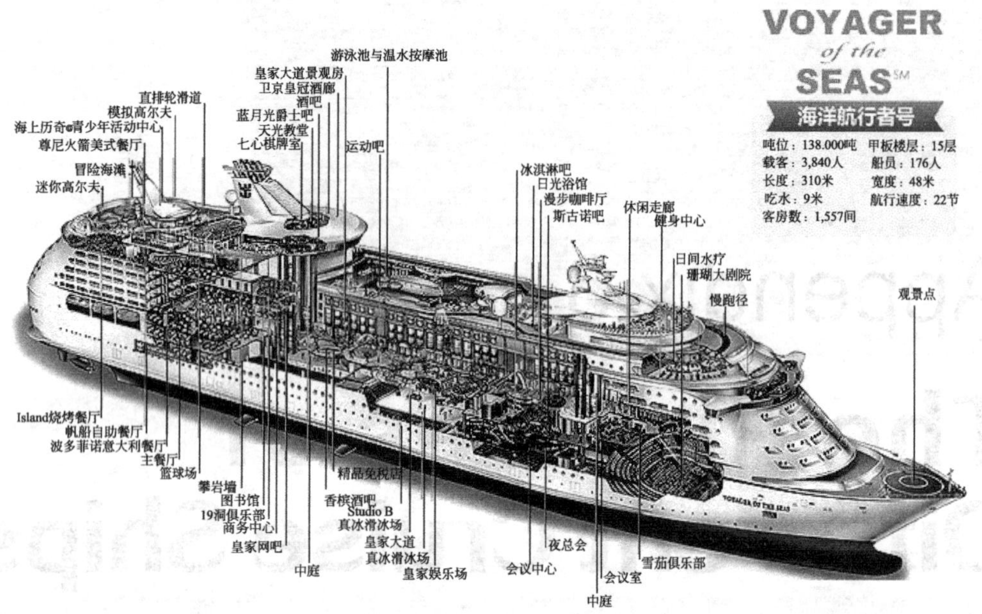

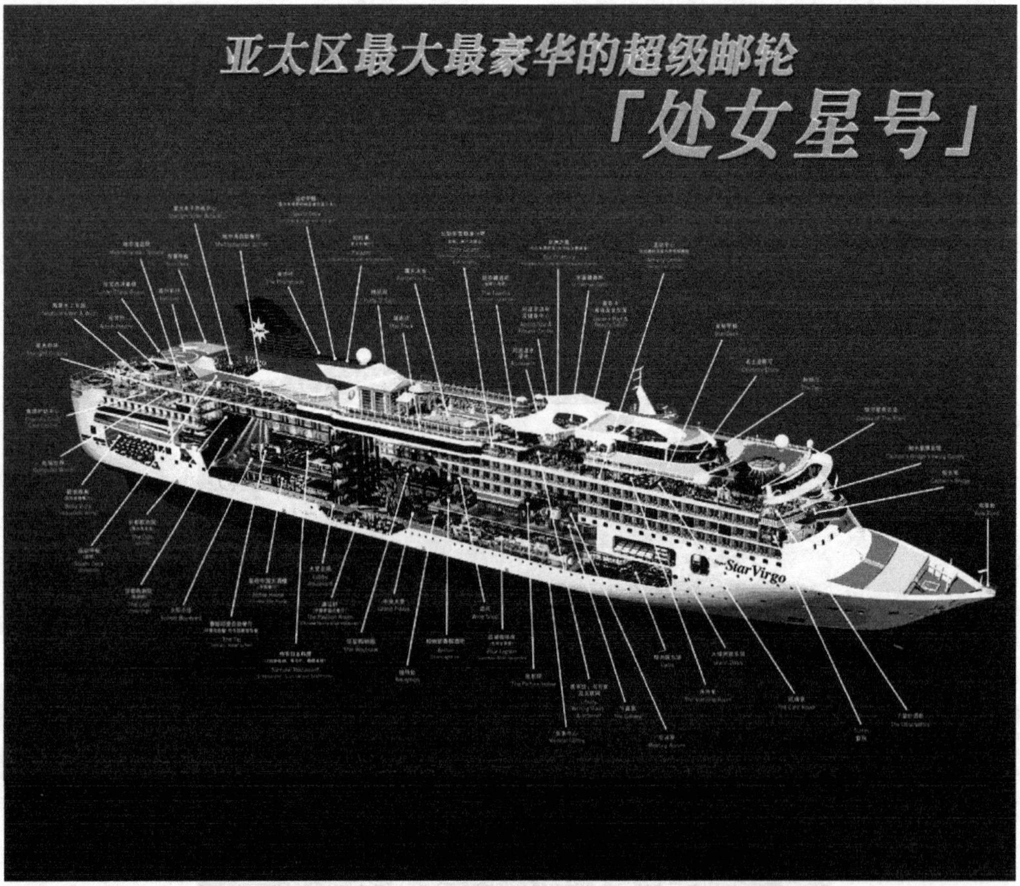

参 考 文 献

[1] Denney G. Rutherford. Hotel Management and Operations. New York：John Wiley & Sons.，2002.

[2] 程丛喜．海上酒店基础知识．武汉：武汉出版社，2004.

[3] 程丛喜，林华英，魏日．发展水上酒店教育，开拓劳务外派新路．武汉：中国水运，2004（6）：47-48.

[4] 程丛喜．发展我国海上酒店教育模式探析．北京：商场现代化，2007（2）：254-255.

[5] 程丛喜．The feasibility and strategy studies on marketing the Yangtze cruising products through Internet. 第六届武汉电子商务国际会议论文集．武汉，2007.

[6] 程丛喜．游船实务与管理．武汉：武汉大学出版社，2009.

[7] 林华英，程丛喜．国际邮轮基础知识．上海：上海交通大学出版社，2015.

[8] 2001 年于伦敦举行的世界海上酒店大会文件．

参考文献

[1] Denney G. Rutherford. Hotel Management and Operations. New York: John Wiley & Sons, [illegible].

[2] [illegible], [illegible]出版社, 200[illegible].

[3] [illegible]. [illegible], 2004, (6): 41-46.

[4] [illegible], 2004 (9): 224-225.

[5] [illegible]. The feasibility and strategy study on marketing the Yangtze cruising products through Internet. [illegible] 2005.

[6] [illegible]. 武汉: 武汉大学出版社, 2009.

[7] [illegible]. 上海: 上海交通大学出版社, 2011.

[8] 2011 年[illegible]大会文件.